The College History Series

South Carolina State University

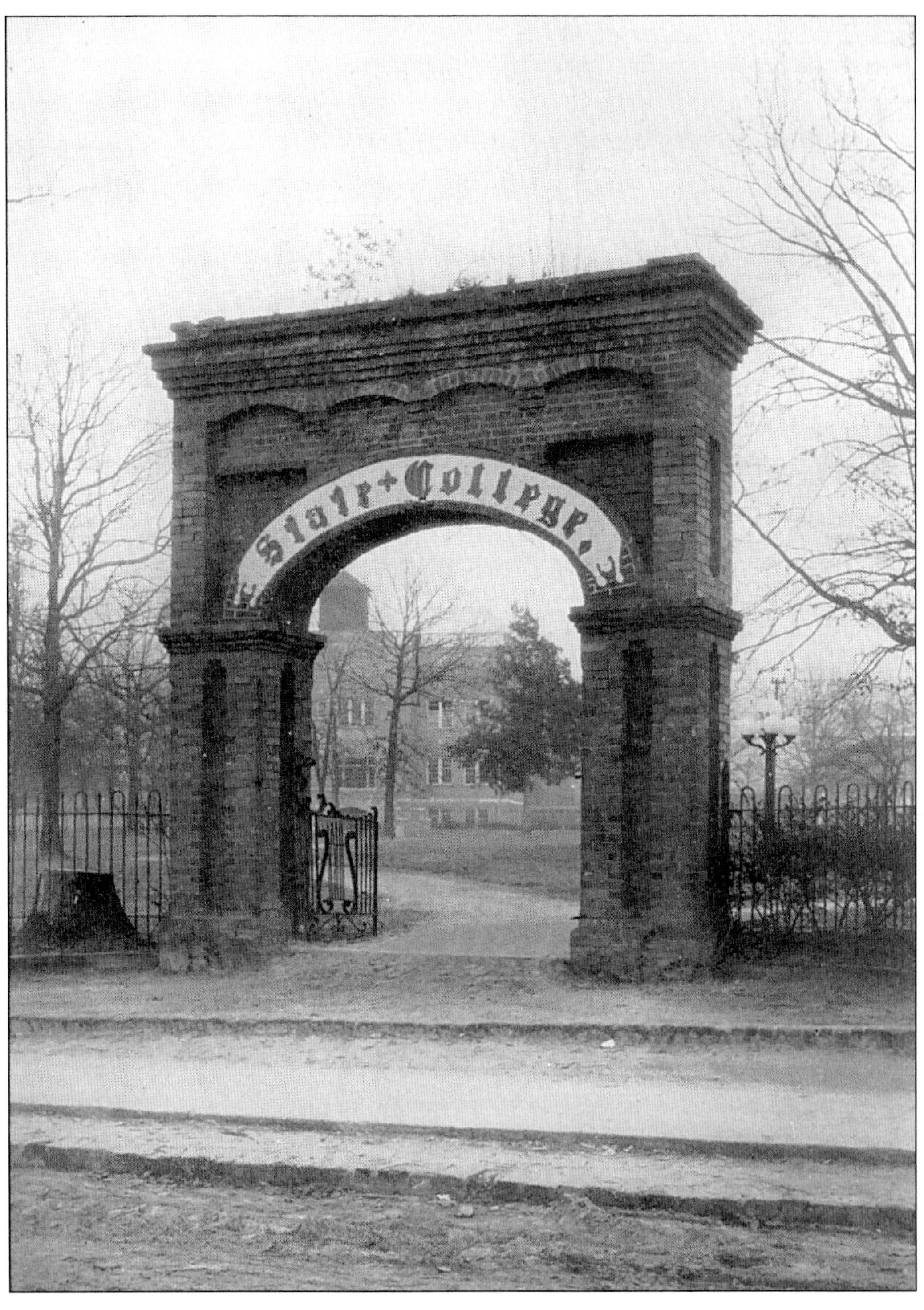
State College

The College History Series

South Carolina State University

Frank C. Martin II, Aimee R. Berry, William C. Hine,
Minnie M. Johnson, and Mary L. Smalls

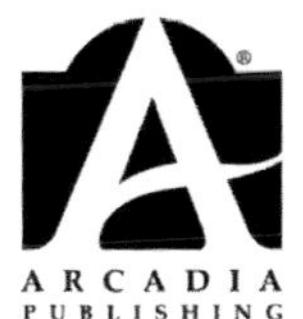

ISBN 978-0-7385-0630-2

Published by Arcadia Publishing
Charleston, South Carolina

Printed in the United States of America

Library of Congress Catalog Card Number: 00-106476

For all general information contact Arcadia Publishing at:
Telephone 843-853-2070
Fax 843-853-0044
E-mail sales@arcadiapublishing.com
For customer service and orders:
Toll-Free 1-888-313-2665

Visit us on the Internet at www.arcadiapublishing.com

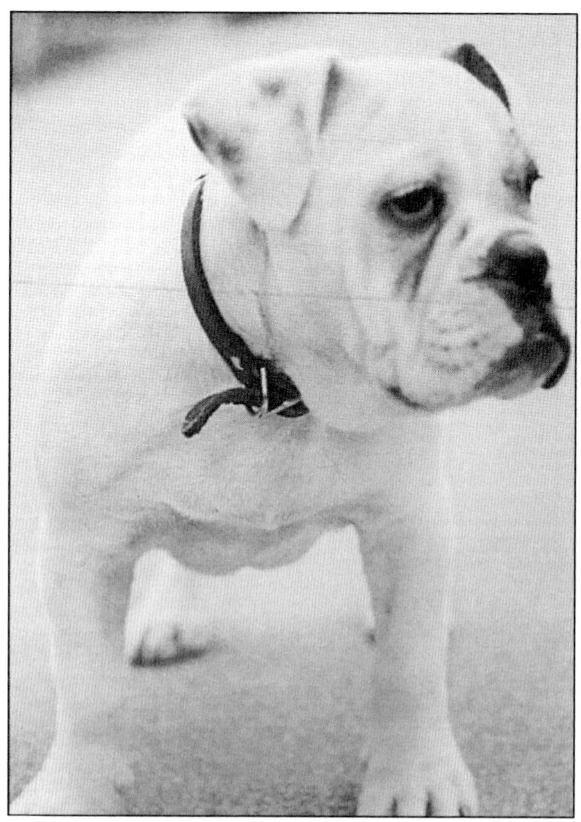

The Bulldog, the University's mascot, symbolizes South Carolina State University's fighting spirit and "bulldog" tenacity.

CONTENTS

ACKNOWLEDGMENTS

Historical research consumes countless hours spent sifting through boxes of photographs, reviewing shelves of books, flipping through folders full of programs, clippings, obituaries, and announcements, and then attempting to assemble a coherent presentation for publication. There is also time spent verifying information, gathering supporting data, culling and weeding excess material, and writing descriptive captions.

It has been our intention to provide a photographic history of the University from 1896 to 2000. We have organized the material by presidential administration. Unfortunately, because of publication limitations, we were unable to include many splendid photographs. The photos selected depict a century's worth of events, activities, and progress. Most importantly, we have tried to highlight the individuals and groups who have contributed so immensely to what was originally known as the Colored Normal, Industrial, Agricultural and Mechanical College of South Carolina, later South Carolina State College, and now South Carolina State University. We hope that this slim volume revives fading memories, gives pause for reflection, provides a chuckle or two, and incites new interest in the history of South Carolina State University.

The authors are indebted to many people for their assistance in providing photographs as well as information from conversations and interviews that were used in the preparation of this book. Our appreciation is extended to Shondra N. Abraham and Jonathan Jamison, Office of News and Communications; the South Carolina State University Historical Collection; Cecil J. Williams; Dr. Miriam Calhoun Hinds; William P. Hamilton, Sports Information Director; Mrs. Gracia Watermann Dawson; Jack Bass; Jack Nelson; the I.P. Stanback Museum and Planetarium; Angela Corbett, 1890 Research and Extension; Larry Mitchell; and Dr. Clemmie E. Webber.

Frank C. Martin II
Aimee R. Berry
William C. Hine
Minnie M. Johnson
Mary L. Smalls

Introduction

The art of photography, a development of the mid-nineteenth century, has provided a timeless measurement of the contributions not only of individuals, but also of whole cultures, races, and peoples. Themes of culture, community, and continuity are intrinsic to this form of visual expression, for, in our culture specifically, the photographer is called upon to synthesize experience into tangible objects, and to document a moment in time which may be viewed by others for reactions, confirmation or dispute, and polemic exchange. The communicative nature of this art form, the act of assessment and transformation of experience, and the resultant intellectual exchange that occurs between photographer and audience is an important source of historical preservation, socio-cultural growth, and renewal in our community.

This publication provides a consideration of more than 100 years of South Carolina State University's history as represented in the visual images assembled for this work by a team composed of a historian, librarians, an archivist, and an art historian.

The attempt, in any publication, to communicate ideas, summarize a historical point of view, document reactions, concepts, or emotions experienced by a selected group for an audience member or spectator, is always only partially successful. Each viewer processes, perceives, and understands the same information differently, as filtered through the veils of experience, perception, interest, political view point, and thousands of diverse active and passive influences that condition the responses that we all are capable of formulating in reaction to exterior (here particularly visual) stimuli.

That active participation of the faculty, staff, and students of the University in the intergenerational transference of enjoyment in the cultural legacy of this institution, using these visual materials, is a part of the educators' function in which we may all take great pride and enjoyment.

The history of South Carolina State University is a triumph of fortitude, perseverance in the face of adversity, transcendence of seemingly insurmountable obstacles (racism, sometimes intentional under-funding, public apathy, political unrest, and disinterest), and simple Bulldog tenacity. The founders of this institution, who greeted severance from sectarian Claflin University more than 100 years ago as a new beginning, hoped for an institution that would prepare Americans of African descent for participation in the mainstream of American society. Unavoidably, and in a very positive sense, the tenor of that function has had to change in many ways, due to the progress in human rights issues in this nation. However, at its core, the University's essential function remains much the same as it was over 100 years ago. We have progressed; yet, we have remained the same. This is part of the paradoxical dilemma of the human condition: we change, the circumstances that engulf us are transformed, and yet, we often remain the same.

In the period of the aftermath of Reconstruction in the South during the 1890s, as part of a power struggle to evict Americans of African descent from meaningful, self-directed participation in the political processes of the state, Dr. Thomas E. Miller was offered leadership of the Colored, Normal, Industrial, Agricultural and Mechanical College of South Carolina on the condition that he withdraw his extremely vocal and highly influential presence from the state legislature. Only some 60 years following this, the graduates of this institution, which had become at that time South Carolina State College, were fighting in the courts to regain the privileges and entitlements that American citizenship and Constitutional assurances had supposedly guaranteed.

Today, alumni of South Carolina State University participate in the national and local political dialogue as major contenders and provide contributions in business and industry, the fine and performing arts, sciences and technology, athletics, and all areas of human endeavor. The dream of Dr. Miller has become a reality within the last century, yet much work remains to be done to assure the character and caliber of inclusive participation and representation in the state and nation. South Carolina State University continues to prepare students to anticipate and face the challenges of the future and to search for new dreams, and perhaps better dreams, which may be transformed into realities in the post-modern age of global communication which surely characterizes the twenty-first century.

Each president of the institution that evolved into modern South Carolina State University made a unique contribution to the on-going process of discovery that has helped the University formulate a sense of its character and direction. Dr. Thomas E. Miller served as the visionary and principal architect of that vision. He laid the foundation that shaped the institution's growth and future. Dr. Robert S. Wilkinson brought the small obscure "colored college" forward, achieving recognition for the school across the country. Dr. Miller F. Whittaker, architect, diplomat, gentleman, and scholar, oversaw the growth and transformation of the school into a true college, providing a vision of the ideal graduate. Dr. Benner C. Turner, a standard-bearer and task-master, elicited a sense of refinement, professionalism, and poise, insuring the accreditation of the college and acceptance as a legitimate institution of higher learning. Dr. M. Maceo Nance Jr. oversaw an unprecedented period of expansion and modernization, firmly establishing the school's character and refining its mission. Dr. Albert E. Smith cultivated the growth begun by Nance as the institution evolved into a comprehensive teaching University. Under the steady leadership of Dr. Carl A. Carpenter, an alumnus, the S.C. Legislature awarded the school official university status. As the seventh president of the University, Dr. Barbara R. Hatton selected the theme of *Culture, Community, and Continuity*. She was the first and, to date, only woman to serve in this capacity. The administrative successes of Hatton's short-lived regime served to clarify the directions of the University: global involvement, community outreach, intensive self-study and assessment, new funding sources, consideration of its intellectual impact, and areas of specialization within the higher education arena. The stable leadership of president Dr. Leroy Davis, an alumnus of the institution like Nance and Carpenter, offers a marvelous sense of hope, continuity, and purpose. The University family can comfortably look forward with optimism and enthusiasm to future developments under his guidance.

The examination of experience, translated into images, is a time-honored expression of our common humanity. South Carolina State University, with its unique history, cultural heritage, and educational achievements, has had an indelible and irreplaceable impact on the complex social systems of the state of South Carolina. No other institution in the state shares precisely the same political, social, traditional, or historical niche.

This publication in celebration of the University's entry into a new millennium provides an excellent example of the interdependent relationships of culture, community, and the continuity these social phenomena must engender to preserve civilization as we know it. Yet simple preservation of the past is not adequate, for we are obligated to transform our culture and ourselves in order to enhance our humanity as well as to improve the quality and character of the world we will bequeath to future generations.

Early History

The founding of this institution has its antecedents in the first Morrill Act passed by the United States Congress in 1862, authorizing the establishment of land-grant colleges which incorporated not only scientific and classical studies, but which also included instruction in military tactics, agriculture, and mechanical arts. This provision was intended specifically to address the practical educational needs of the masses and to assure that higher educational opportunities were not reserved solely for the upper classes. The fundamental idea of these land-grant institutions was in part to provide the educational, cultural, and intellectual opportunities for the general populace of the nation with the intention of providing a process of socialization that would serve to maintain the integrity and equality inherent in the American ideal of democracy.

Prior to the South Carolina Constitutional Convention of 1895, which authorized the creation of the institution that evolved into modern South Carolina State University, an act of 1872 had already established the South Carolina Agricultural College and Mechanics' Institute in association with Claflin College (later Claflin University, founded in 1869) as a branch of the University of South Carolina, located in the city of Orangeburg. The Morrill Land Grant Act of 1890 required all states that did not equally admit African Americans to their educational institutions to maintain comparable, separate institutions for blacks. Clemson University, founded in 1889, prohibited the admission of Americans of African descent. Due to this act and other related developments within the state of South Carolina, Representative Thomas E. Miller, later first president of what became the autonomous South Carolina State University, proposed that the Agricultural College and Mechanics' Institute sever its association with Methodist-affiliated Claflin College and establish a state-supported, non-sectarian institution of higher learning to serve the state's African-American populace. Thus, on March 3, 1896, an act was passed by the South Carolina Legislature to found the "Normal, Industrial, Agricultural and Mechanical College for the Colored Race."

Following many years of successful administration as the Normal, Industrial, Agricultural and Mechanical College for the Colored Race, first under Miller, then Robert Shaw Wilkinson, and Miller F. Whittaker, in 1954, during the regime of the institution's fifth president, Benner C. Turner, the name of the college was officially changed to South Carolina State College. In that same year, following the historic *Brown vs. Board of Education* decision by the United States Supreme Court, the groundwork was laid for the traditional function of this significant state-supported institution to be transformed and expanded. South Carolina State College had originally been founded to provide higher educational opportunities to the African-American citizens of South Carolina and, indeed, South Carolina State University's legacy as a historically black institution provides a source of great pride and esteem to the University family. In accordance with the legal and social advances of the last four decades, beginning with the administration of President M. Maceo Nance Jr., the contemporary University now serves a student population representative of the full spectrum of cultural diversity within the state, nation, and international community. Its unique history within the state of South Carolina provides it with a distinguished and irreplaceable intellectual and cultural legacy unlike that of any other institution within the state-supported or state-assisted university system.

In its first 100 years, South Carolina State University has provided a proud legacy to the state and nation as exemplified in the contributions of its faculty, students, staff, and alumni, who include prominent local, national, and international figures in all areas of human endeavor, including, but not limited to, contributors in education, government, religion, the fine and performing arts, technology, natural science, military science, athletics, industry, medicine, and all other aspects of the intellectual, social, and political community. These exceptional products of the University experience continue into the new millennium the dream initiated by the founders of South Carolina State University

One

Thomas E. Miller 1896–1911

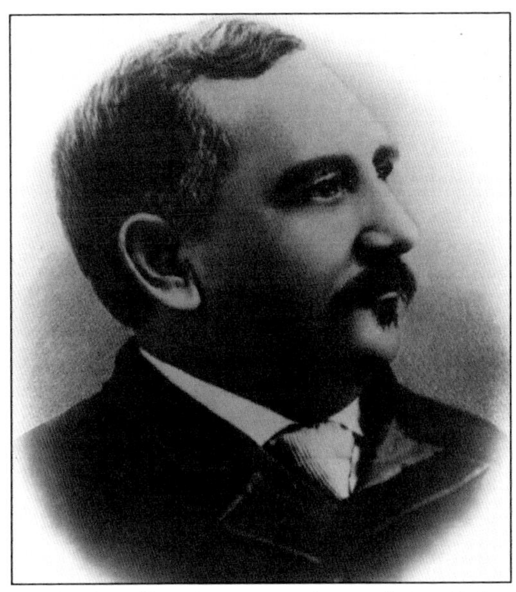

This image of Thomas Ezekiel Miller, first president of the Colored Normal, Industrial, Agricultural and Mechanical College of South Carolina, was made by noted African-American photographer Addison Scurlock of Washington, *c.* 1880. An 1872 graduate of Lincoln University, Miller served as school commissioner for Beaufort County, from 1873 to 1874, and later studied law at the University of South Carolina. He was admitted to the bar in 1875. From 1876 to 1879, he served in the House of Representatives of South Carolina and was returned to the House in 1894. In 1895, Miller was elected to the State Constitutional Convention.

President Miller was a man of rare intellectual and political abilities. Despite his fair complexion, Miller was of African descent. The son of free blacks, he and his family were quite prominent in Beaufort County, and indeed, his mother's maiden name, Ferrebee, was the root of the name of the town in Beaufort County where Miller was born, Ferrebeeville. Miller's dream was to found a state-supported institution of higher learning for Americans of African descent in South Carolina that would train and employ the African-American populace of the state. This dream has been greatly expanded due to the changes in the perception of human rights issues in America in the last 40 years, yet the essentials of President Miller's dream remain a significant part of the reality of South Carolina State University's function, role, and tradition in our culture since the student population remains largely African-American.

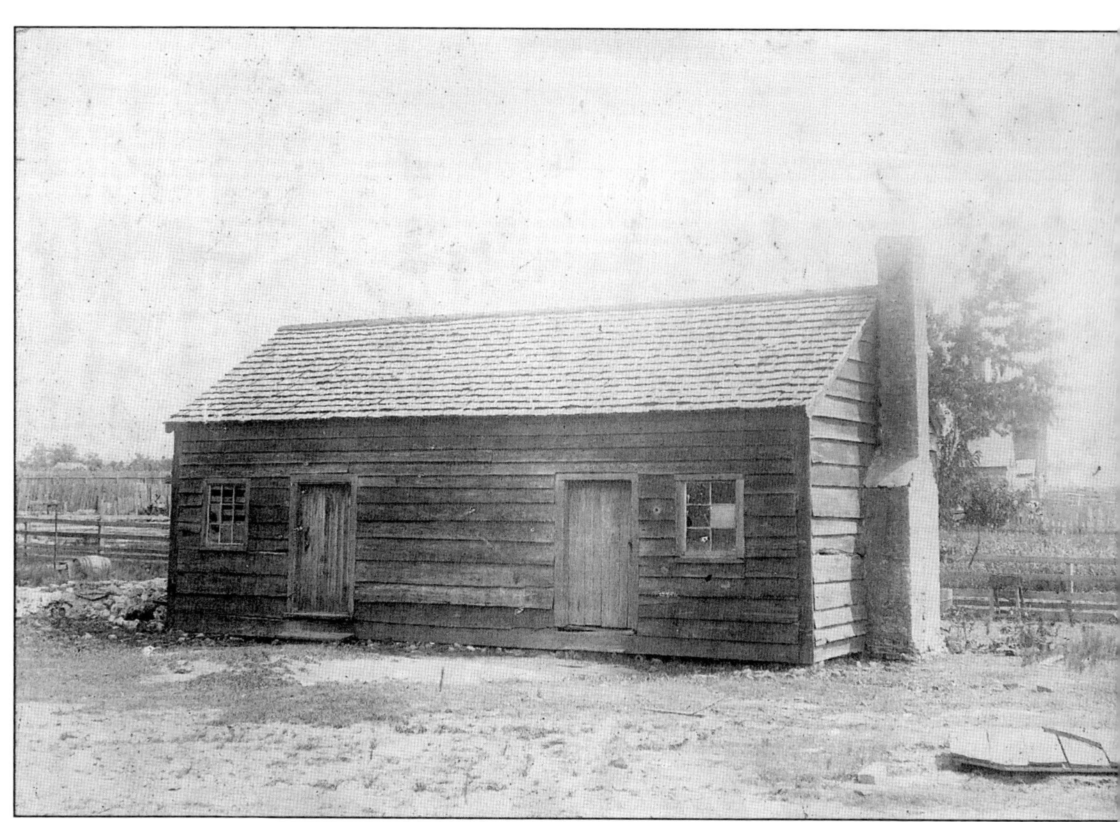

Dean Nelson C. Nix identified the Old Red Inn as the original dormitory for the boys of the college department, which was used for the first three months of the fall of 1896. James A. Pierce, one of the earliest graduates of the Colored Normal, Industrial, Agricultural and Mechanical College of South Carolina, described the Red Inn as having been located in the area directly behind Manning Hall on the campus of what is now South Carolina State University.

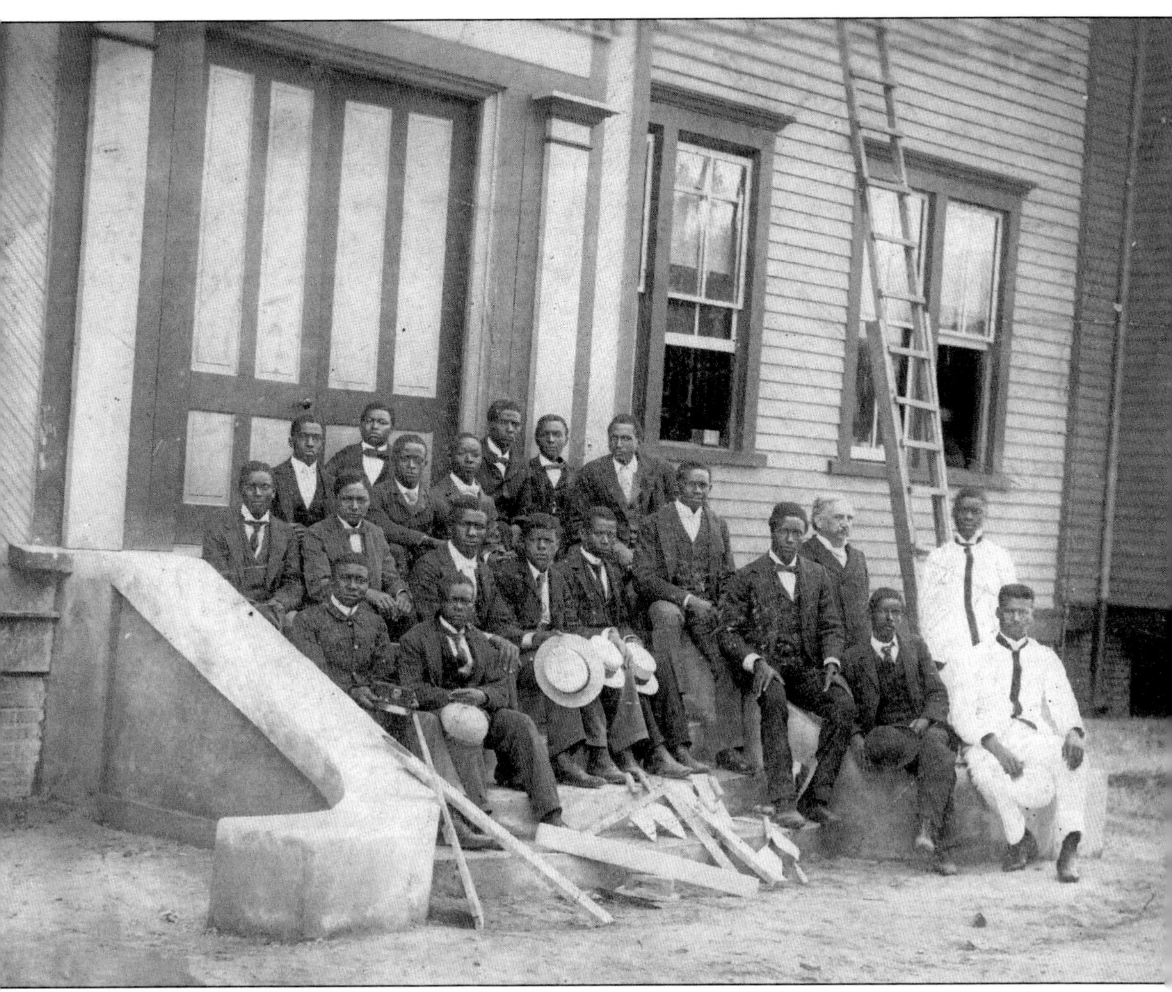

This image, *c.* 1898, shows the first president of the institution, Thomas E. Miller (standing left of the ladder on the viewer's right), outside of the earliest version of Bradham Hall, which was constructed under the supervision of the president and his master mechanics, William W. Gruber, ? Mingo, Henry Ferebe, Eugene Lewis, E.P. Hume, ? Shuler, and Lewis Collier. This photograph may have been taken shortly after or during the actual process of construction of the building, documenting the progress of the work and early growth of the school.

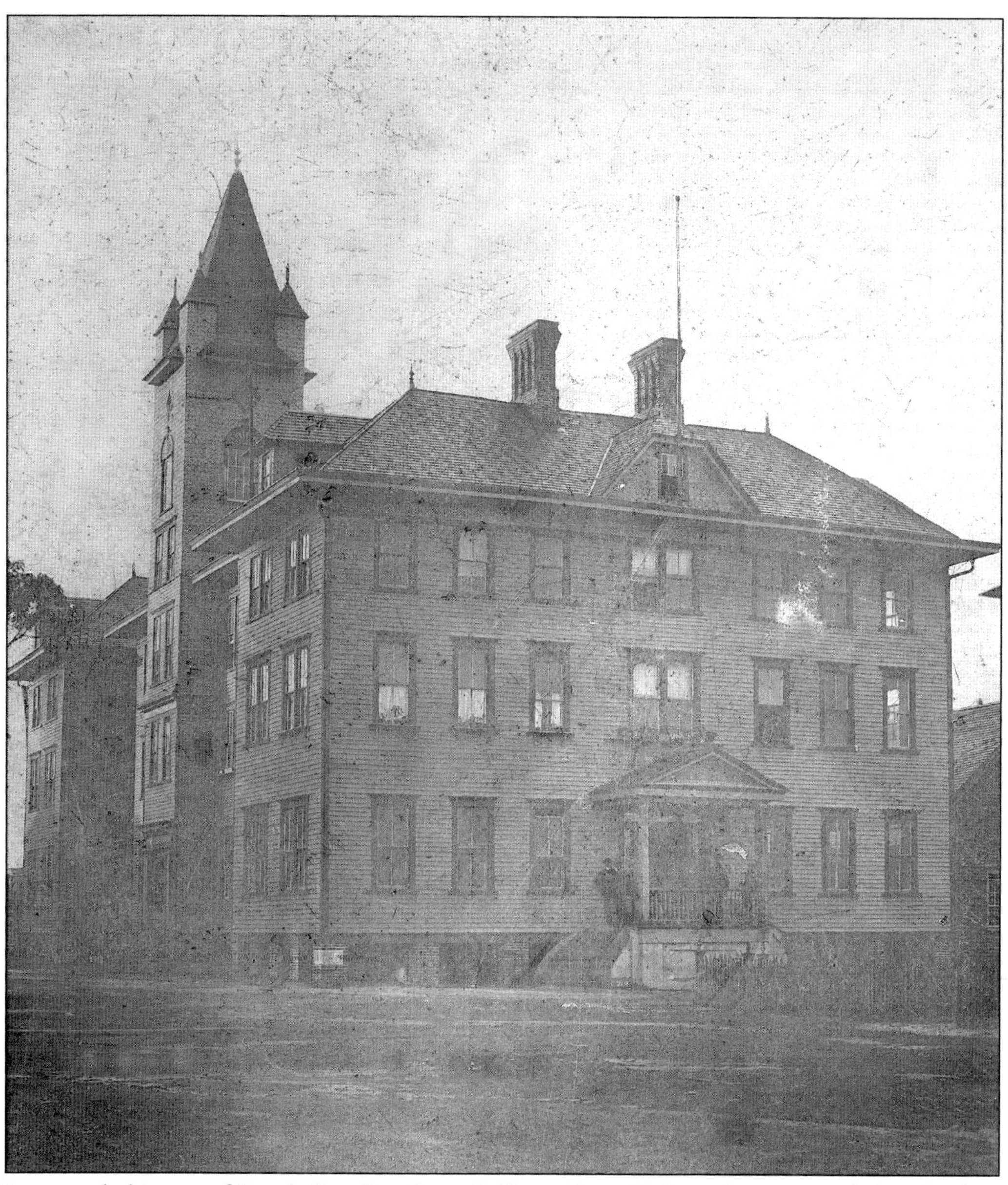

In an early history of South Carolina State College, Dean Nelson C. Nix noted that the first major structure on the college campus, Bradham Hall, was completed only a few months after the school opened on September 27, 1896. This image shows the first of three structures called Bradham Hall, all of which were named in honor of Major D.J. Bradham, a member of the Board of Trustees. Bradham Hall served as a dormitory for men and women. It also contained the President's office, classrooms, a chapel, dining hall, and the accountant's office. President Thomas E. Miller moved into Bradham Hall with his family and occupied the front wing of the first floor on the men's side of the dormitory. This edifice was destroyed by fire on November 24, 1909. It was rebuilt in brick in 1910, burned a second time in 1916, and was rebuilt that same year. This final structure provides the foundation of the present building, which exists in a renovated form on the campus.

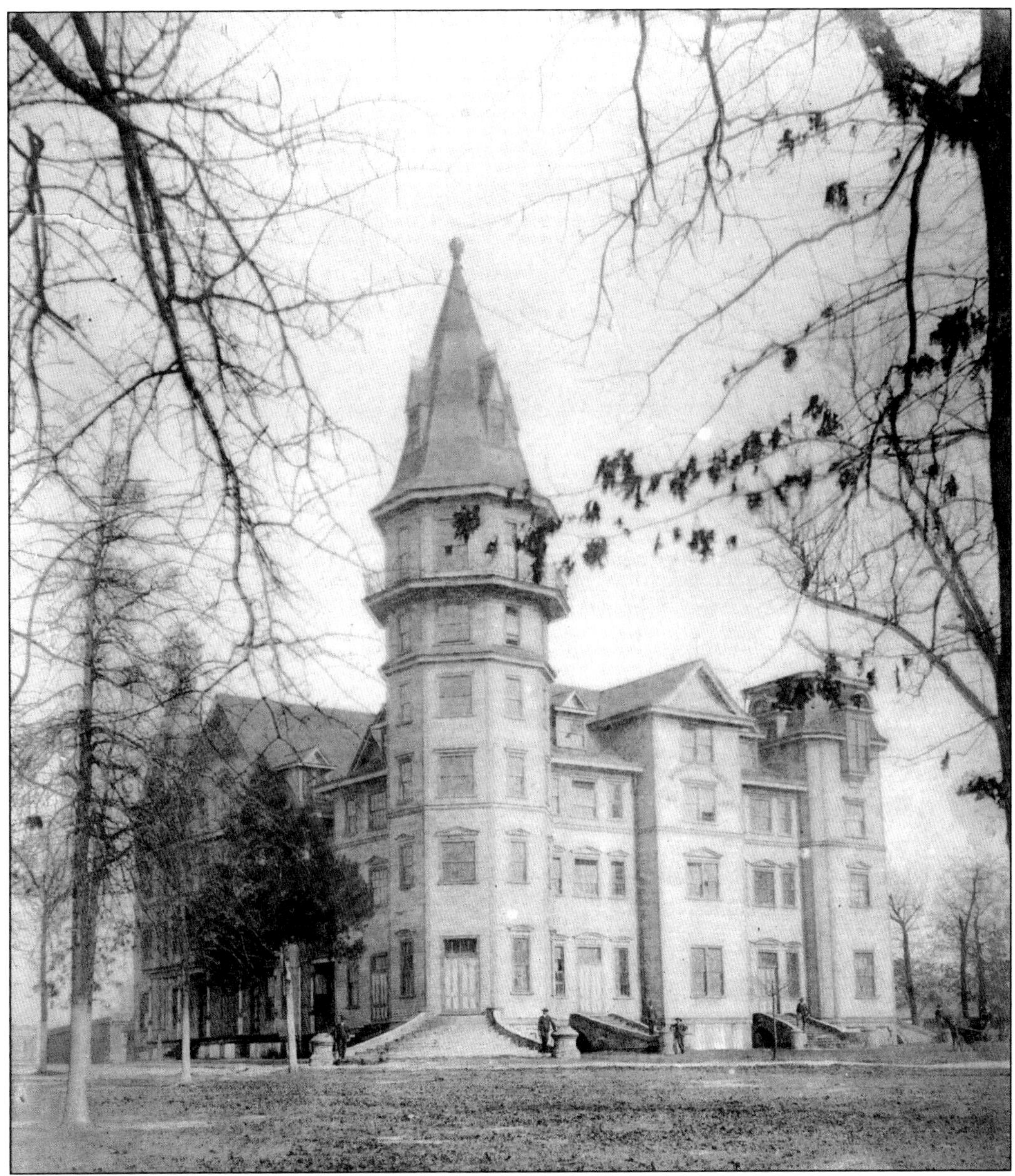

According to Dean Nelson C. Nix, Morrill Hall was designed by William Gruber and erected with the assistance of Henry Ferebe and Mssrs. Mingo and Steele. The six-story building, shown here *c.* 1899, contained a chapel, 16 classrooms, 52 apartments, and rooms for astronomical and observatory purposes. The building, a wooden frame structure, was destroyed by fire on October 21, 1916.

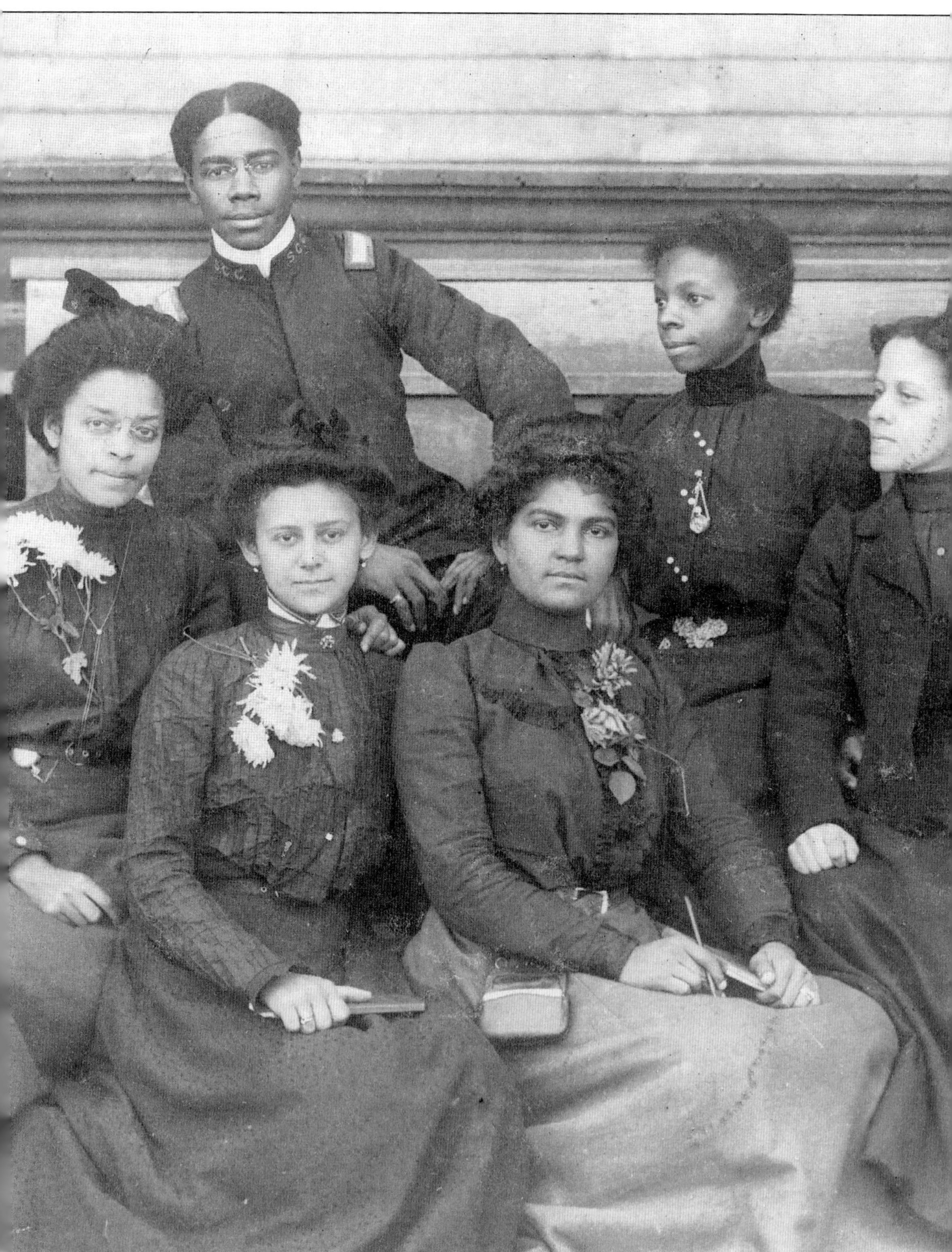

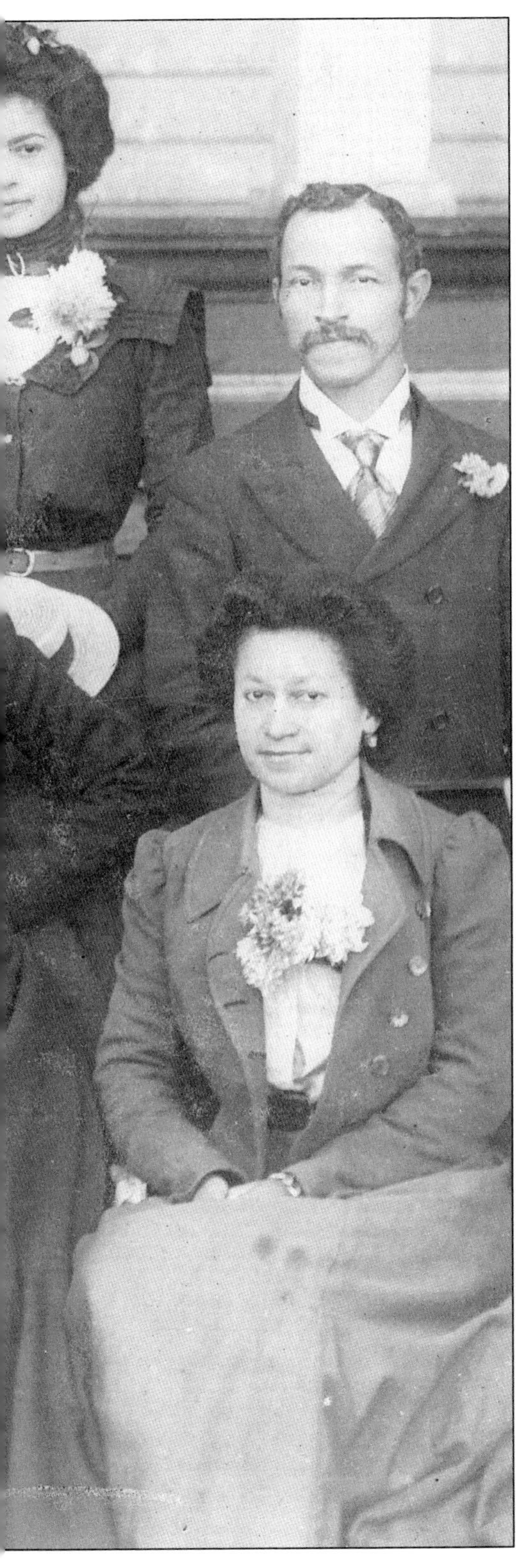

This photograph of nine members of the early faculty of the college was taken *c.* 1901–1903 by W.A. Reckling Studios of Columbia during President Thomas E. Miller's administration. It captures the pride, elegance, sense of purpose, and self-assurance of the dedicated young educators who pioneered the institution that has endured for more than a century. Shown are, from left to right, (top row) Eugene F. Mikell, instructor in band and orchestra, employed in 1897; at his elbow, Alice B. McCloud, instructor in English, employed in 1900; Lillian C. Mack, instructor in English, employed in 1901; and Johnson C. Whittaker, employed in 1900 as professor of mathematics and commandant, providing instruction in military science, a state function of the land-grant title of the school. Whittaker, a native of Camden, had been among the first Americans of African descent to attend West Point Military Academy from 1877 to 1881, but had been wrongfully expelled and was posthumously awarded his commission in 1995 by President Bill Clinton. Shown on the bottom row, from left to right, are Otis Cecil Davenport Council, assistant teacher (Model School), employed in 1896; Louise B. Forham Holmes, instructor in art, employed in 1896; Julia A. McClain Douglass, instructor in kindergarten methods, employed in 1896; and Olive Sasportas. Sasportas had been admitted to the college as a senior on the first day of its opening and soon after her admission became assistant instructor in English. Ms. Sasportas was the first person to receive a Bachelor of Arts degree from the Colored Normal, Industrial, Agricultural and Mechanical College of South Carolina. An early appreciation by the college founders of the benefits of artistic and cultural curriculum offerings is implied by the presence of instructors Mikell and Holmes. This early appreciation is noteworthy in an institution that was designed to have an agricultural, mechanical, scientific, and industrial emphasis. It is clear that the founders of this exceptional institution understood that the intellect must be developed, cultivated, and refined with an appreciation of the arts, philosophy, and cultural activities regardless of the students' menial or vocational training.

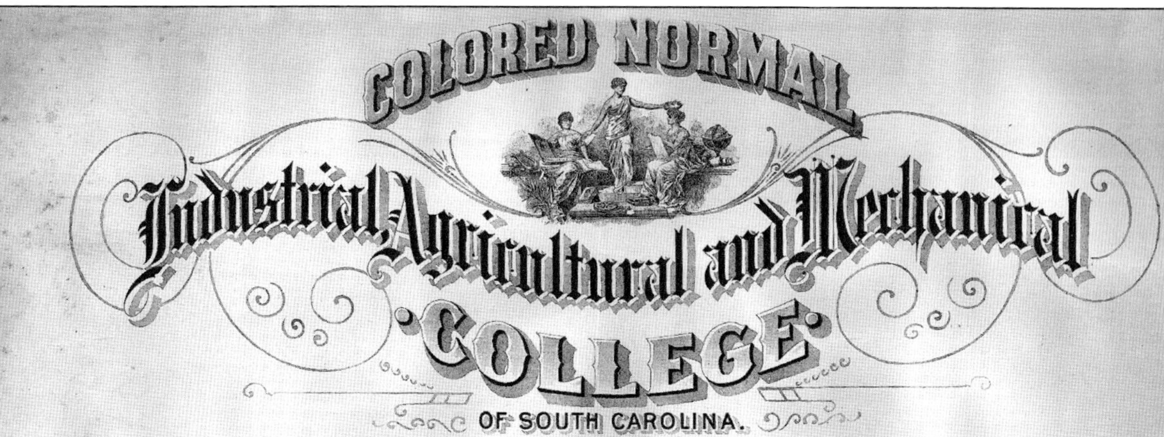

COLORED NORMAL

Industrial, Agricultural and Mechanical

·COLLEGE·

OF SOUTH CAROLINA.

It is Hereby Certified, That Felicia A. Sasportas

honorably completed the Normal Course of Study prescribed by this Institution, and proficiency in scholarship and integrity of character has merited the degree

LICENTIATE OF INSTRUCTION

Therefore, that upon the recommendation of the Faculty the aforesaid title and deg with all the rights, privileges and honors pertaining thereto, are hereby conferred.

In Witness Whereof The Trustees have caused the proper signatures and the seal of the Institution to be affixed.

Done at Orangeburg, S. C., this twelfth day of May one thousand eight hundred and ninety eight

On March 3, 1898, the "Degree of Licentiate of Instruction" was established by an act of the General Assembly of South Carolina. In accordance with the Legislative enactment, the president and faculty of State College were given authority to confer the "Degree of Licentiate of Instruction" on students who would be entitled to receive it at the coming commencement. Above is a copy of Miss Felicia A. Sasportas's degree. Sasportas went on to teach at Delaware State College in Dover, Delaware.

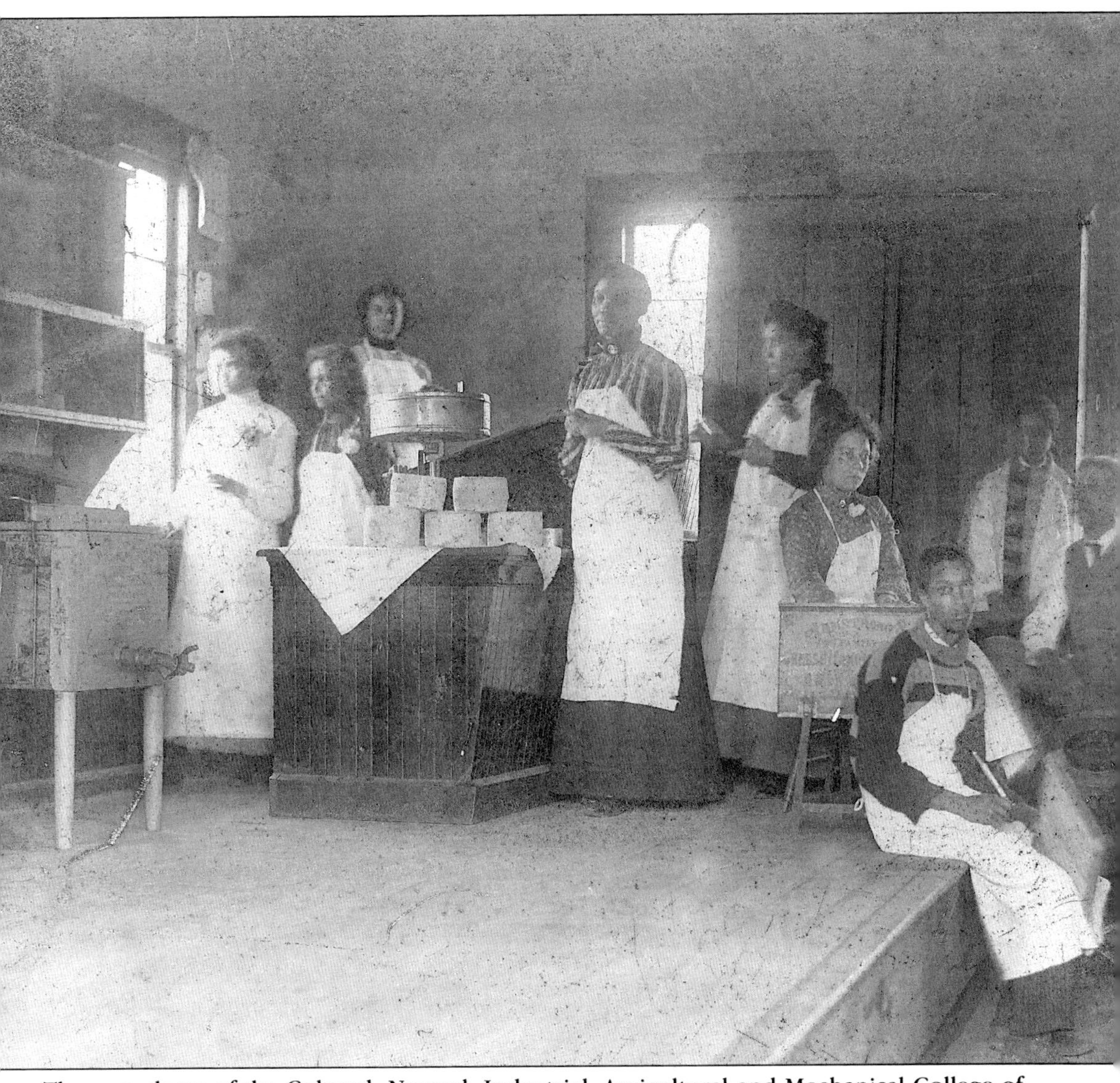

These students of the Colored, Normal, Industrial, Agricultural and Mechanical College of South Carolina are shown participating in a class that underscores an aspect of the school's agricultural mission; practical arts such as cheesemaking, dairy production, and animal husbandry were important components of the early curriculum of the institution. W.H. Adams was superintendent of agriculture. The above image depicts students in a cheese-making class.

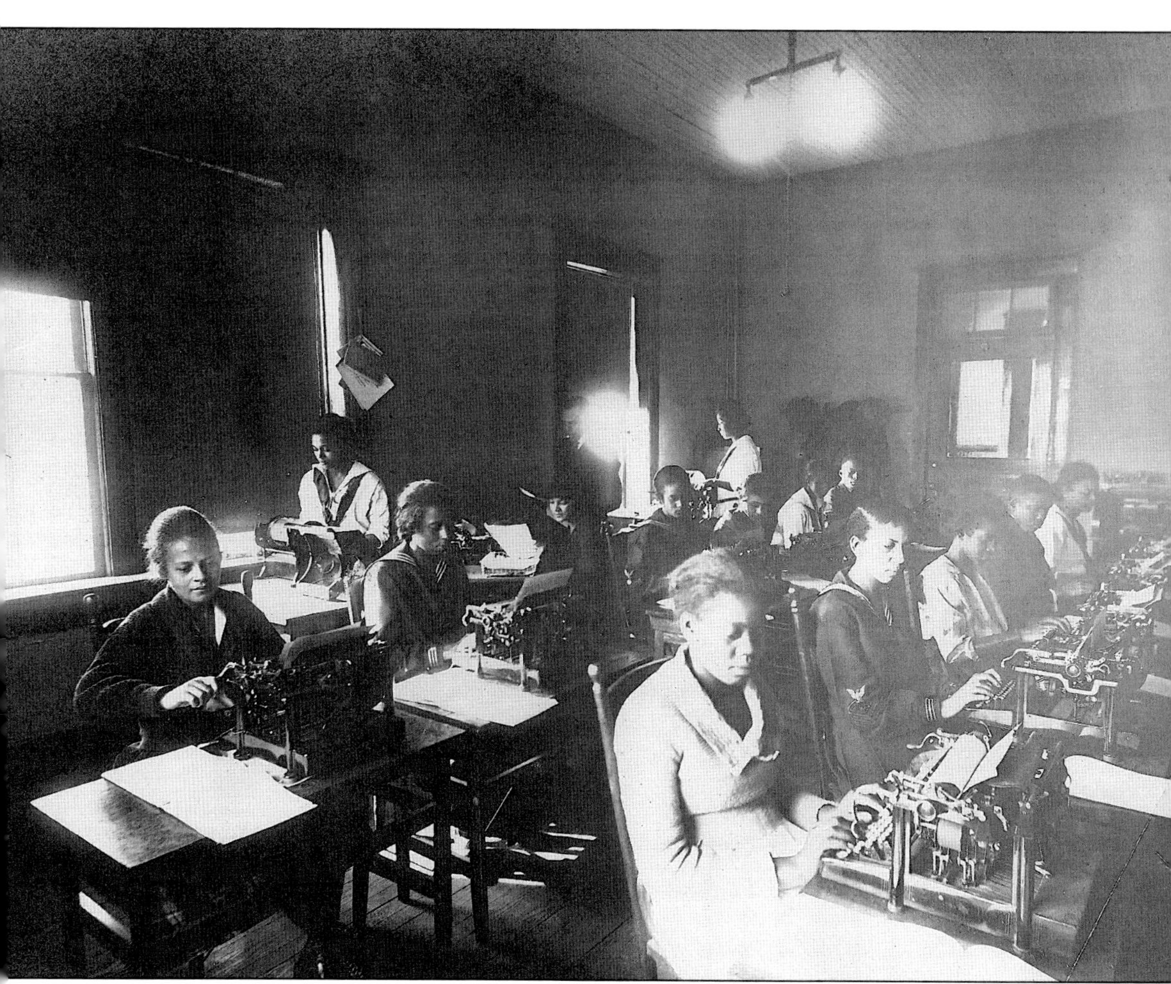

Courses offering instruction in practical and clerical skills, such as typing, formed an important component of the curriculum intended to provide students with the abilities that would assure gainful employment upon completion of the school's program of study.

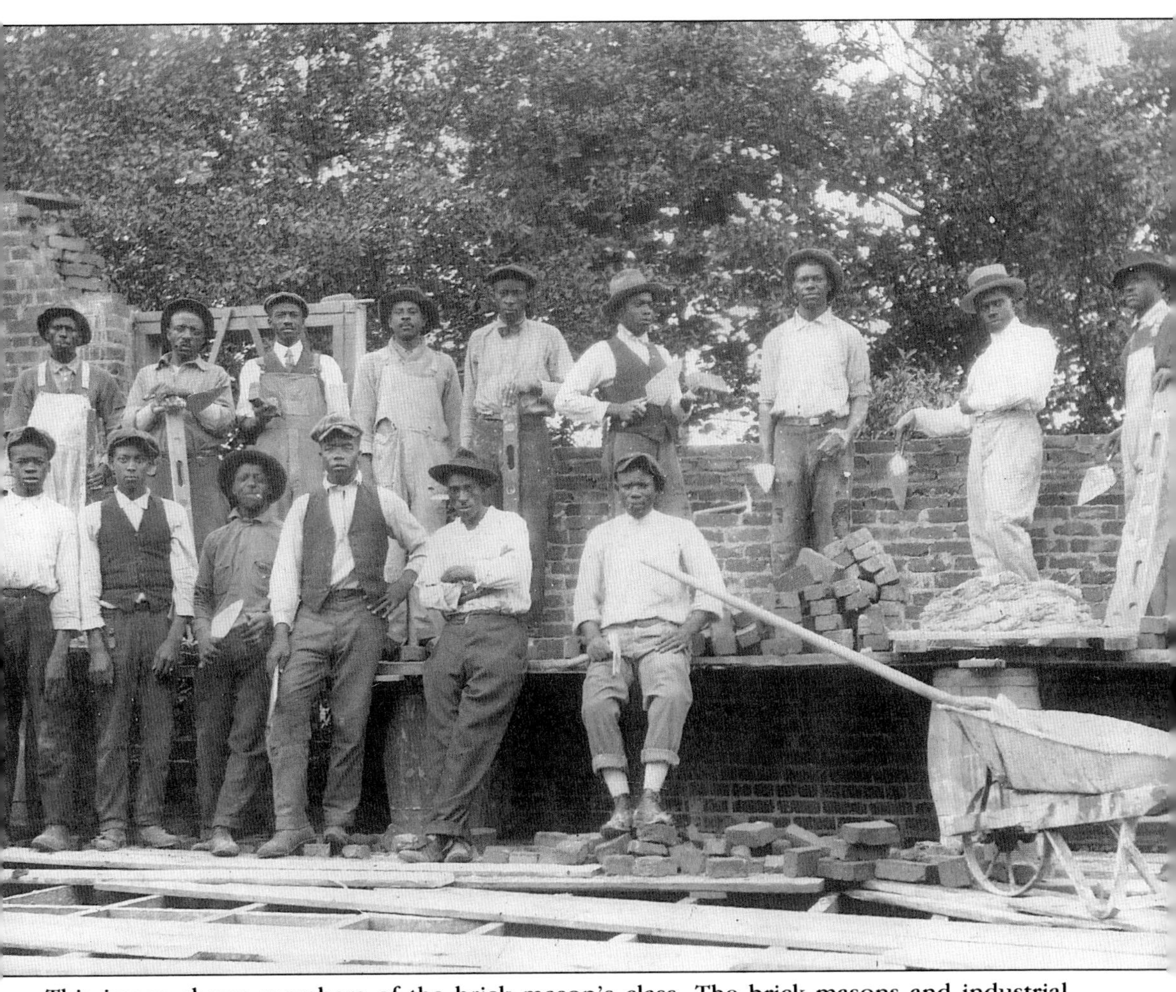

This image shows members of the brick mason's class. The brick masons and industrial education specialists at the college had a formidable reputation. According to Thomas E. Miller, the college's students performed work on the cotton factory in Orangeburg so well that the contractor engaged them for three successive summers to go to Indiana, Michigan, and Illinois to continue their services as bricklayers. Later, when students were installing the heating plant in Morrill Hall, the inspector from the heating plant company was so pleased with their work that he engaged their services to go to Savannah, Georgia, to install the heating plant at the DeSoto Hotel.

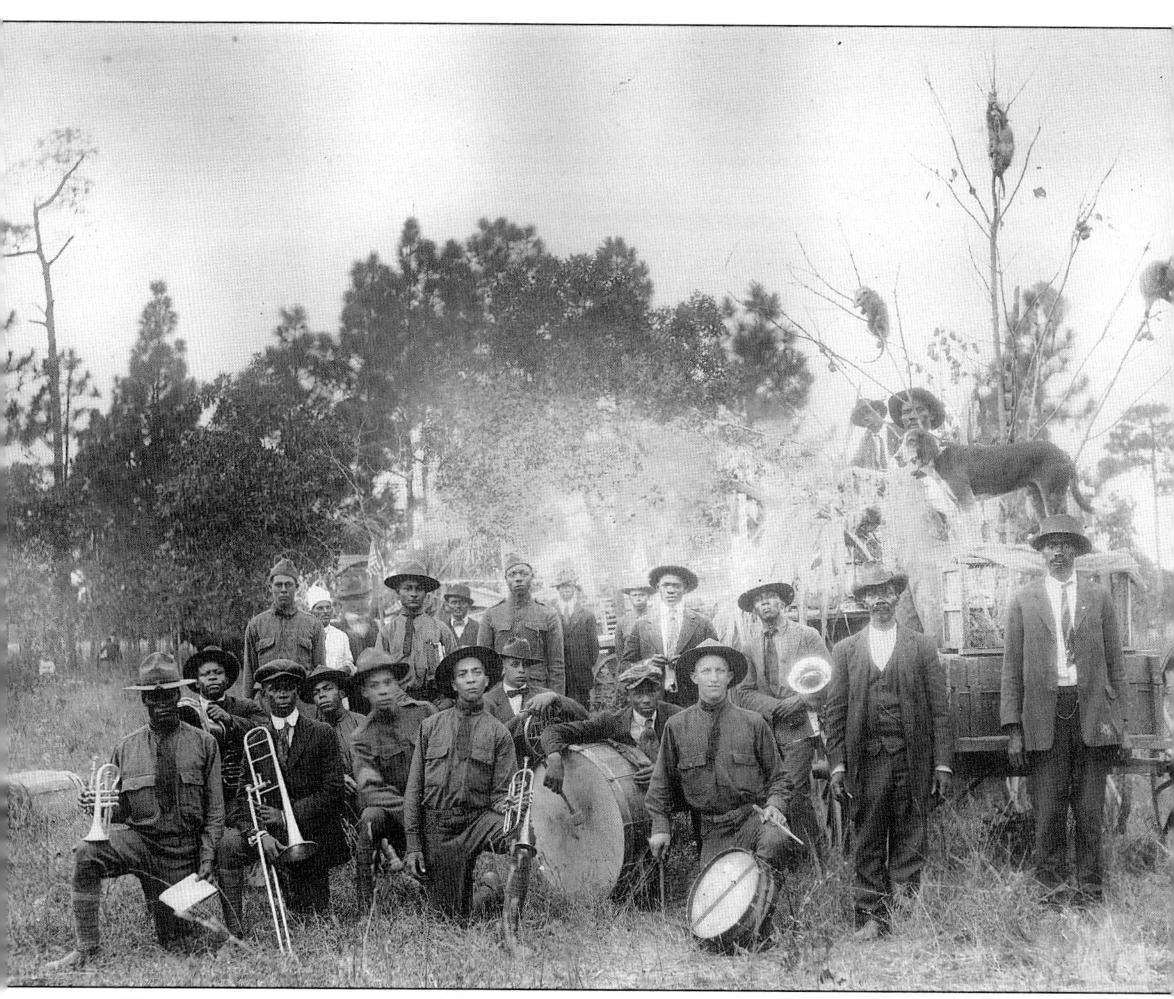

While the young men and older adults shown here appear to be band members, some in military-style dress, they may be Free Masons on a hunting trip or some other campus organization. Note the opossums clinging to the branches of the trees placed on the wagon and the presence of hunting hounds. This image is probably from the period just some years following World War I, for James Edmundreaux Prioleau of Georgetown, South Carolina, a 1925 graduate, is shown standing fourth from the left.

Nelson C. Nix, in whose honor Nix Hall is named, served as dean, professor of mathematics, and early historian of the institution. Dean Nix served the college from 1896 to 1944, having been a part of the college from the day of its inception. Nix Hall has been used as a dormitory for faculty men, the Speech, Hearing, and Language Clinic, and female student housing.

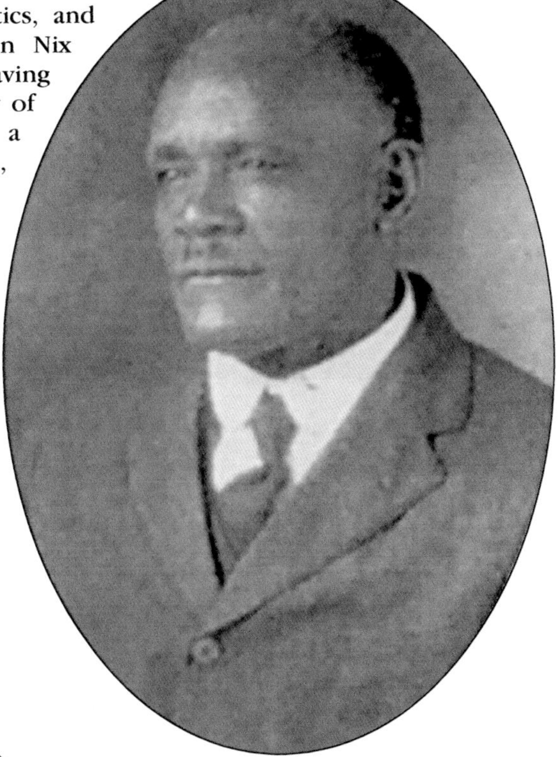

Zoologist and educator Ernest Everett Just was born in Charleston, South Carolina, and later graduated from the preparatory school associated with the Colored Normal, Industrial, Agricultural and Mechanical College of South Carolina in 1899 in anticipation of going on to a college program. One among the many students mentored by Dean Nelson C. Nix, Just later receive his BA degree from Dartmouth College in Hanover, New Hampshire, and the Ph.D. from the University of Chicago in 1916. In addition to his extensive research activities centering on fertilization and parthenogenesis of marine eggs, Just served with distinction on the faculty of Howard University in Washington, D.C., where he was also a founder of the Omega Psi Phi fraternity in 1911.

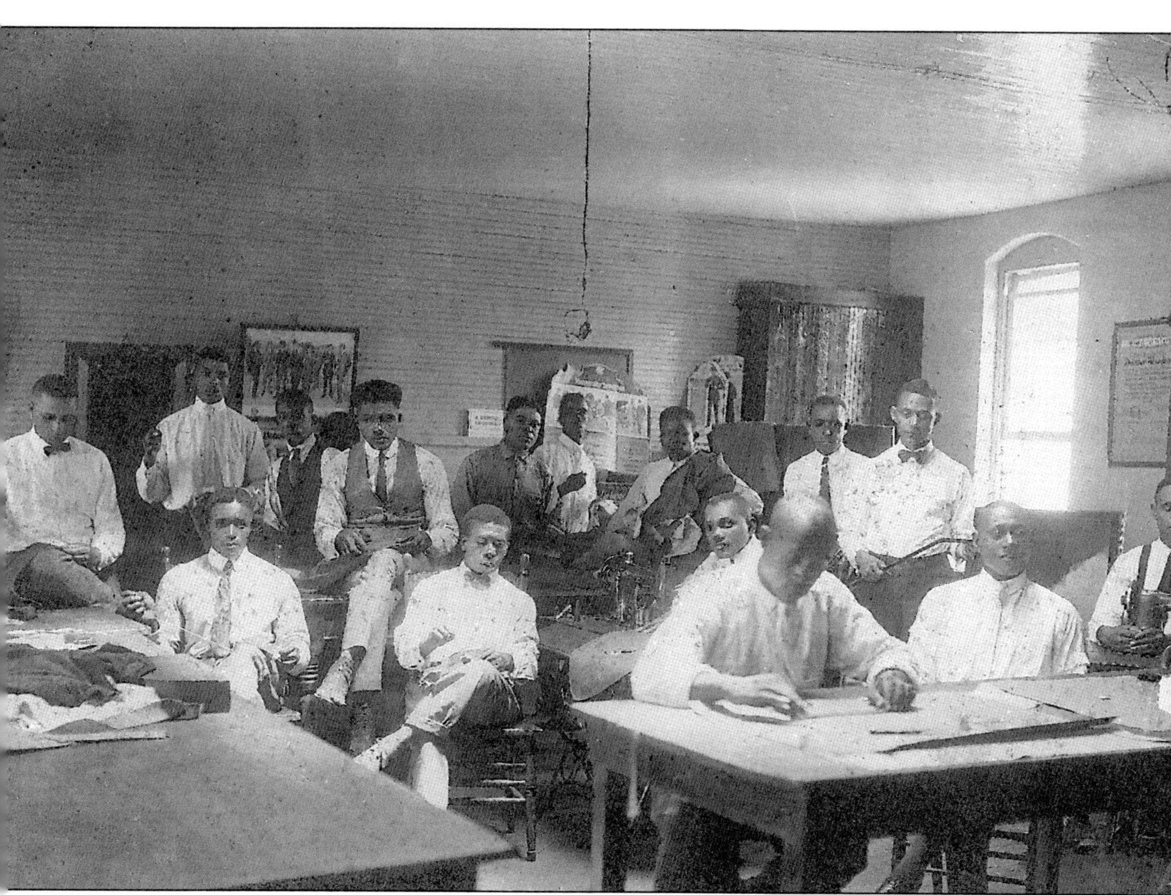

Charles Watermann's tailoring class is shown participating in the practical and industrial educational curriculum of the college, *c.* 1912. Young Watermann, shown standing on the right next to the window, provided instruction in the cutting, fitting, and completion of garments for men. The tailor shop was located in Industrial Hall, which had been constructed in 1902. Watermann's exceptional talent for fitting and assembling garments was recognized by South Carolina's elite, and he was commissioned to provide suits to state governors from Coleman Blease to Strom Thurmond.

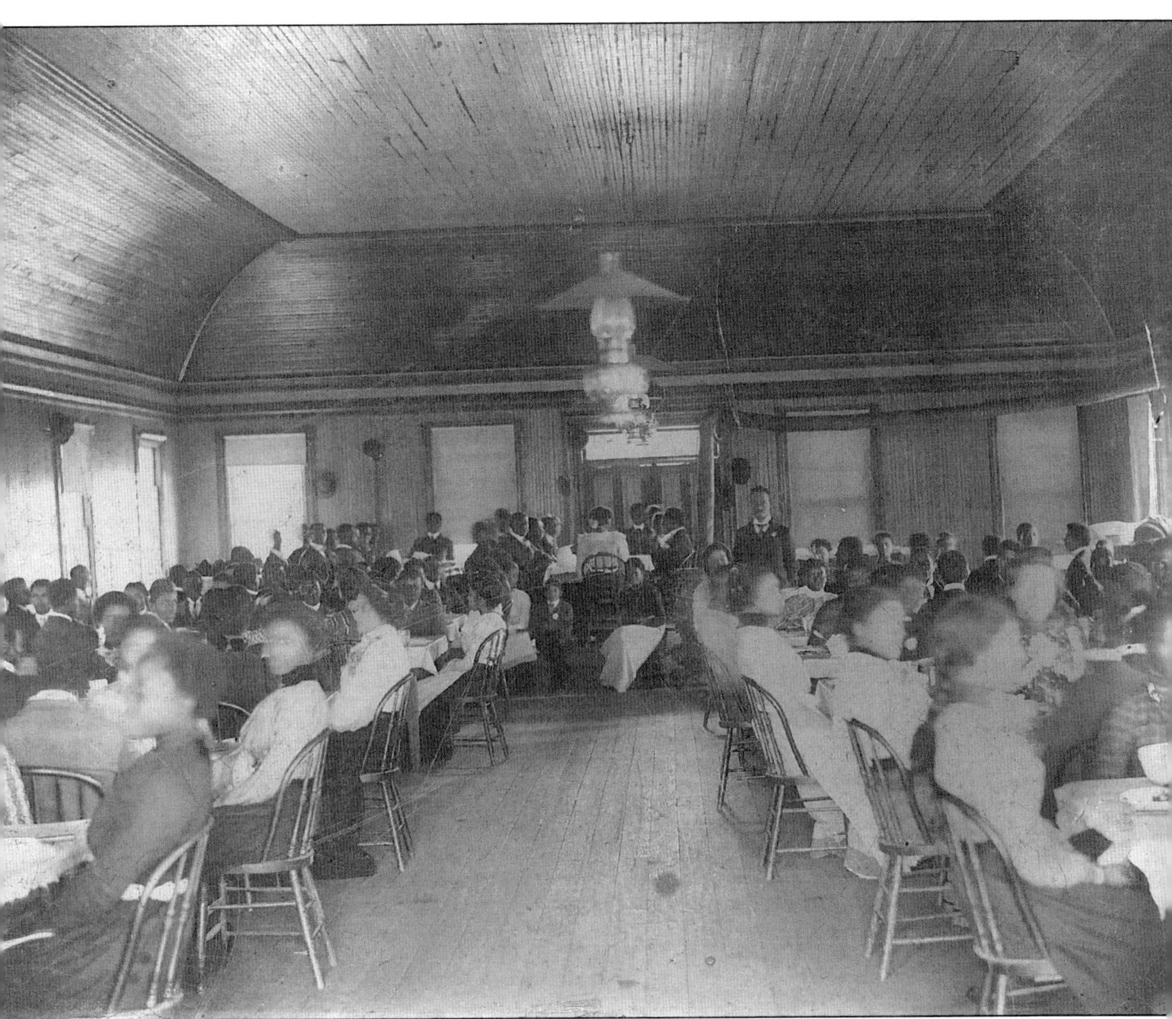

In the early years of the school, students were provided with waiter service (as a practicum in professional service etiquette) and formal dining procedures were used. According to Nelson C. Nix, Floyd Hall, which served as the dining hall, was completed during 1897. The structure was destroyed by fire in 1909 and rebuilt in 1910. Floyd Dining Hall and Kitchen, with a serving hall and rooms attached, was a spacious brick building with seating accommodations for 800 students.

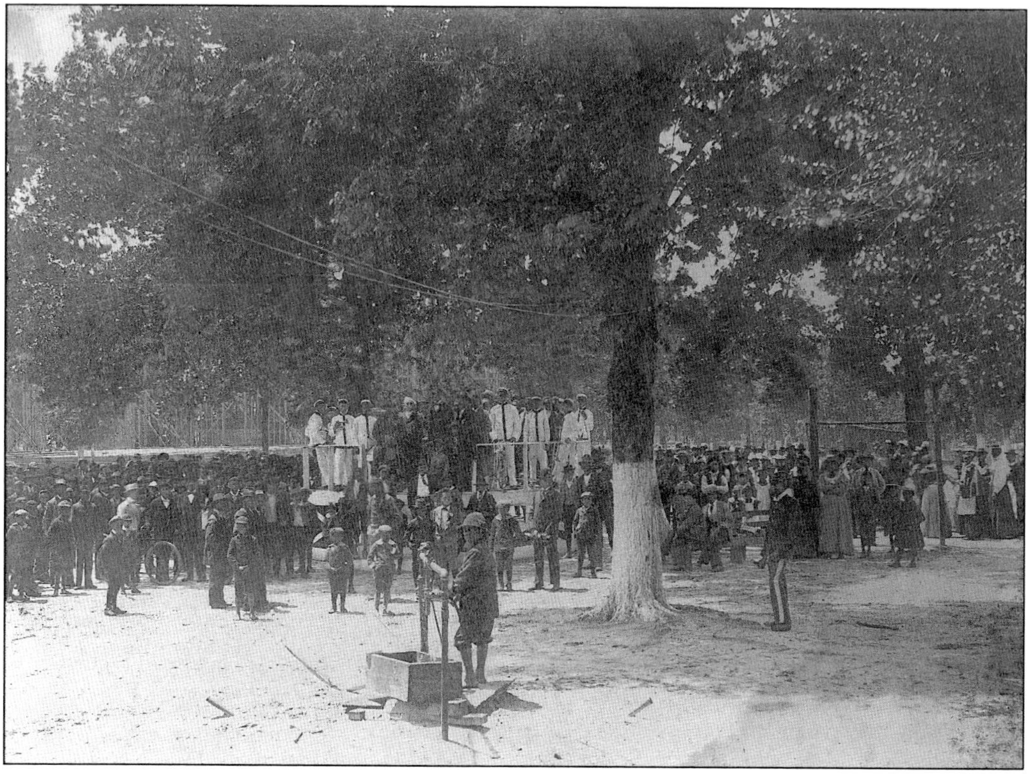

Shown above at a farmer's conference organized in 1898 and below, among the dairy herd of Jersey milkers, President Thomas E. Miller served as the conceptualist and visionary for the establishment of the institution's early mission. This aspect of the university's contribution to the community is continued in the contemporary 1890 Research and Extension programs which provide services to the rural community.

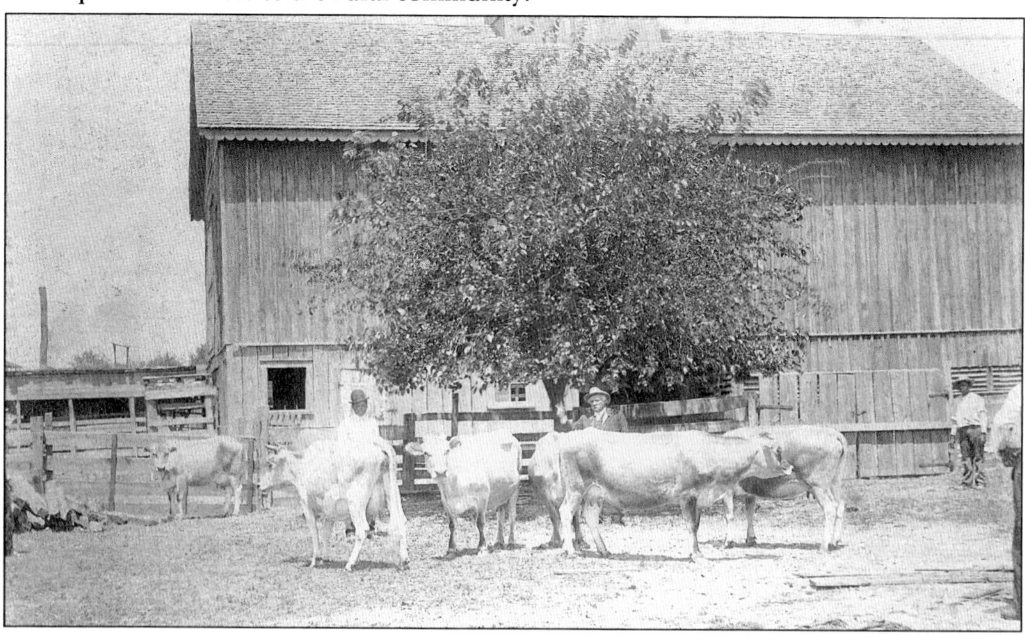

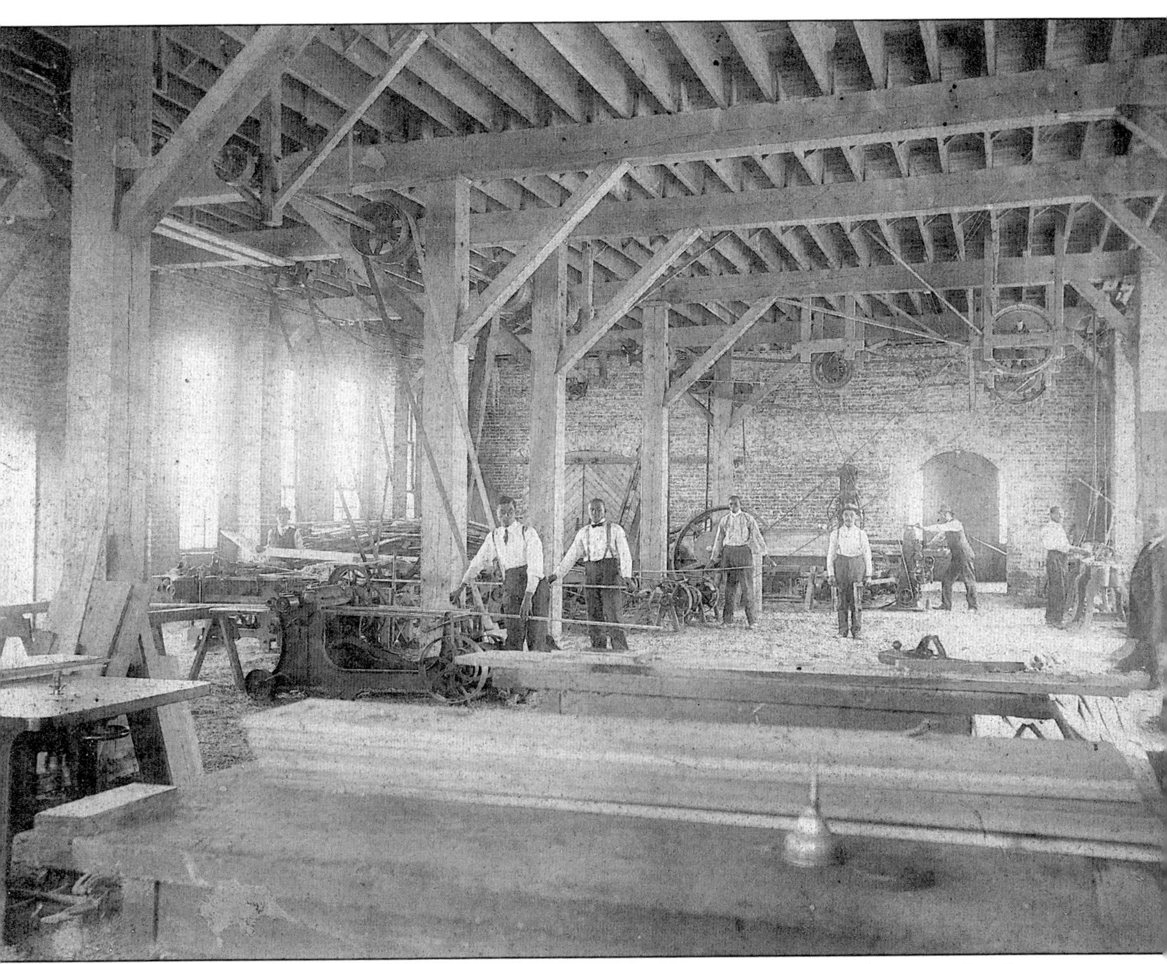

The sawmill was an essential facility on the campus in the college's early years. Students, with faculty assistance, processed thousands of board feet of lumber that were used in the construction of campus buildings, including Bradham Hall and Morrill Hall. In this image, President Thomas E. Miller is standing on the right.

GENERAL PROGRAM

Commencement Week, May 1-6, 1897,

Colored Normal, Industrial, Agricultural and Mechanical College, Orangeburg, S. C.

MONDAY, MAY 3, 12 M.

Prize Recitations,........Kindergartens....1, 2, 3 and 4 Grades,

PROGRAM.

Part I..........Kindergarten.

1 Music,..........Band.
2 Prayer.
3 Music,..........."The Sparrow and the Cat."..........
4 Recitation,........"Welcome Friends."........Flossie Glover.
5 Motion Recitation,.......... ..Little Housekeepers.
6 Recitation,............."Be Polite.".............William Jeffcoat.
7 Recitation,.........."Liberty,"........William Patton Palmer.
8 Music,..............."The Owl," (Motion Song.)
9 Recitation,....."The Lost Kitten,"....Julia May Williams.
10 Concert Recitation,............."Our Work."
11 Recitation,........"Our Banner,"......William Wigg Smalls
12 Recitation,.........."To My Dolly,".............Louisa Seward.
13 Music, Chorus,.........."The Choo Choo Car."
14 Recitation,..."The Farm Boys' Song,"..A Class of Boys.
15 Recitation,......"Catch the Sunshine,".....Mary Williams.
16 Recitation,..............."The Owl,"...............Felicia Palmer.
17 Recitation,........"The Warrior's Wreath,"..........Ida Cain.
18 Song and Fairy Drill..........Class of Little Girls.

PART SECOND.

1 Music,..........Band.
2 Concert Recitation,..."Angels of Buena Vista,".....Class.
3 Recitation,...."A Graduating Essay,"....Elnora Brunson.
4 Instrumental Solo,........"Brier Waltz".........May Stewart.
5 Recitation,..............."A Rhymlet"...............Hyce Zeigler.
6 Music, Chorus,.........."The Raindrops,"........First Grade.
7 Recitation,...."Going after the Cows,"....Serena Ancrum.
8 Recitation,..........."Tale of the Tramp,"........Leon Steele.
9 Music................."Sing Merrily,"..................Second Grade.
10 Recitation,........"Keeping His Word,"..........Rosa Judson.
11 Recitation..............."A Visit,"...............Rosa Lee Miley.
12 Music,............."Say Pretty Rover,"............Third Grade.
13 Recitation..........."If we Knew,"...........Maggie Stephens.
14 Recitation,..........."Aunt Tabitho,"..............May Stewart.
15 Music..........."Bright be each Face,"..........Fourth Grade.
16 Composite Declamation..........Class.
17 Decision of Judges.
18 Music,.........."Quaker Song,"..........Class
10 Benediction.

In the late nineteenth and early twentieth centuries, college commencements lasted more than a few hours. Commencement at most institutions continued several days and involved lengthy and extravagant exercises and religious observances that attracted large numbers of people. The first commencement at South Carolina State consumed almost an entire week in 1897 as students demonstrated their musical and literary skills.

Two

ROBERT S. WILKINSON 1911–1932

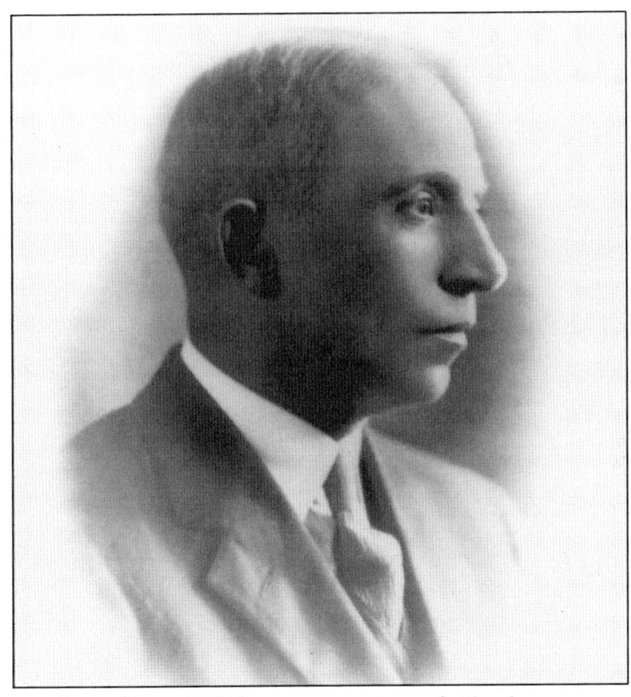

On March 29, 1911, Robert Shaw Wilkinson, a native of Charleston, was chosen by the Board of Trustees as the second president of the Colored Normal, Industrial, Agricultural, and Mechanical College of South Carolina. He had attended Shaw Memorial School and the Avery Institute, which had been founded on the premise of W.E.B. Dubois's concept of a "talented tenth," an elite group that would serve to lead Americans of African descent into the mainstream of participation in this nation. Appointed to the prestigious military academy at West Point in 1884, Wilkinson won first place in the competitive examination. He later withdrew from West Point for reasons pertaining to his health and entered Oberlin College in Ohio, where he graduated in 1891 as class valedictorian. He was invited to serve as an instructor at Kentucky State University and later was one of the first faculty members of the Colored Normal, Industrial, Agricultural and Mechanical College of South Carolina. He served as a professor of physics and head of the department of science for 16 years before becoming president. He also wrote the alma mater, which is still sung by the school.

When he eventually assumed the presidency of the school, after Thomas E. Miller was forced into early retirement for political reasons, Wilkinson was well equipped to build upon the foundation established by Miller. He successfully brought national attention to the college through his extraordinary abilities as an educator and administrator. A brilliant and tireless worker, Wilkinson traveled extensively throughout the state and country, advancing the goals of the college and of meaningful education for Americans of African descent. He possessed special expertise in public relations and provided leadership to other educational institutions and organizations, which resulted in his rise to national prominence. Some of his accomplishments include establishing a centralized business office to improve the management of fiscal affairs under the supervision of J.I. Washington; reorganizing the faculty into departments and unifying the faculty under one centralized office, the Dean of the Faculty; reorganizing and enlarging the Extension Program; developing a cooperative arrangement with Clemson College under the terms of the Smith-Lever Act that provided for the appointment of Negro agents to serve in the state; establishing four-year programs for home economics, commercial, mechanical, and teacher-training departments; organizing the State Teachers Summer School in 1914; receiving designation as the pre-medical college of South Carolina by the American Association of Medical Colleges; organizing a unit of the Reserve Officers Training Corps in 1919; making a cooperative arrangement with Claflin University in 1928;and adding 11 buildings to the campus (Lowman Hall—1917, White Hall—1920, Jacob W. Lowman Hospital—1920, Felton Training School and Teacherage—1924, Marion Birnie Wilkinson YWCA Hut—1925, Home Economics Practice Home—1928, Hodge Hall—1928, the creamery—1929, garage and poultry plant—1930, Dukes Gymnasium—1931, and the cafeteria 1932). He was married to Mrs. Marion Birnie Wilkinson. In 1938 Wilkinson Hall was built and named in his honor.

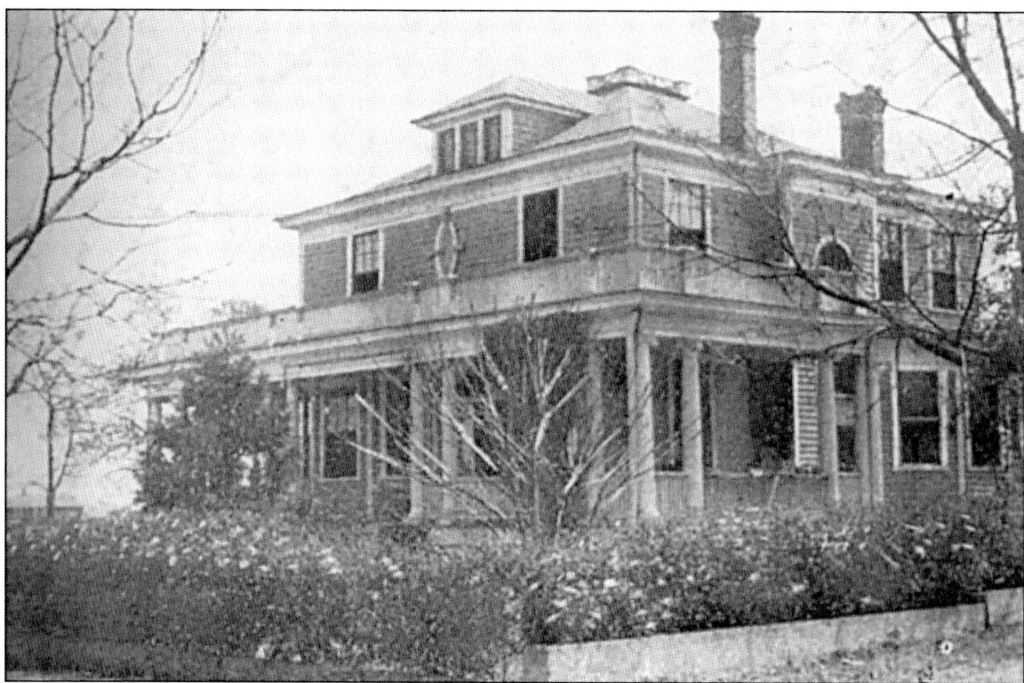

The President's Residence (1918), a two-and-a-half-story, commodious framed building, was built in 1905 and was known to several generations as the "White House." It was built next to Wilkinson Hall (1938) and was demolished to make way for the present J.I. Washington Dining Hall in 1962.

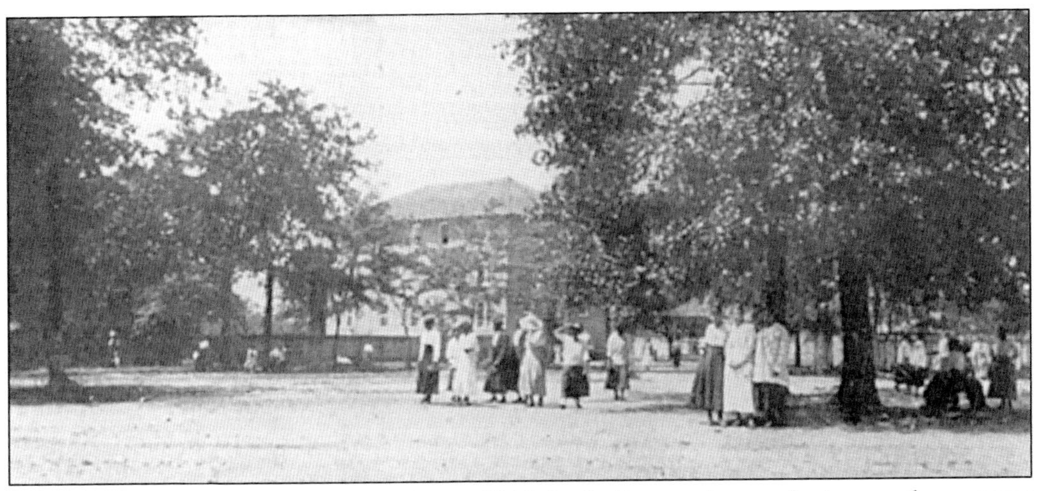

These images depict campus activities, *c.* 1918, including students relaxing on the campus and marching to dinner.

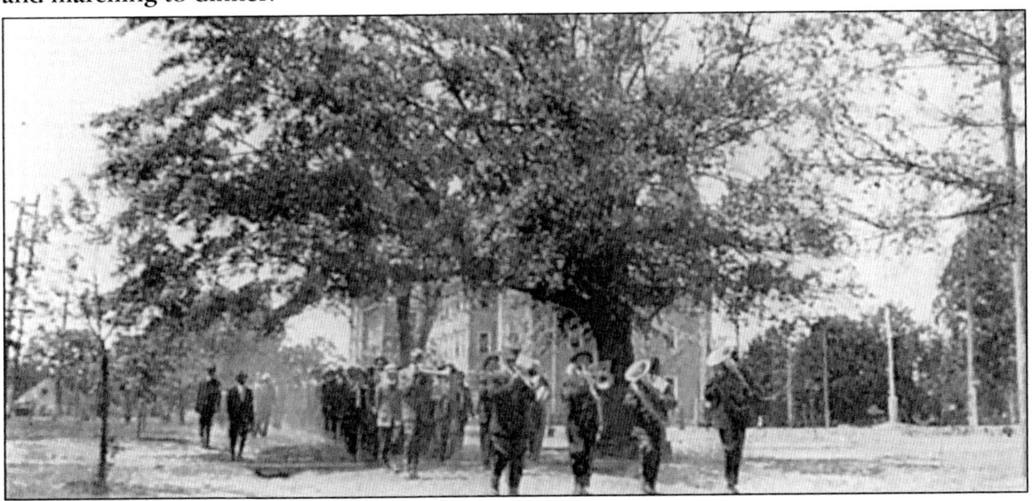

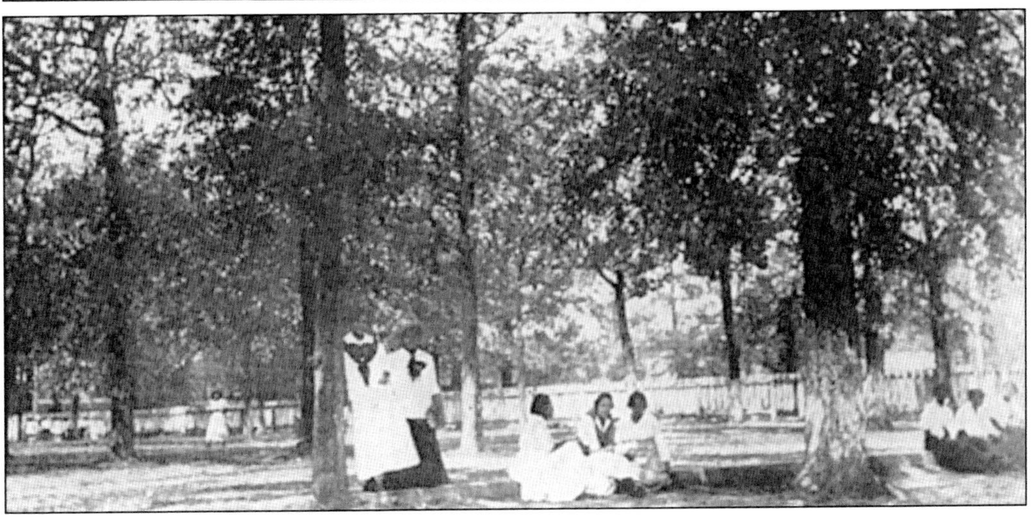

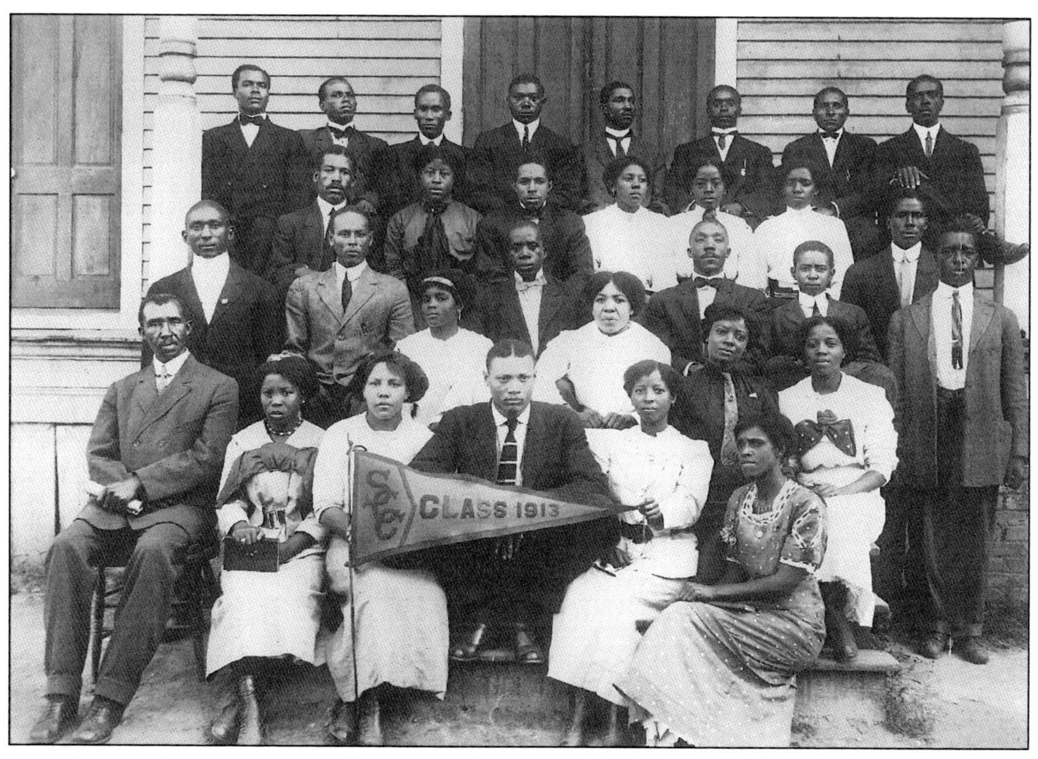

The Reverend Bollie Levister and the graduating class of 1913 sit on the steps of Morrill Hall on the brink of students receiving their degrees.

Alma Mater

Hail, Hail Carolina!
Loyal and true;
Thy sons are gathered
To Cheer for you,
And whether victor or
Vanquished we,
Still we'll be cheering for S. C. C.

Hail, Hail Carolina!
E'er for the right;
Like valiant soldiers
Serving with might
Beacons forever shall firmly stand,
Changeless and held by
God's right hand.

Hail, Hail Carolina!
Garnet and Blue;
Undaunted we shall
Defend you
With colors flying,
On land and sea
Still we'll be cheering
For S. C. C.

These are the words to the original college Alma Mater.

In 1925 President Wilkinson wrote the lyrics to the current alma mater. Mr. Ted Phillips, an alumnus, wrote the music in 1927. Reginald R. Thomasson, a longtime member of the music faculty, wrote "The Evening Song" in 1939 to remind students, staff, faculty, and alumni that eventide is a time to reflect on their loyalty and dedication to their school.

Alma Mater

Sing the praise of Alma Mater,
Let us rally to her call,
Lift the voices, send them ringing
Through the groves and classic halls

Hail, Hail! Dear Alma Mater,
Hail, Hail! Dear S. C. C.
We'll defend and honor,
Love and cherish thee.

We are loyal sons and daughters,
Proud to own the names we bear.
For the truth that thou has taught us,
Ready all to do and dare.

Hail, Hail! Dear Alma Mater,
Hail, Hail! Dear S. C. C.
We'll defend and honor,
Love and cherish thee.

EVENING SONG

When shadows steal across the way
Our love for thee turns night to day
A love that's true, as oceans' blue
And ever will abide.
We pledge ourselves with loyalty.
Dear Alma Mater still for thee;
We hear thy call; we give our all
To thee at even-tide.

—R. THOMASSON, '36

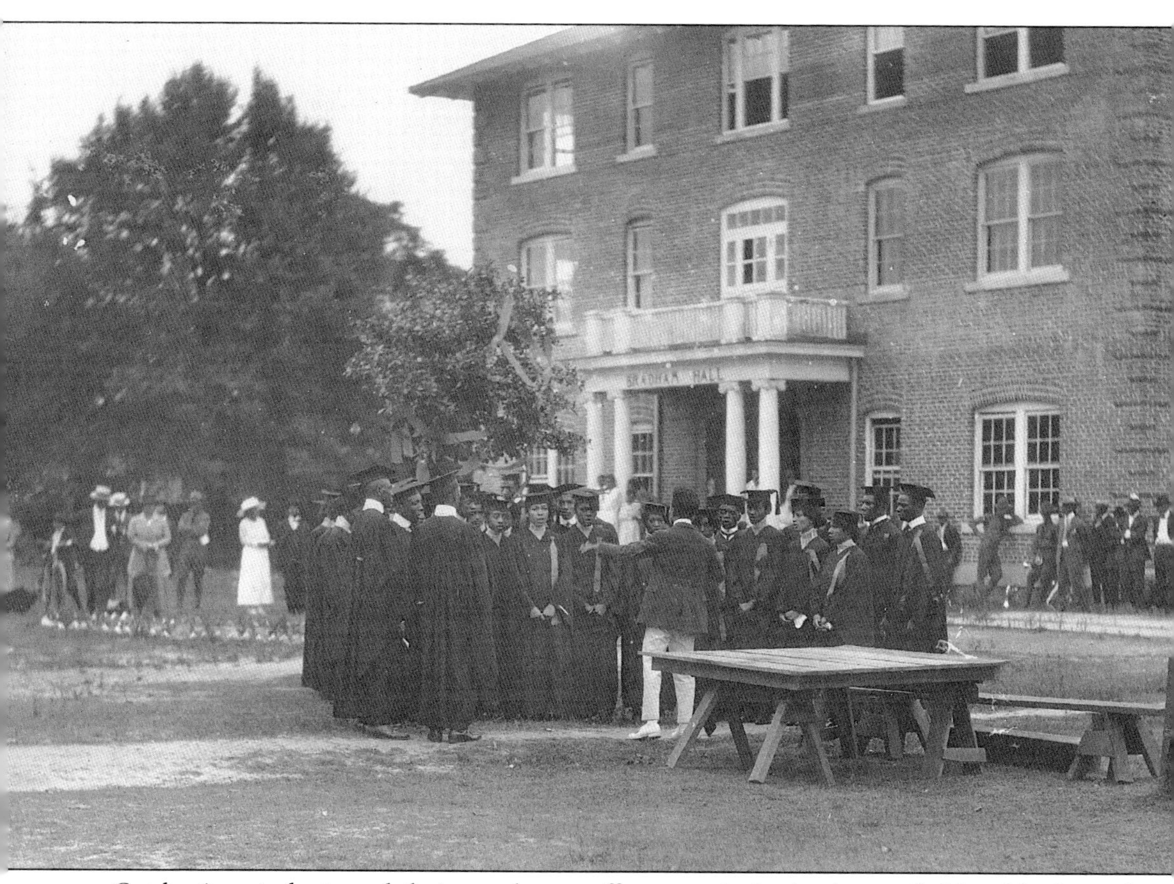

Graduating students and their conductor offer a musical selection as fashionably dressed well-wishers look on, *c.*1916–1917. The assembly is depicted before the newly rebuilt Bradham Hall, designed by Miller F. Whittaker, college architect and later president of the college from 1932 to 1949. The architectural character of Bradham and its twin structure, Manning Hall, was transformed in later years, deleting the classical details of its Greek-revival, ionic columns, and columnated porches. The first building was erected in 1896, destroyed by fire in 1909, rebuilt in 1910, and destroyed by fire again in 1916. It was named for the late Mayor D.J. Bradham of Clarendon, South Carolina, a member of the first board of trustees. President Miller and his entire family occupied the front end of the first floor on the boys' side of the dormitory. It also housed the students' dining hall, college chapel, classrooms, president's office, and the office of the college accountant.

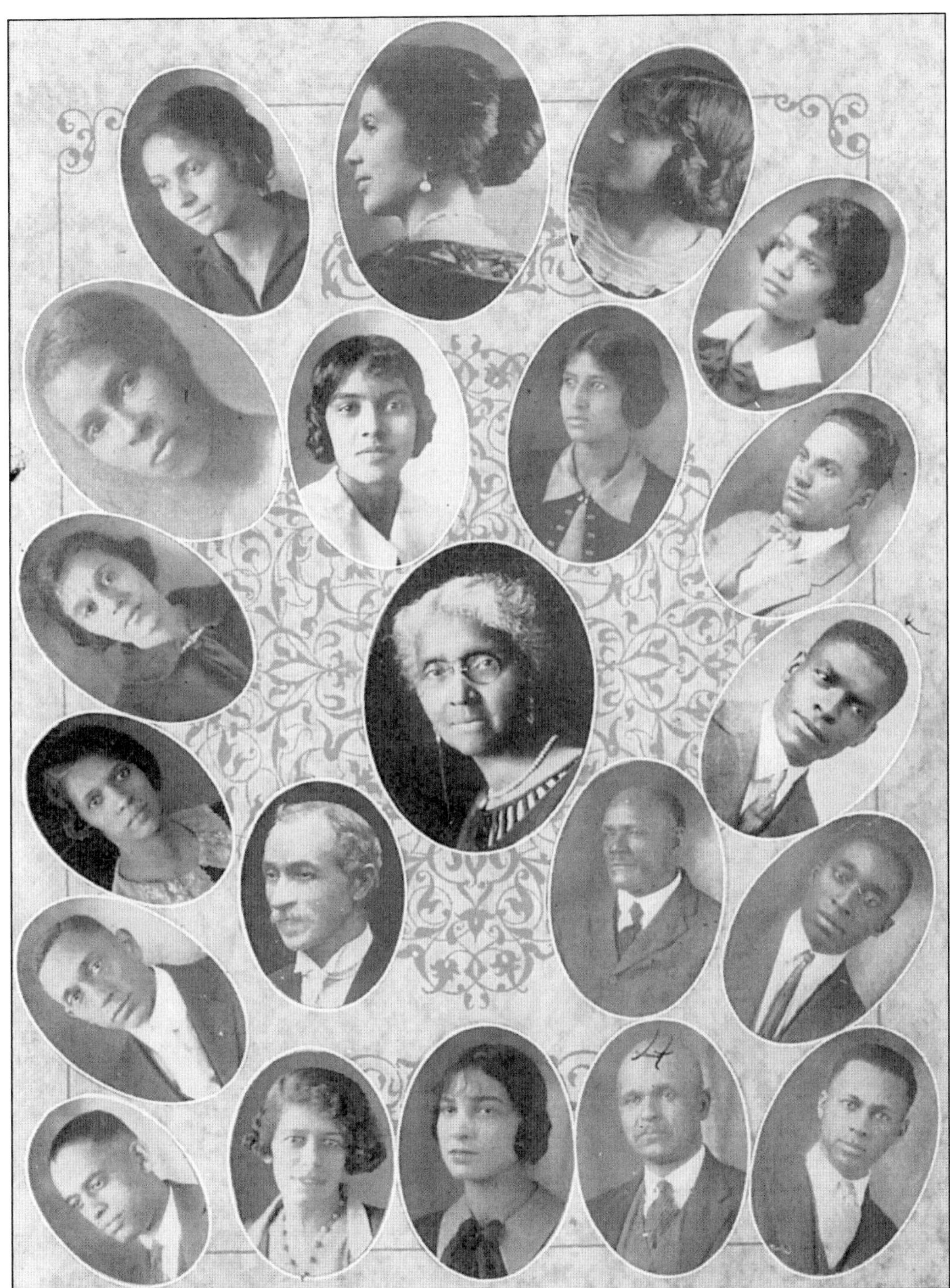

Dr. Benjamin E. Mays (pictured directly right of center), an Epworth, South Carolina native, graduated as class valedictorian from the high school department of the college in 1916. He graduated from Bates College in 1920 and taught at The Colored Normal, Industrial, Agricultural and Mechanical College of South Carolina from 1925 to 1926 as an instructor of English. He was also the alumni association president in 1925.

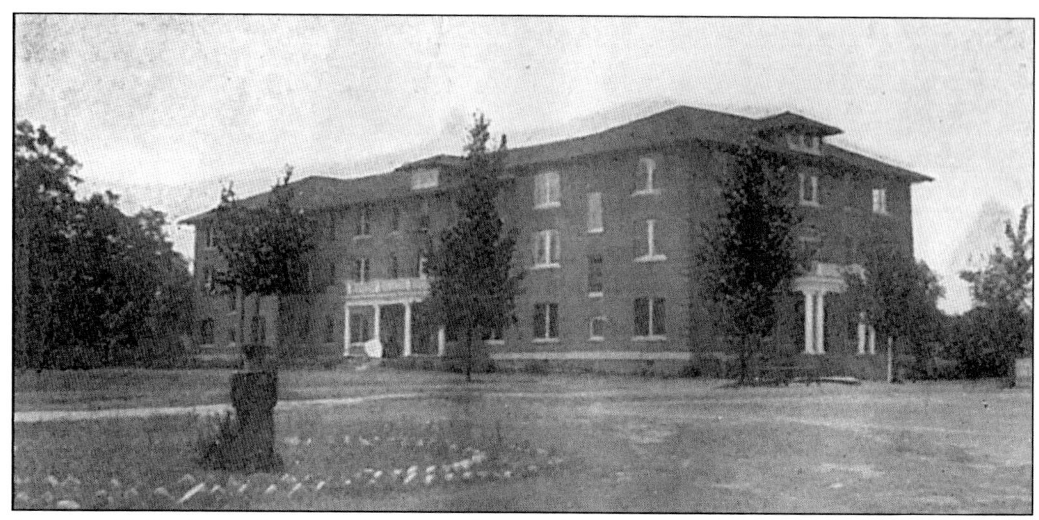

Lowman Hall, shown here *c.* 1921, was designed by Miller F. Whittaker, college architect, who later became president of the college. Formerly a dormitory for male students and male faculty members, Lowman Hall, built in 1917, was named for William R. Lowman, a former board member and trustee of the college. It later became a male students dormitory only. Lowman Hall is the oldest existing building in its original design on the campus and is listed in the National Register of Historic Places.

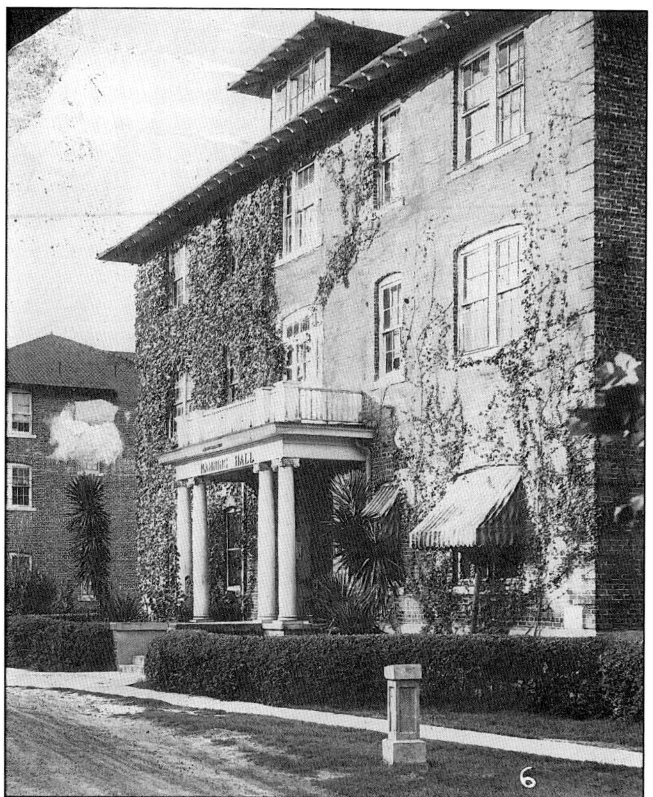

This photograph documents the original appearance of Manning Hall, a three-story dormitory built in 1916 and designed by Miller F. Whittaker, former instructor in architecture and later president of the college. It presently houses first-year female students. Its floor plan is quite similar to that of the third version of Bradham Hall, located opposite this building. At present, both are used as dormitories for young women who reside on campus at South Carolina State University; however, the historic character and integrity of this structure and similar Bradham Hall have been greatly altered due to their historical restoration. Manning Hall was renovated in 1981.

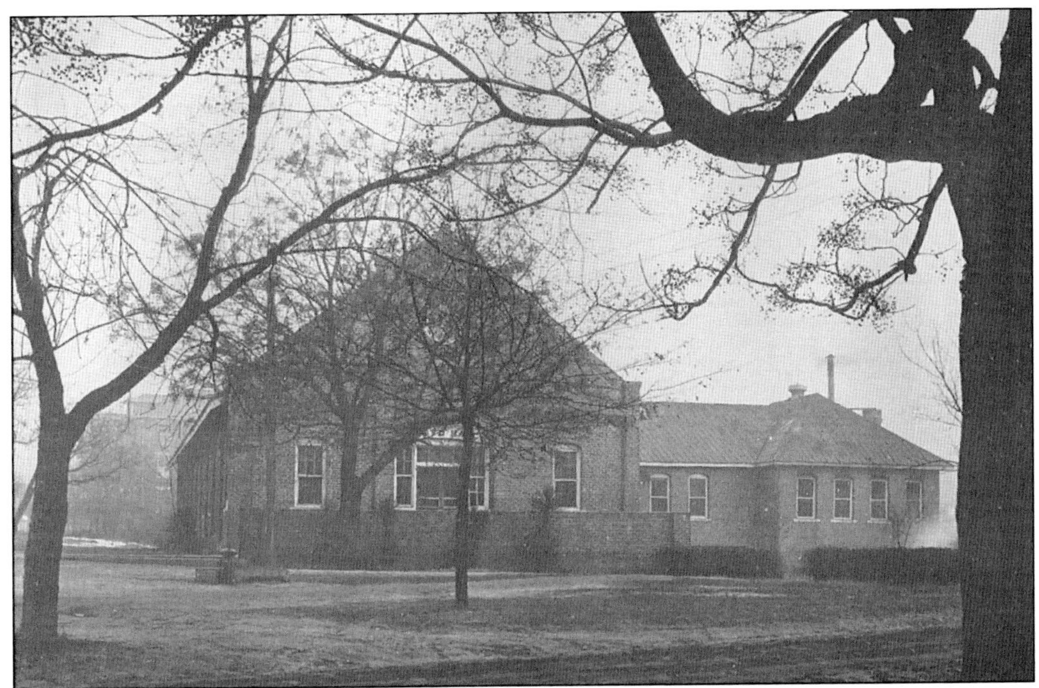

Floyd Hall, shown here *c.* 1925, was built in 1910. It housed a baking department and served as the dining hall. The original dining hall, which was connected to Bradham Hall, was destroyed in the Bradham Hall fire in 1909. Floyd Dining Hall and Kitchen was a serving hall with rooms attached and seating accommodations for students.

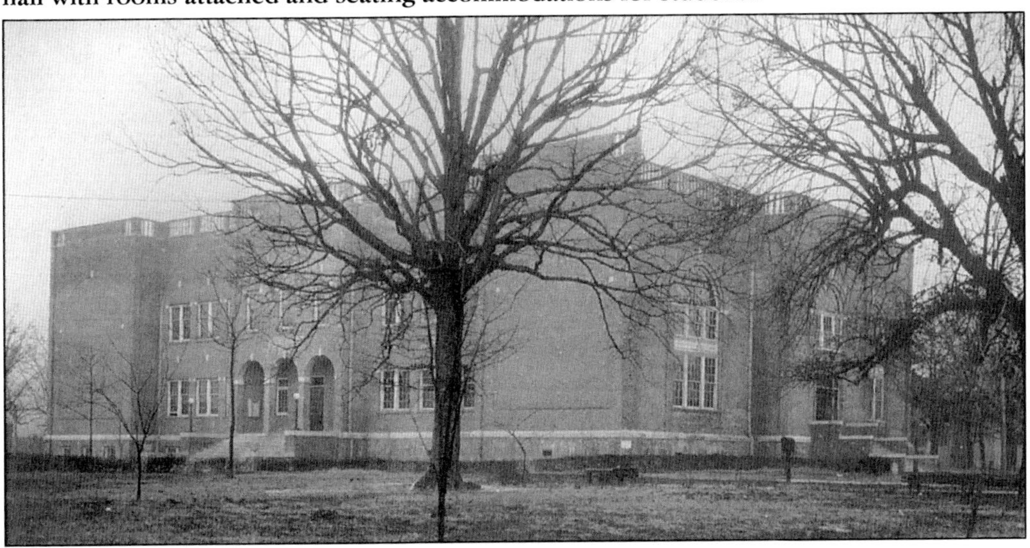

White Hall, shown here *c.* 1925, was constructed with student labor in 1920 as the main academic building in the location where Morrill Hall burned in 1916. White Hall was named for the late C.B. White of Chester, a former board of trustees member. The Annual Easter Service, with Dr. Benjamin E. Mays as speaker, was held in the auditorium for 27 years, as well as statewide educational and cultural events. It was considered "a new academic building" with 12 well-equipped classrooms and an auditorium capacity for about 1,000 people. The parking lot adjacent to Nance Hall presently occupies this space.

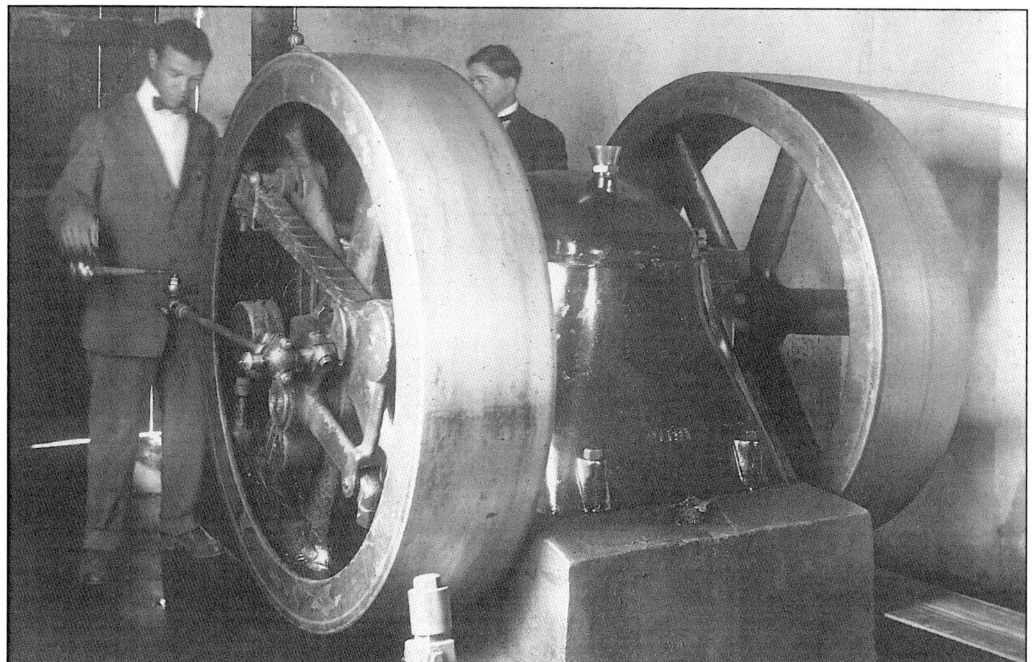

The Men's Trade Building or Industrial Hall, shown here *c.* 1916, was constructed in 1902. Here, two male students are shown in what may be an image of the new power plant. According to Dean Nelson C. Nix's history of the college, from 1914 to 1915, a machine shop and power plant with two 125 horsepower boilers were completed and equipped. The device shown in this image appears to be some form of electrical generator or other equipment associated with the power plant of the school.

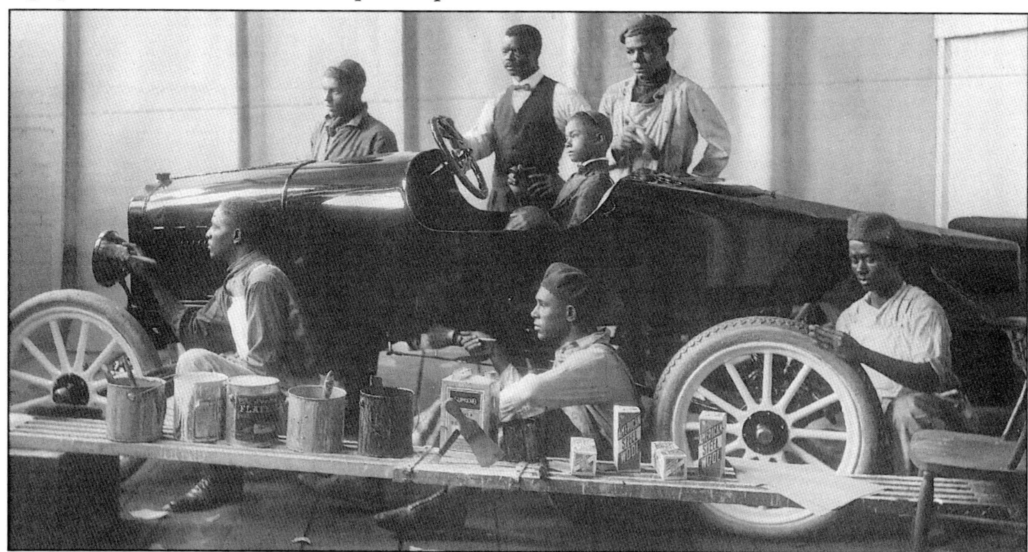

As part of the Mechanical Arts and Industries curriculum established as the result of the land-grant mission of the institution, trade skills such as automotive repair were part of the instructional program offered at the college. Mr. Elliott Jamison, instructor of painting, and students are shown in a 1924 photo in the automotive workshop in the mechanical arts department.

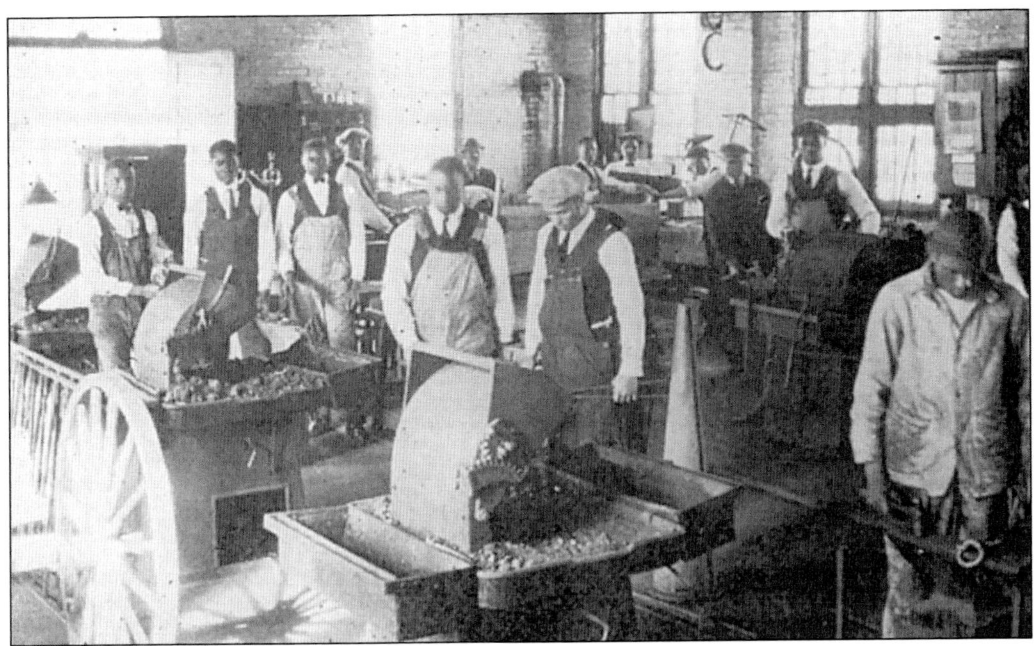

Students in a blacksmithing class were taught practical, general shop work techniques with emphasis as a practicing blacksmith and helper. Mr. Willie W. Williams was the instructor. The class was taught in Industrial Hall, which was also known as the Men's Trade Building. Mr. Williams was originally hired at the college in 1897 in the iron works department.

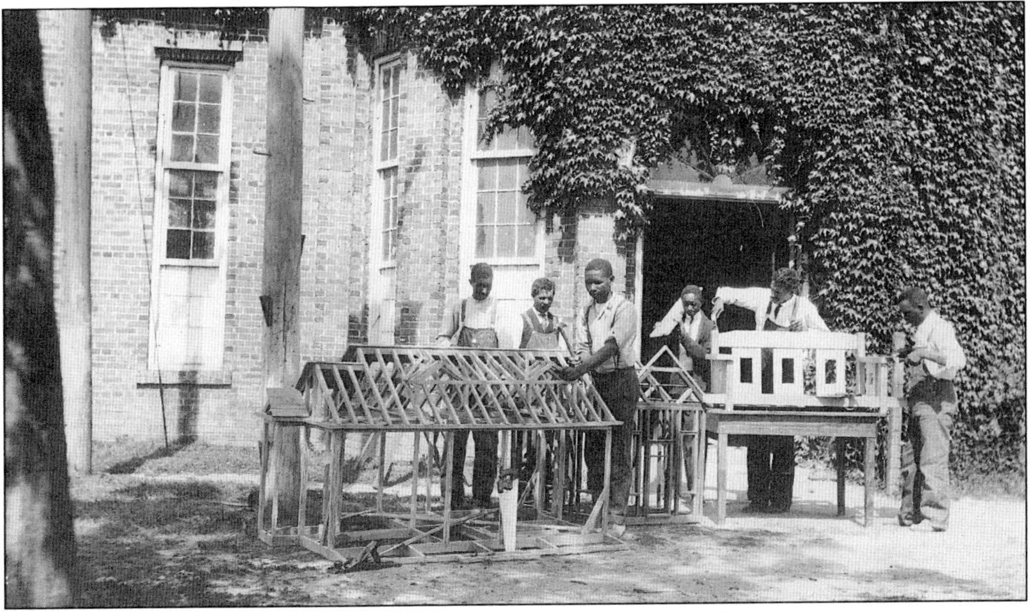

The 1925 photo of Industrial Hall shows students studying building construction. The students often gained invaluable practical experience while constructing buildings that would serve the campus. Indeed, Industrial Hall, the early mechanical industries building, shown covered with ivy in this photograph, had been erected using student labor. For this class in construction, the college was fortunate to have a certified architect, Dr. Miller F. Whittaker, who designed and oversaw the erection of many campus structures.

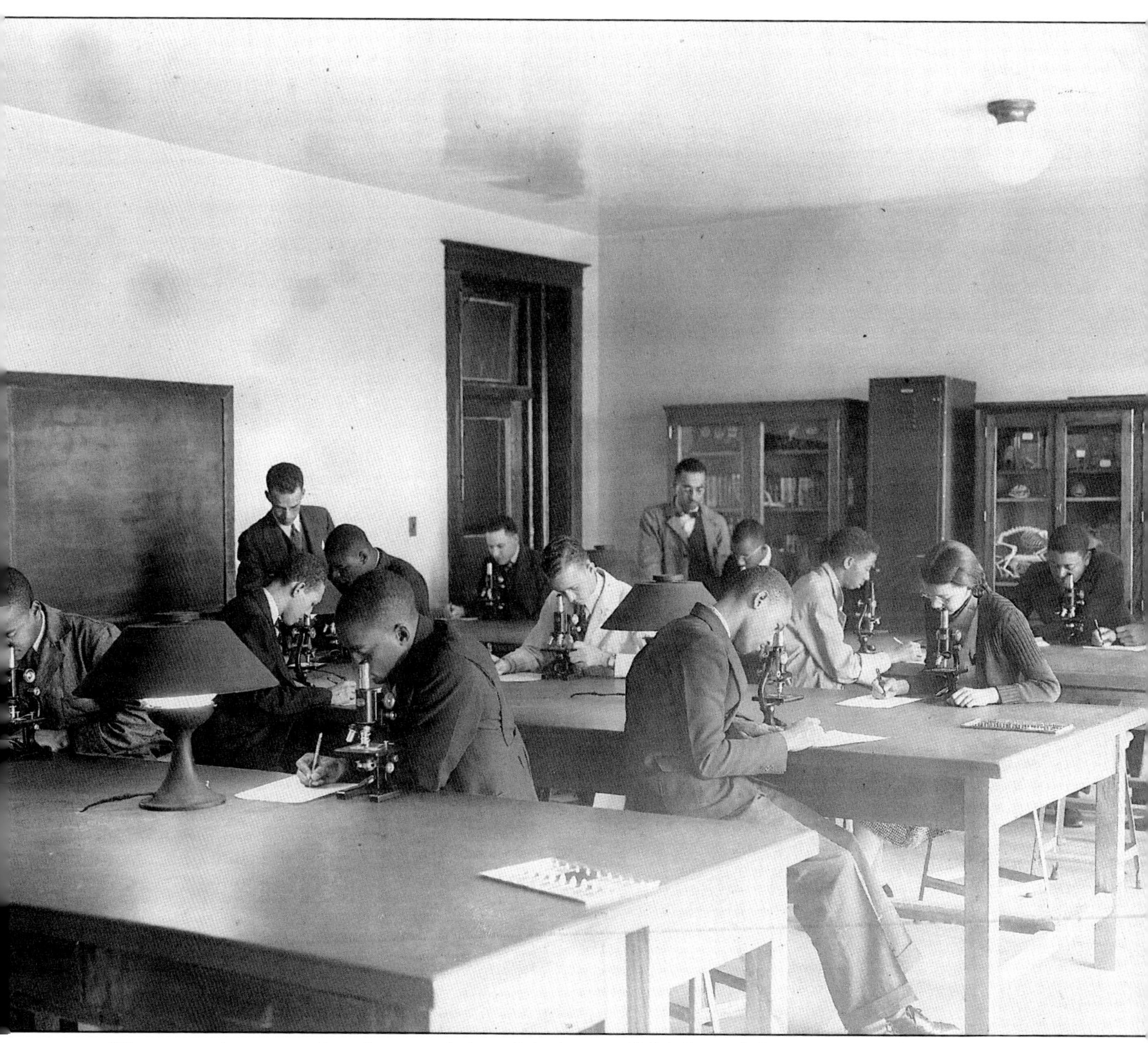

These students are hard at work in a Hodge Hall biology laboratory in the 1930s. They are working under the supervision of highly respected biologist James H. Birnie, who is standing to the left. Standing near the center in the background is T.J. Crawford, who spent nearly 70 years as a student, faculty member, and administrator at South Carolina State University

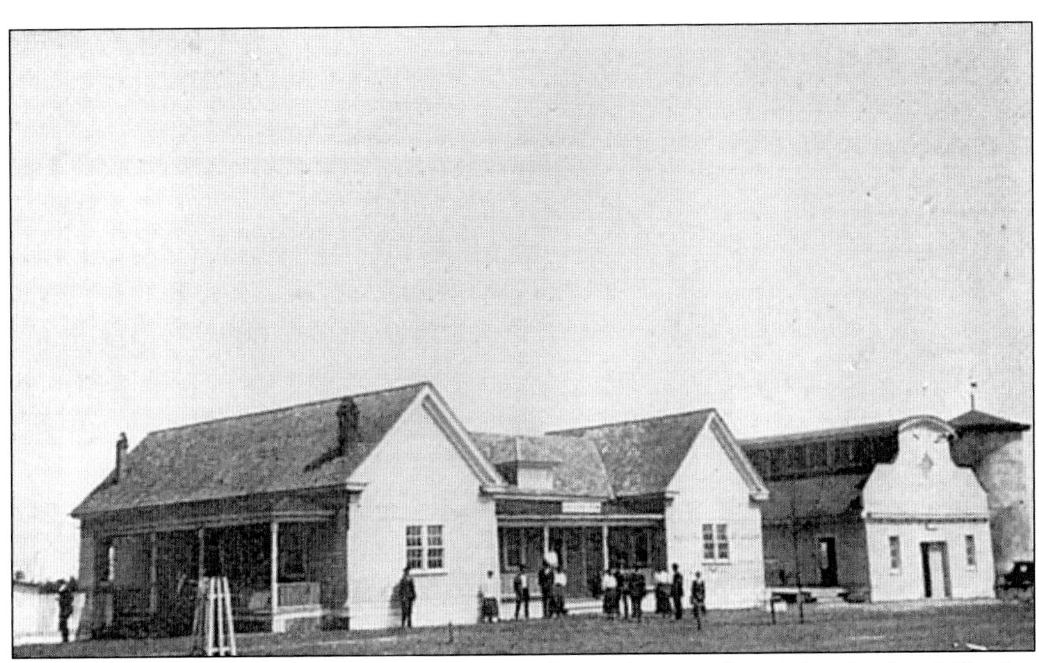

The emphasis on agriculture was to provide the students with training in the skills that would prepare them to go back to their communities and become actual demonstrators of what had been learned in school. The dairy buildings and the poultry yards, *c.* 1918, were located on the college farm and housed the livestock and poultry that provided the practical laboratory experiences for students taking courses in these disciplines. County and state fairs, as well as large poultry farms in the immediate vicinity of the college were used for poultry judging experiences.

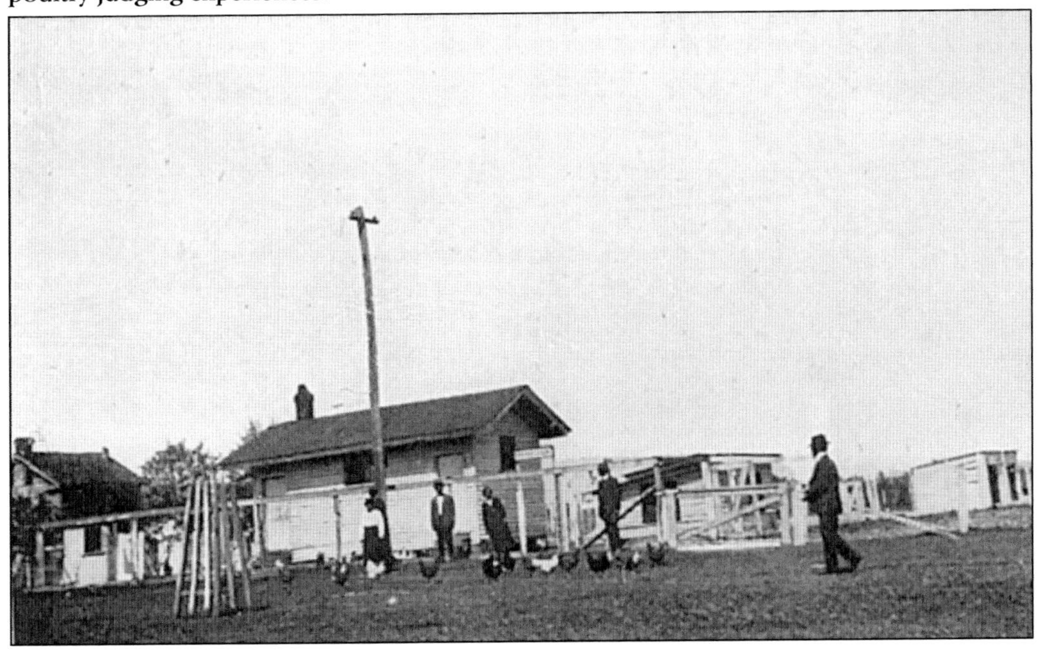

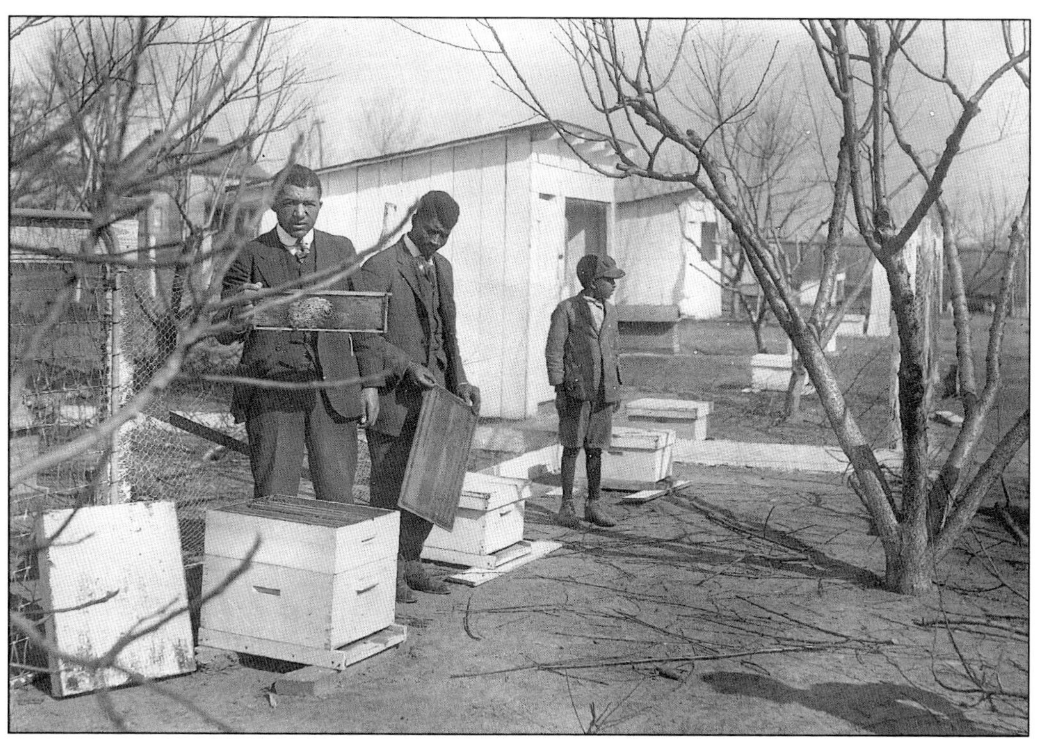

The beekeeping area on the college farm, shown here *c*. 1919 or 1920, served as a laboratory for the course in beekeeping taught at the college. Students studied the biology of the honeybee and received firsthand, practical experience. In the forefront, Mr. Benjamin F. Hubert, director and professor of the agricultural department, exhibits his hive of bees.

ANNUAL SUMMER SESSION

State Agricultural and Mechanical College

ORANGEBURG, S. C.

Courses in Elementary, High School, College, Religious Education and Vocational Subjects. Agriculture, Home Economics Trades, Theory and Practice of Athletic Coaching.

Thirty Days Session

BEGINNING JUNE 15 ENDING JULY 18

For Information and Bulletin address
R. S. WILKINSON, President

Shown here is a 1925 advertisement for the college's summer school session, highlighting offerings in education, vocational skills, agriculture, home economics, trades, and athletic coaching.

First Annual Meeting South Carolina

NEGRO BUSINESS LEAGUE

STATE AGRICULTURAL & MECHANICAL COLLEGE

ORANGEBURG, JULY 10, 1928

MORNING SESSION 10:30, College Auditorium
Mr. I. S. Leevy, Vice President, Columbia, Presiding

MUSIC—

INVOCATION—

REPORT OF THE SECRETARY—
Prof. J. E. Blanton, Denmark

MUSIC—

ANNUAL ADDRESS—
President R. S. Wilkinson

DISCUSSIONS—

1. Why so many Negro Business Failures?
   Mr. J. M. Maxwell, Orangeburg (10 Minutes)
   Mr. Fred Bacote, Timmonsville (10 Minutes)
2. What Business Occupations Offer Widest Opportunities to our Group?
   Mr. J. H. Rodolph, Charleston (10 Minutes)
   Mr. S. E. Clemmons, Charleston (10 Minutes)
   Fifteen minutes of General Discussion of each Topic.

RECESS—Luncheon in the College Dining Hall will be announced.

AFTERNOON SESSION—3:00, College Auditorium
Mr. W. H. Harvey, Columbia, Presiding

MUSIC—

TEN MINUTE

DISCOURSES—

1. The Present Outlook for Negro Business Men and Women.
   President D. H. Sims, Allen University, Columbia
2. The Present Status of Commercial Training in Negro Schools.
   Prof. J. Irwin Washington, Director of Commerce, State A. & M. College, Orangeburg.
3. How May a Deeper Interest in the State Business League be Aroused?
   Mr. J. H. Goode, Columbia.

ADDRESS—By a Representative of the National Business League.

BUSINESS SESSION

ELECTION OF OFFICERS

APPOINTMENT OF COMMITTEES

ADJOURNMENT

OFFICERS

R. S. Wilkinson, Orangeburg, President
I. S. Leevy, Columbia, Vice President
J. E. Blanton, Denmark, Corresponding Secretary
P. M. Bowling, Columbia, Recording Secretary
J. J. Starks, Sumter, Treasurer

The first annual meeting of the Negro Business League of South Carolina was held in 1928. The program depicts the agenda, which contains topics that are still being discussed more than seven decades later. President Wilkinson served as president for this group.

THE OMEGA PSI PHI FRATERNITY

EPSILON OMEGA CHAPTER

PRESENTS

JUNE AND HIS ROYAL COLLEGIANS

STATE COLLEGE AUDITORIUM

February 11, 1929 **Eight P. M.**

June and His Collegians on the Stage

I. Scarf Dance—Fox Trot....................................C. C. Chaminade
  2. Just a Memory—Fox Trot ....R. Henderson
II. Saxophone Solo—Ripples .. ..King
  (Mr. Herbert Reeder)
III. Sally Of My Dreams—Fox Trot...........................W. Kernel
  2. Mighty Lak a Rose—Waltz....................Nevin and McKee
IV. Girls Quartette in Two Selections—Selected
  (Misses Frasier, Campbell, Nelson and Williams)
V. Waters of Minnetonka—Fox Trot ....T. Tieurance
  2. Blue Danube—Waltz.................... ....G. F. Briegel
VI. Cornet Solo—Marguerite (Polka)...... .... C. W. Smith
  (Mr. Harold June)
VII. Jo-Anne—Fox Trot ....Silver, Ward, Pinkard
  2. I'll Get By—Fox Trot..... ....Tunk and Ahlert
VIII. Piano Solo—Selected
  (Mr. Cornelius Jenkins)
IX. Roses of Picardy—Fox Trot ....Hadyn Wood
  2. Chlo-e--Fox Trot................ ....Kahn and Monet
  3. When Day Is Done—Fox Trot..................Robert Katscher

June and His Collegians in the Ball Room

1. Constantinople
2. Pickin' Cotton
3. Where the Shy Little Violets Grow
4. Milenberg Joys
5. Me and the Man in the Moon
6. I Ain't Got Nobody
7. Tain't So, Honey, Tain't So
8. East St. Louis Toodle-o
9. I Must Have That Man
10. My Weakness

Final——Goodnight

PERSONS OF THE ORCHESTRA

Herbert Reeder..........................1st E Flat Saxophone
Paul Stewart ....B Flat Tenor Saxophone
John Blanche........ ....2nd E Flat Saxophone
Harold H. June ....1st Trumpet
Ernest Shaw......................... ....2nd Trumpet
Henry Butler ....Trombone
John Jones.............. ....Tuba
Cornelius Jenkins ....Piano
Morris McDuffie .. ..Banjo
Postell Brown..Drums
Richard Kennard...Entertainer
Harold H. June......... ....Leader

Richard (Dick) Kennard-directing

W. F. Cannon, Printer, Orangeburg, S. C.

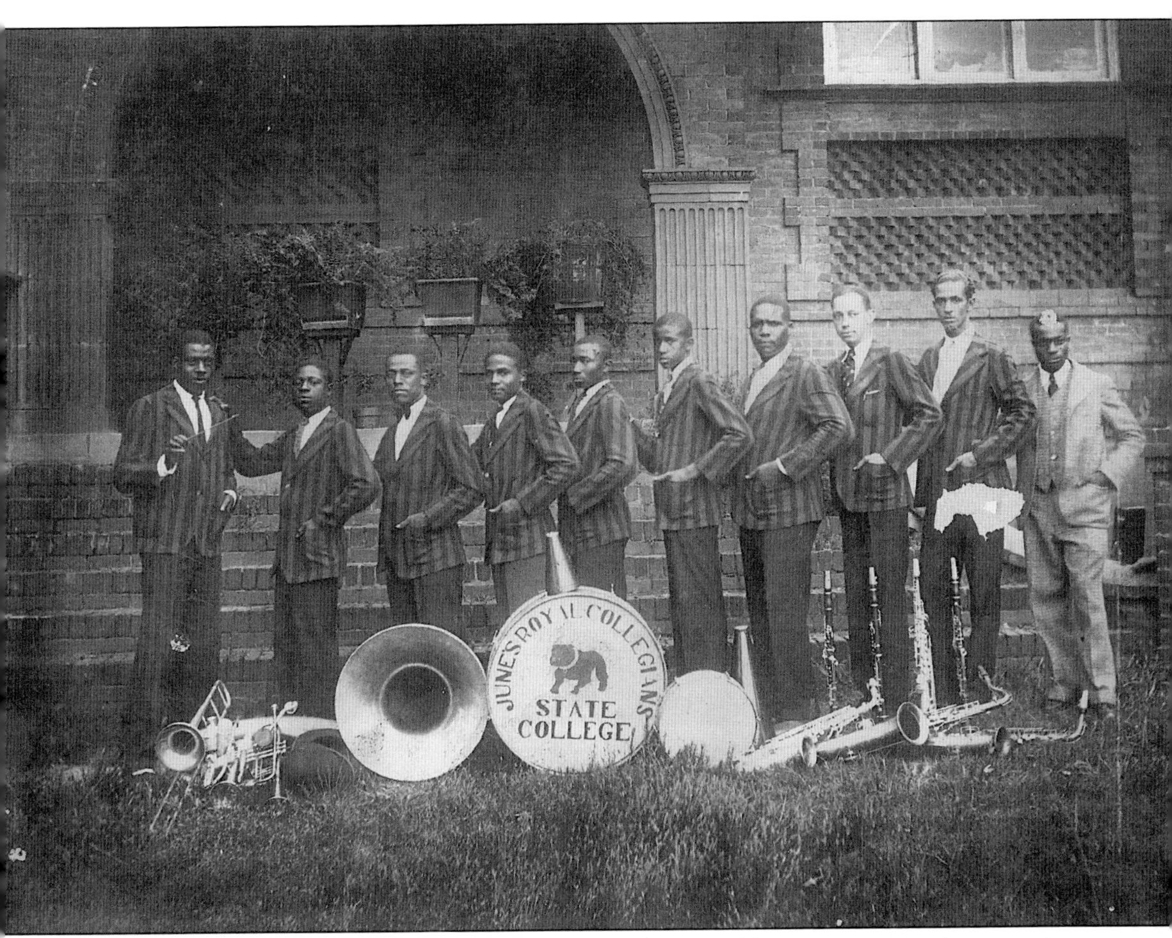

June and the Royal Collegians, shown above in 1930 photo and in a program on the opposite page, were students at the college who performed the "music of the day" at many college events and the surrounding areas. They were known for the garnet- and blue-striped jackets they wore to performances. June, an outstanding catcher on the baseball team, was very popular and would sit in his window in Lowman Hall every night at 10:00 p.m. to play "Taps." Members are, from left to right, Harold H. June, unidentified, John Blanche, Herbert Reeder, unidentified, Paul Stewart, unidentified, Henry Butler, Richard Kennard, and unidentified. The opposite image depicts a program from a June and His Royal Collegians performance presented by the Epsilon Omega Chapter of Omega Psi Phi Fraternity in 1929.

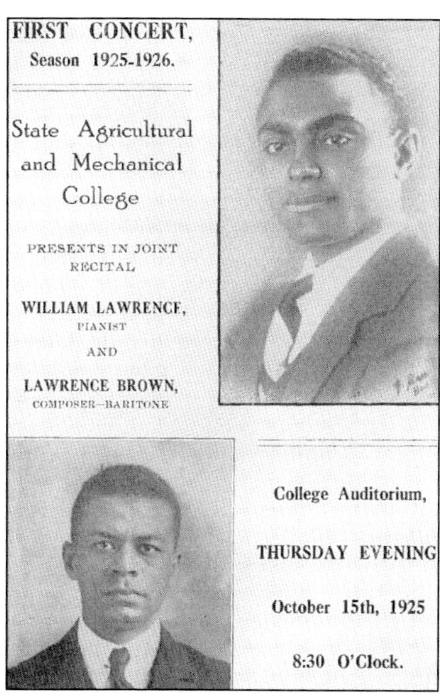
FIRST CONCERT,
Season 1925-1926.

State Agricultural
and Mechanical
College

PRESENTS IN JOINT
RECITAL

WILLIAM LAWRENCE,
PIANIST

AND

LAWRENCE BROWN,
COMPOSER—BARITONE

College Auditorium,

THURSDAY EVENING

October 15th, 1925

8:30 O'Clock.

The first musical concert of the 1925–1926 academic year presented students an evening of music with William Lawrence on piano and Lawrence Brown, composer, on the baritone in the White Hall auditorium.

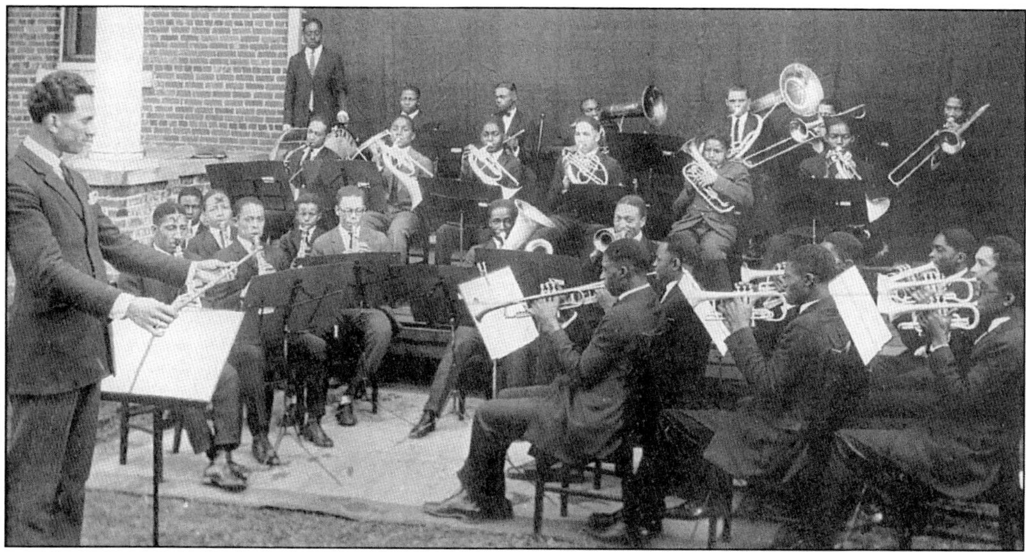

The Band and Orchestra were responsible for the music at the college. The band was composed of 27 men under the direction of Frederic Burgard Payton, and provided proper training for students who showed any talent. It appeared in concert bimonthly on Sunday afternoons and for other formations during the week. The orchestra was composed of 12 men, directed by Frederick Franciuel Mayson, and played for all socials, rhetoricals, Sunday chapel services, and other public exercises. The roster included on clarinet Benjamin Sanders, John Blanch, Walter Barno, Paul Stewart, Preston Stewart, and Rendall Harper; cornet, Harold June, Thomas Dansby, Frederick F. Mayson, James Morrison, Ernest Shaw, George Cohn, Theodore DeLarge, and Pinkney Davis; horn, Timothy Stewart, Glenwood Perry, Vincent Moses, and William Harper; euphonium, Michael Jackson; baritone, Seymore Howard; trombone, Isaac White and Earle Davis; bass, Francis Brown and Samual Foxworth; drum, Isaac Fraiser, Herman Livingston, and Theodore Parler; and piano, Walter Hunter.

This football souvenir programme of 1928 highlights the season game between A&T College of North Carolina and State College. The score was State 32, A&T 27.

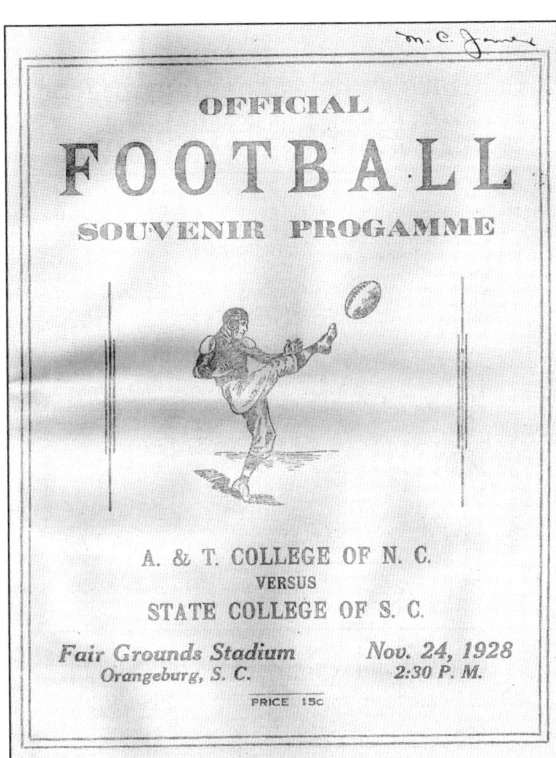

This photograph dates to the period prior to the 1920s, showing the early Bulldog spirit at South Carolina State College. The absence of shoulder pads and style of the helmets suggest that this early team photograph was taken about 1916 or 1917. By 1919, athletic programs were available for women as well as men, and the interest in physical activity and sports has always been an important part of the school's tradition. The college yearbook, *The Bulldog*, 1975 (p. 13), suggests that SCSC was the originator of women's basketball in the Southeast, under the direction of Coach Frank M. Staley.

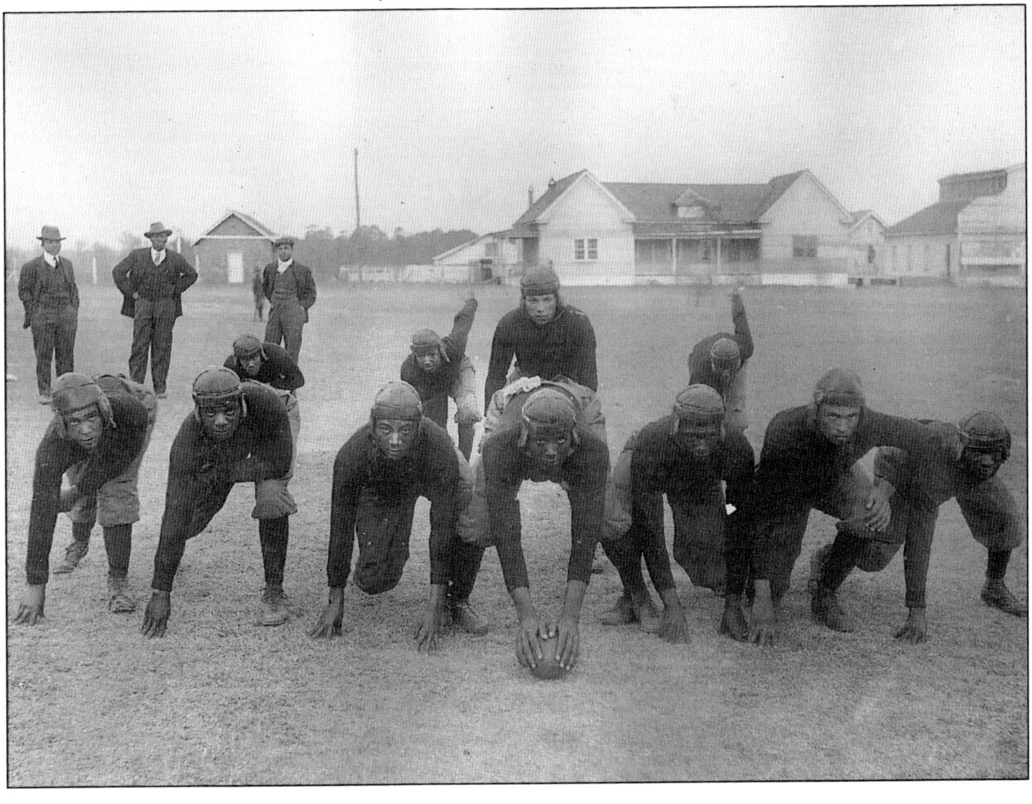

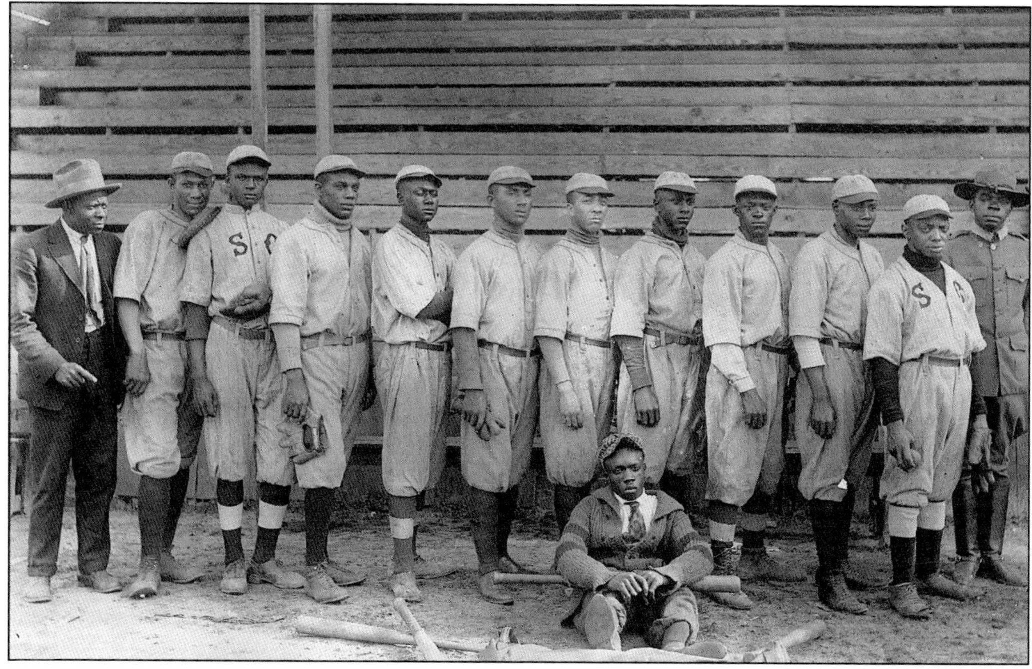

The two primary athletic activities offered at SCSC were baseball and football in the period before 1925. This image documents the 1917 baseball team during the era just prior to World War I with Coach W.C. Lewis exhorting his students to discipline and determination.

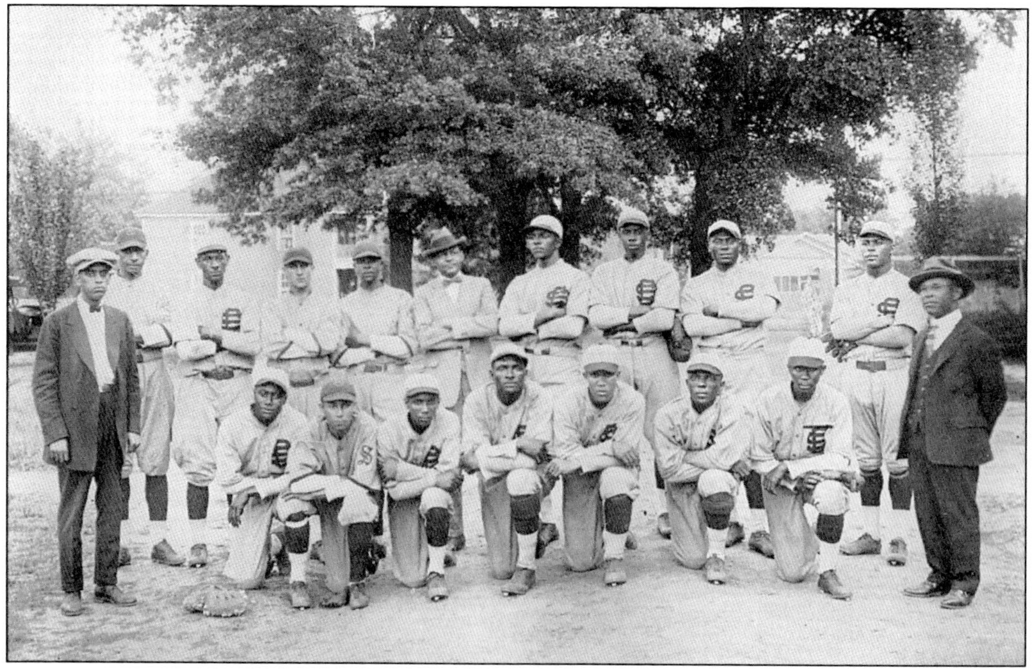

The varsity baseball team is shown in a 1925 photo. The college always had a good baseball team, giving competition to any of the Southeastern Nines. Having one of the best fields in the South to add to the convenience of the players, she was always a terror at home. Coaches were Frederick M. Sheffield and Frank M. Staley.

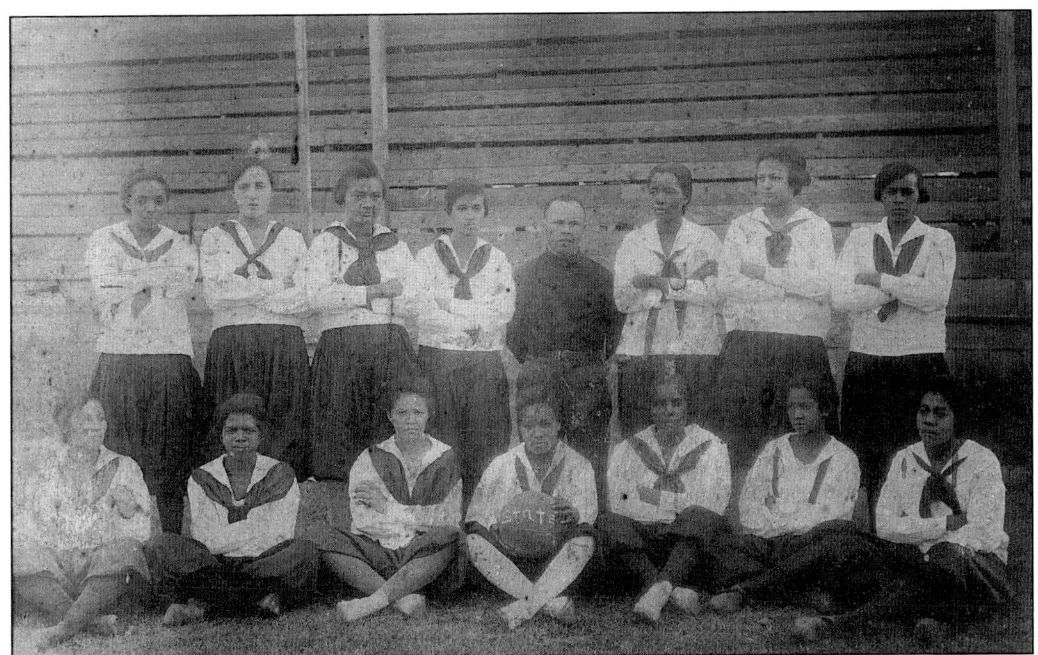

The girls' basketball teams of 1919 and 1921 boasted a record in basketball which no other school in the Southeast can share. Under the direction of Coach Frank M. Staley, the originator of girls' basketball, beginning in 1919, the college passed through a period of eight years with only three defeats. For five years, the team played without a defeat. The team never lost a game until they invaded Alabama and met Tuskegee. In 1922, the Sextette succeeded in winning a silver loving cup, given by Mrs. Marion B. Wilkinson, being the first team to win the championship for three consecutive years. In 1924, the squad lost only one game to Paine College of Augusta, Georgia, downing every other foe who they met. In 1925, the team opened the gates once more with a whirlwind, losing only one time before Paine College in Augusta. The coaches in 1925 were Isabelle M. Hurlong and ? Belton.

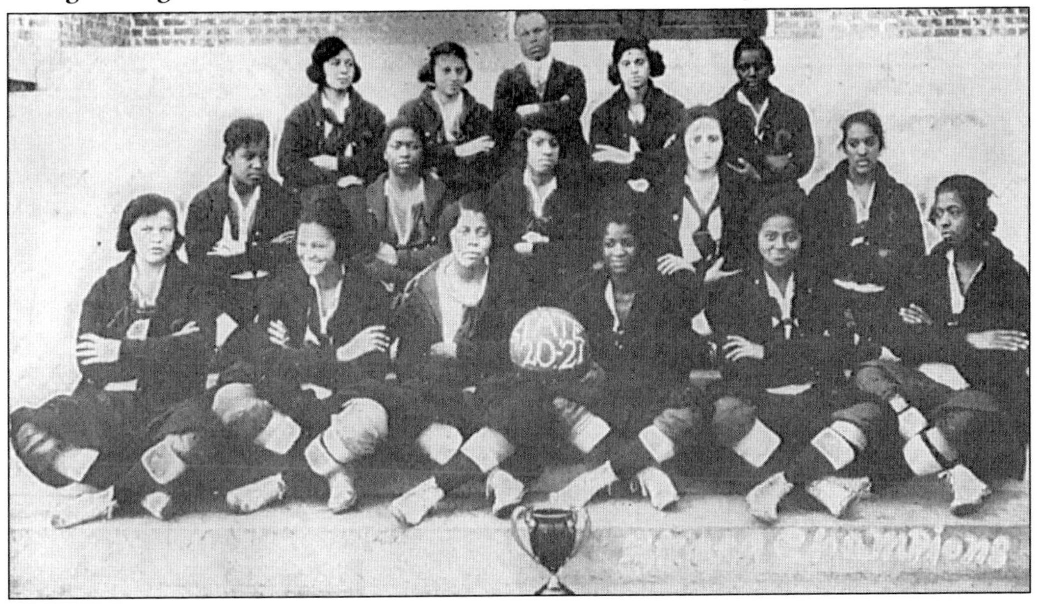

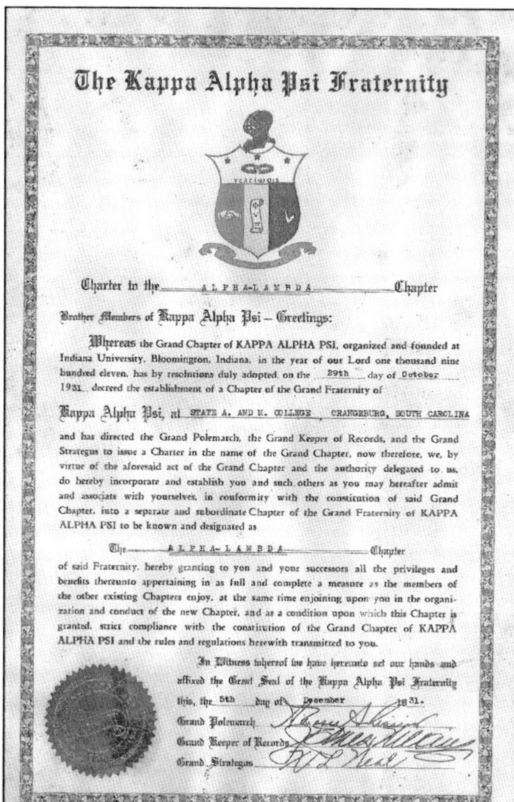

The Kappa Alpha Psi Fraternity

Charter to the ALPHA-LAMBDA Chapter

Brother Members of Kappa Alpha Psi – Greetings:

Whereas the Grand Chapter of KAPPA ALPHA PSI, organized and founded at Indiana University, Bloomington, Indiana, in the year of our Lord one thousand nine hundred eleven, has by resolutions duly adopted, on the 29th day of October 1931 decreed the establishment of a Chapter of the Grand Fraternity of

Kappa Alpha Psi, at STATE A. AND M. COLLEGE, ORANGEBURG, SOUTH CAROLINA

and has directed the Grand Polemarch, the Grand Keeper of Records, and the Grand Strategus to issue a Charter in the name of the Grand Chapter, now therefore, we, by virtue of the aforesaid act of the Grand Chapter and the authority delegated to us, do hereby incorporate and establish you and such others as you may hereafter admit and associate with yourselves, in conformity with the constitution of said Grand Chapter, into a separate and subordinate Chapter of the Grand Fraternity of KAPPA ALPHA PSI to be known and designated as

The ALPHA-LAMBDA Chapter

of said Fraternity, hereby granting to you and your successors all the privileges and benefits thereunto appertaining in as full and complete a measure as the members of the other existing Chapters enjoy, at the same time enjoining upon you in the organization and conduct of the new Chapter, and as a condition upon which this Chapter is granted, strict compliance with the constitution of the Grand Chapter of KAPPA ALPHA PSI and the rules and regulations herewith transmitted to you.

In Witness whereof we have hereunto set our hands and affixed the Great Seal of the Kappa Alpha Psi Fraternity this, the 5th day of December 1931.

Grand Polemarch

Grand Keeper of Records

Grand Strategus

Pictured here is the 1931 charter of Kappa Alpha Psi Fraternity.

President Wilkinson died on March 13, 1932. To the right is the program from the memorial services held on campus for Wilkinson.

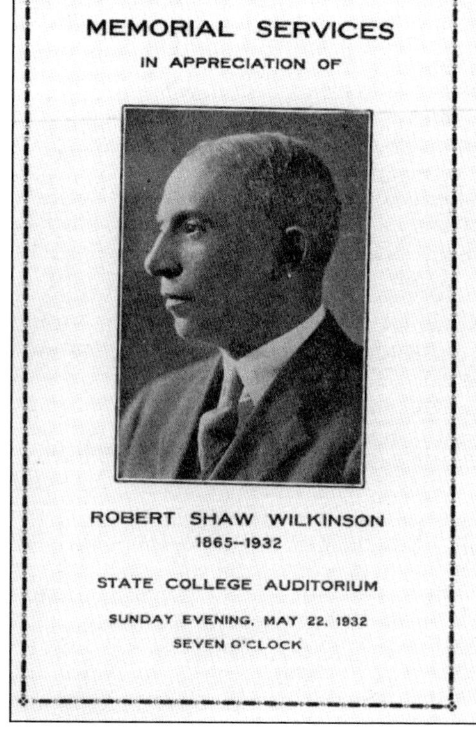

MEMORIAL SERVICES

IN APPRECIATION OF

ROBERT SHAW WILKINSON

1865--1932

STATE COLLEGE AUDITORIUM

SUNDAY EVENING, MAY 22, 1932

SEVEN O'CLOCK

Three

Miller F. Whittaker 1932–1949

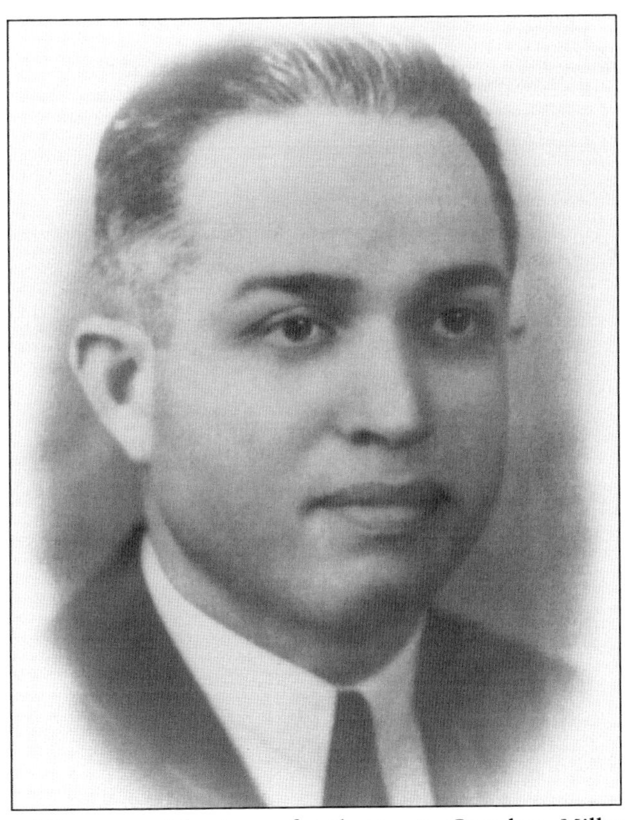

A former resident of Sumter, with strong family ties to Camden, Miller Fulton Whittaker was the youngest of the chief executive officers to assume the presidency of the college. Whittaker was only 39 when he took on the enormous task of overseeing the growing school, following the death of Robert Shaw Wilkinson. Whittaker was also the first student who had attended the school he was later to lead. He attended the college's preparatory school. Dean Nelson C. Nix records in his history of the college, covering the period from 1896 until 1937, that Whittaker worked on the construction of the first residence for the president while he was a student at the school.

The first home for the president was built in 1905 and demolished during the Turner administration. Whittaker is noted in the 1925 edition of *The Wilkinsonian*, the first college yearbook, as having obtained part of his training at State Agricultural and Mechanical College; however, he evidently concluded his studies at Kansas State, where he completed a master's degree in architecture. Whittaker designed or oversaw the completion of many buildings on the university campus. Hodge Hall was his master's thesis project. A distinguished, diplomatic, and unassuming bachelor, Whittaker had a vision for the type of graduate he felt that the college should produce:

> I have an ideal for the College. It is this: That each student shall give evidence of high moral character and personal worth, serious intellectual effort, and an understanding of his obligation to society. Things of the spirit, the common virtues of courtesy, honesty, integrity, and tolerance are just as important as the training of the intellect. To this end we would have this college print an indelible stamp of culture and refinement on its students.

Such goals are worthy of renewal in the ideal of the university's mission. Under Whittaker's leadership the "little colored school" actually became a college approved for the first time by the Southern Association of Colleges and Secondary Schools in 1932. Whittaker's considerable abilities as an administrator are evidenced by the fact that he led the school intact through the worst stages of the Great Depression. It was his ideal to make the institution truly serve the people of the state of South Carolina and of the nation.

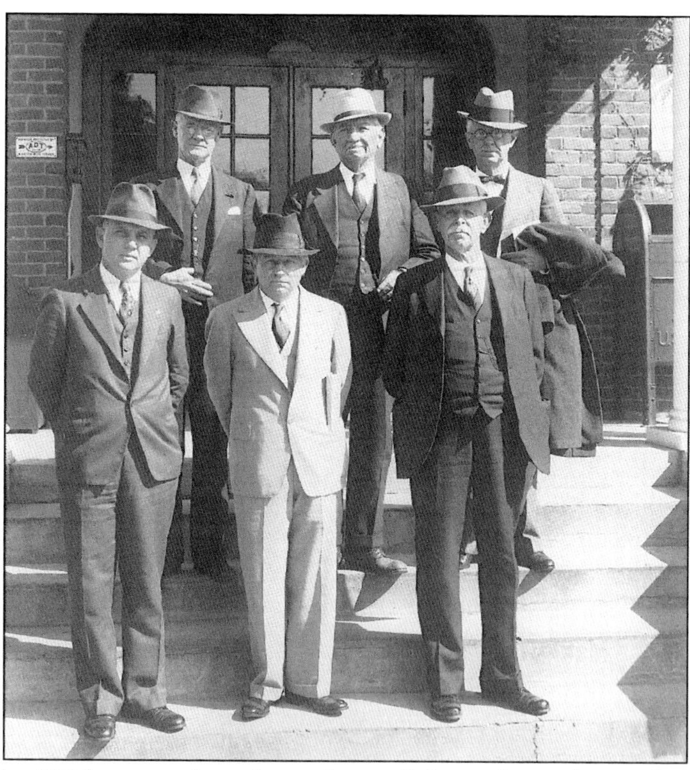

A portrait of the 1934 trustee board members of the college shows, from left to right, the following: (front row) W.C. Bethea, Secretary, Orangeburg; E.D. Hodge, Alcolu; and W.P. Mason, Westminister; (back row) C.F. Brooks, Chairman, Gray Court; A.L. Dukes, Orangeburg; and A.H. Moss, Orangeburg.

The deans of the college from 1937 to 1938 were, from left to right, (top) Dean of the College N.C. Nix; Dean K.W. Green, arts and sciences; (center) Dean M. J. Gardiner, home economics; (bottom) Dean W.M. Buchanan, agriculture, and Dean P.V. Jewell, mechanic arts.

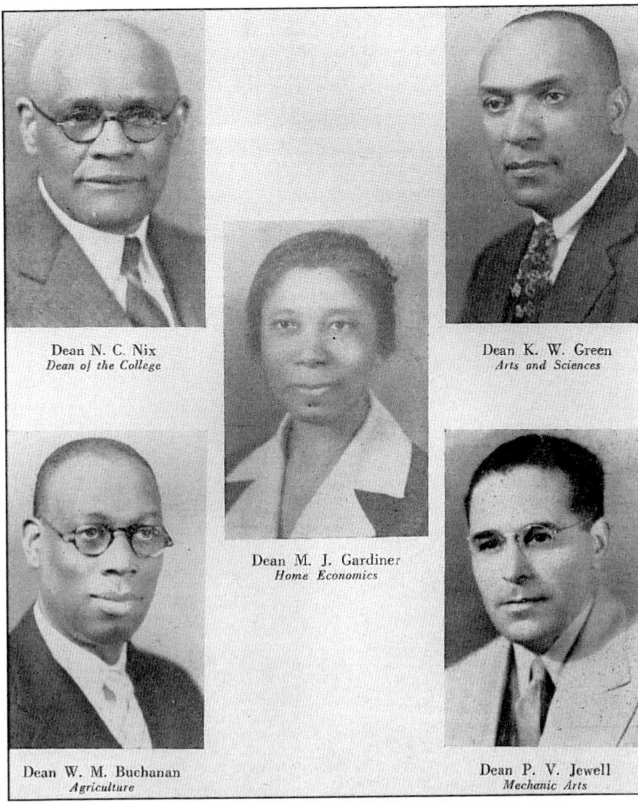

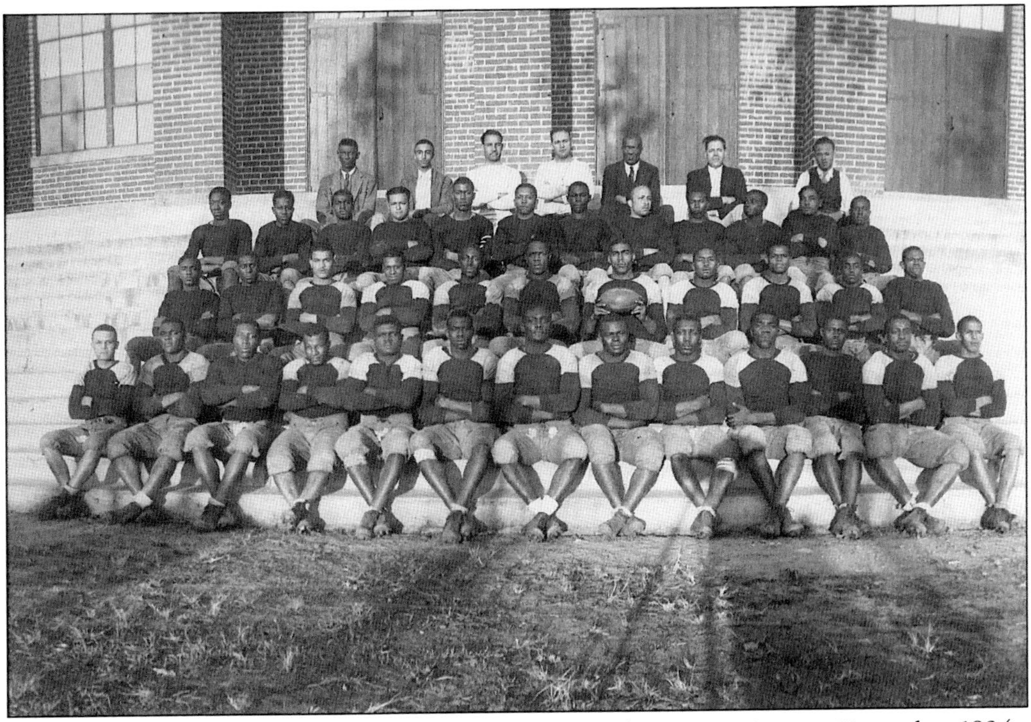

Pictured is the 1934 football team. The earliest record of Homecoming was November 1934.

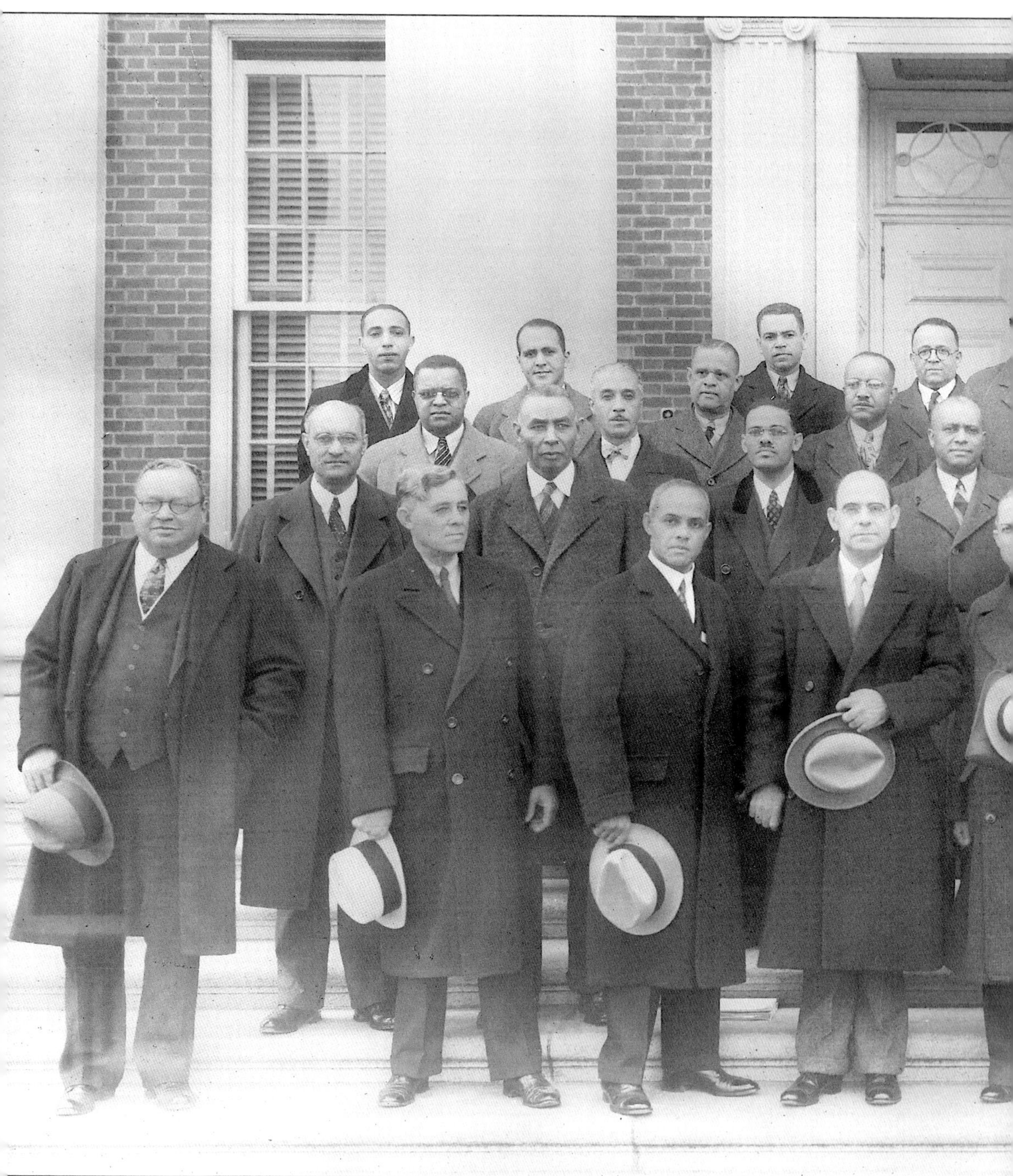

This photograph shows the Conference of Presidents of Negro Land-Grant Colleges, 15th Annual Convention, held at Howard University, Washington, D.C., November 15–17, 1937.

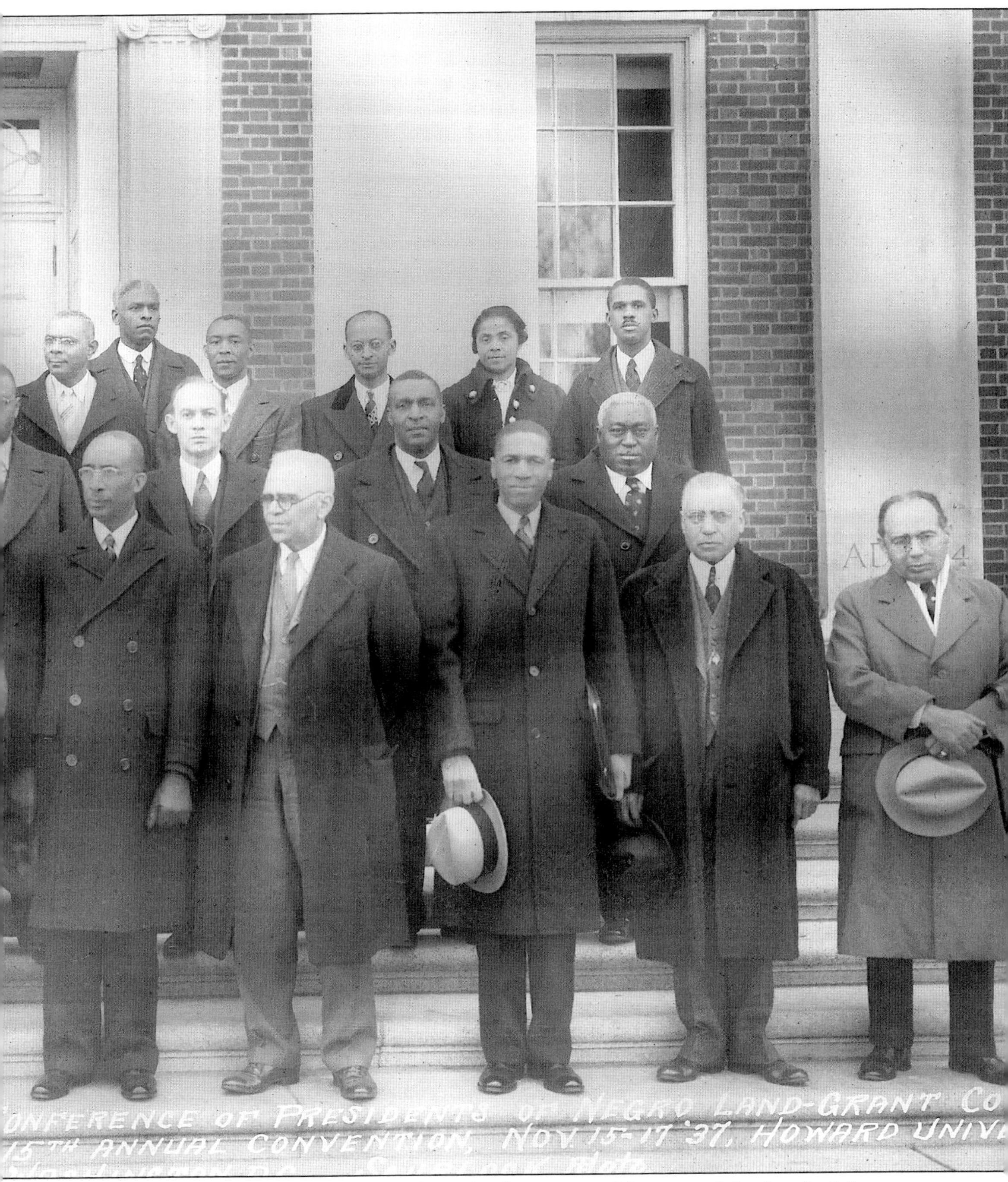

President Whittaker is fifth from the left on the front row. (Photograph by Scurlock.)

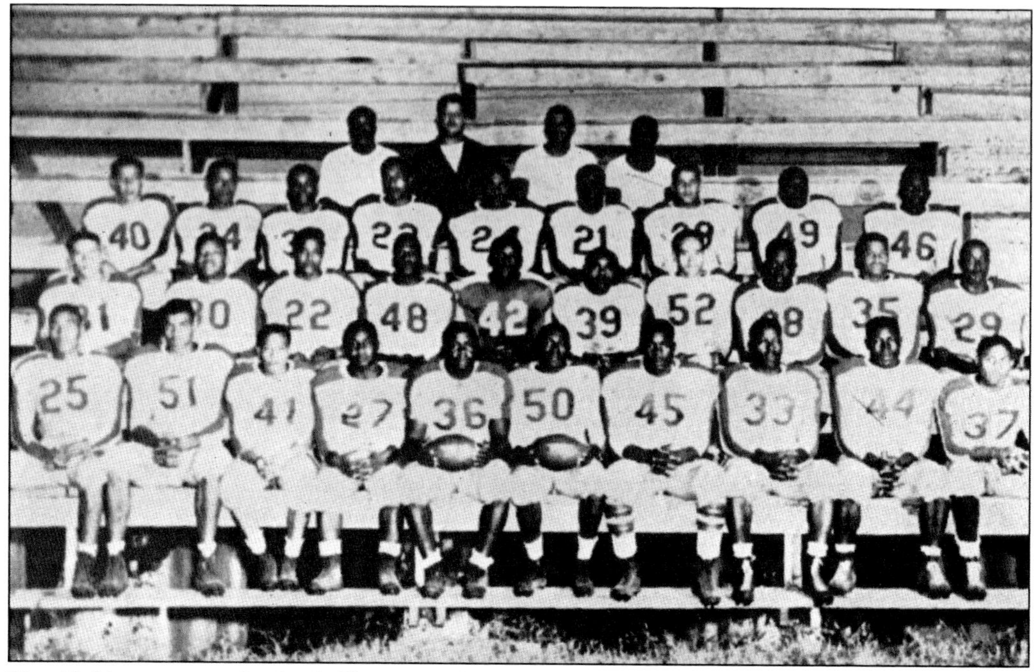

The 1947 team won the SIAC Championship. They defeated Shaw University 7-6 in the Black National Championship in Washington, D.C.

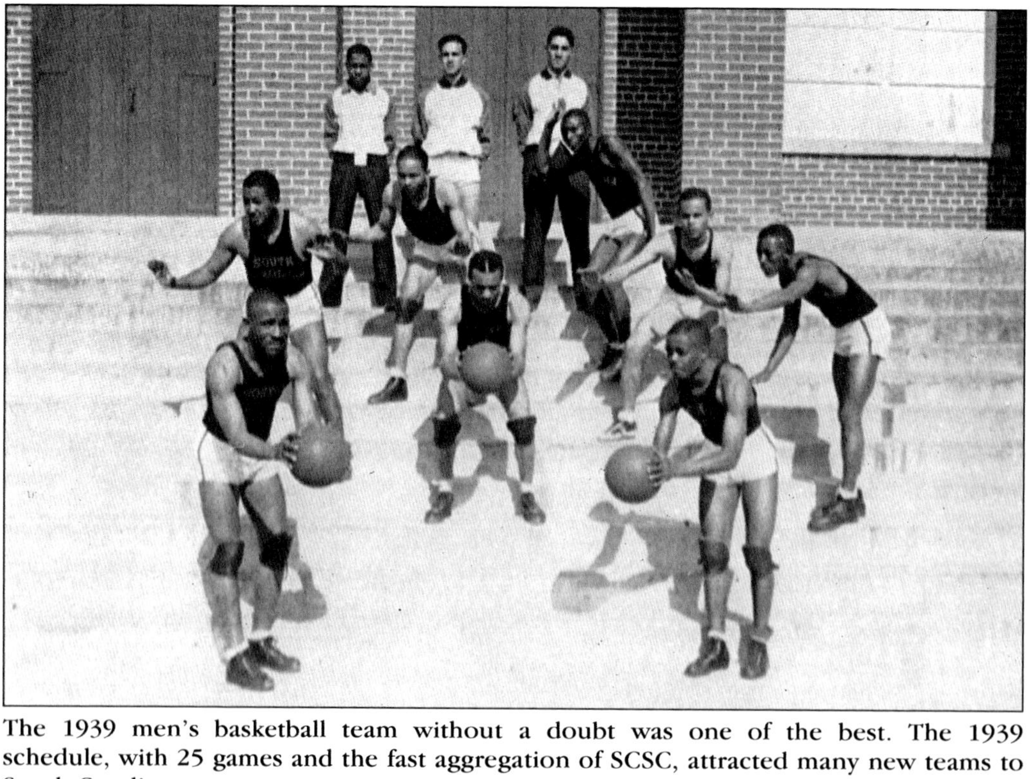

The 1939 men's basketball team without a doubt was one of the best. The 1939 schedule, with 25 games and the fast aggregation of SCSC, attracted many new teams to South Carolina.

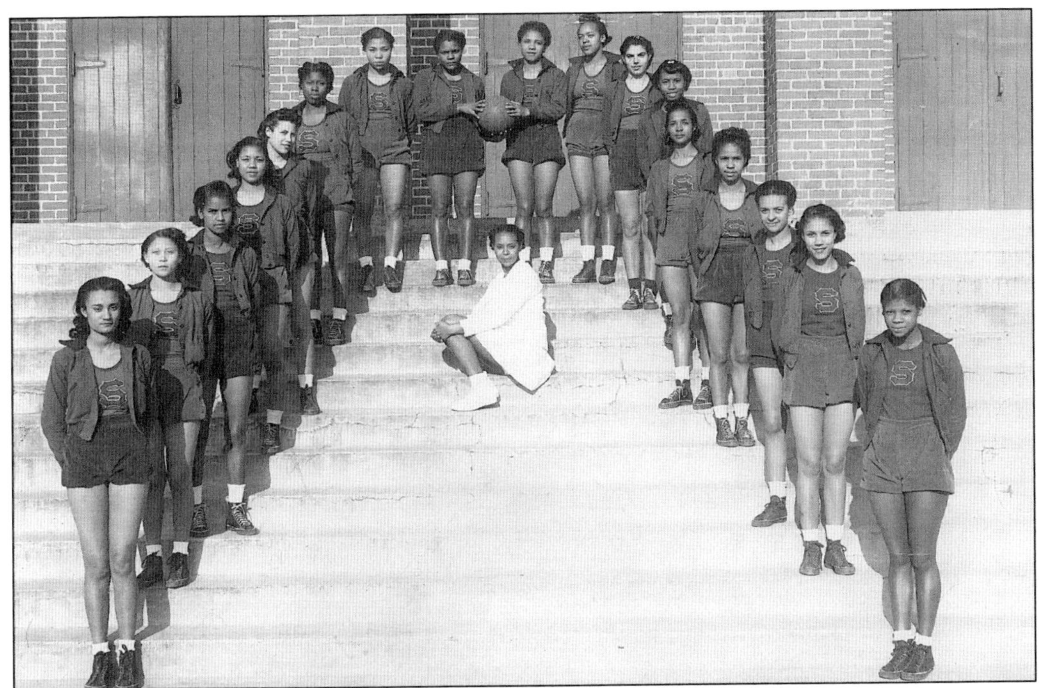

The women's basketball team in 1940 showed unusual strength during the 1939–1940 basketball season in which they competed against 14 schools, losing only two games. Pictured left to right are Mattie Waymer, Mattie Dingle, Elease Belton, Odessa Joyner, Geneva Williams, Lillie S. Simmons, Alease Gardner, Katherine Jackson, Johnnye Taylor, M. Louise Smith, Ruby Bates, Daisy Gordin, Lillian Green, Eugenia Dean, Bertha Collins, Francis Williams, and Gladys Malloy. The coach, seated, is Mamye E. Thompson.

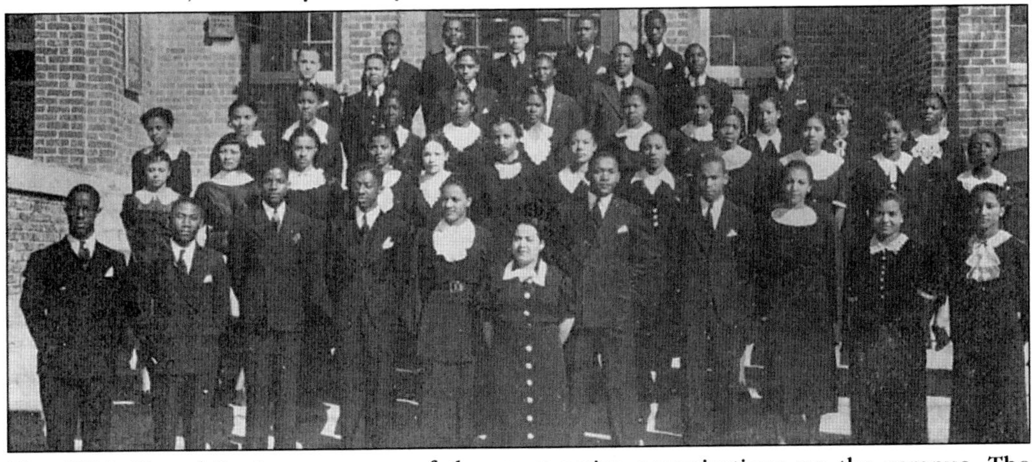

The 1938 Choral Society was one of the most active organizations on the campus. The three major parts of the society were Trio (female), Quartet (male), and the College Choir. This society won a significant place in the hearts of music lovers throughout this region. Among its achievements for the session were a special broadcast from Columbia over station WIS radio on November 23, 1937; a Christmas cantata; some musical contributions at the Palmetto State Teachers' Association; an Easter cantata; a series of weekly broadcasts beginning March 26, 1938, and ending May 21, 1938; a musical comedy on May 4, 1938; and varied programs at local churches.

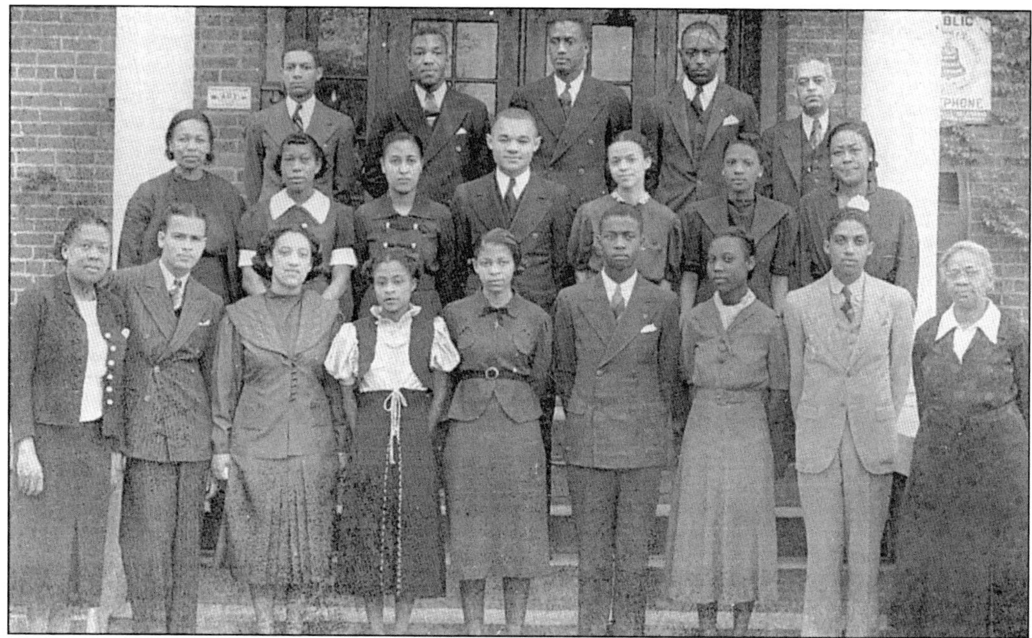

The Cabot Lodge Debating Union of 1938 was one of the oldest organizations on the campus. This union sponsored forensic contests annually between South Carolina State College and other colleges. One of its major events was the annual Tri-State Debate, in which it engaged Virginia State College, North Carolina A&T College, and South Carolina A. & M. College. The team winning both the affirmative and negative sides of the debate for three consecutive years became permanent possessor of a silver loving cup. This union also sponsored contests between South Carolina State College and Florida A.& M. College, as well as occasional debates with Georgia State and Talladega Colleges.

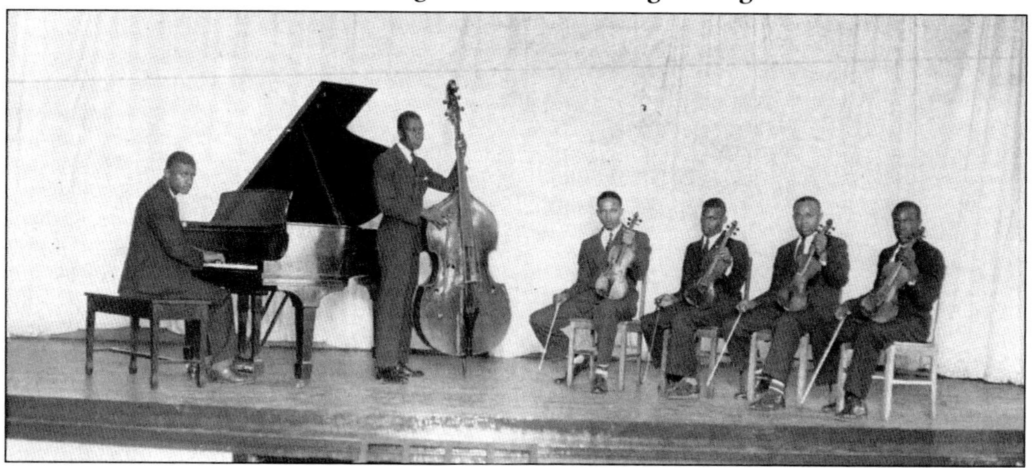

The mixed ensemble (1939) was organized November 1937 as an experiment with the grouping of stringed instruments played by the students. Its accomplishments with the Sunday school, and augmented with brass and wood-wind, accompanying the choral works in the two years of its experience, makes us feel that the organization deserves a permanent place in the life of the college. Shown, from left to right, are as follows: John Motley, piano; William Muldrow, double bass; Ranzy Weston, violin; Homer Jackson, violin; Walter Bennett, violin; and Ernest Roper, violin.

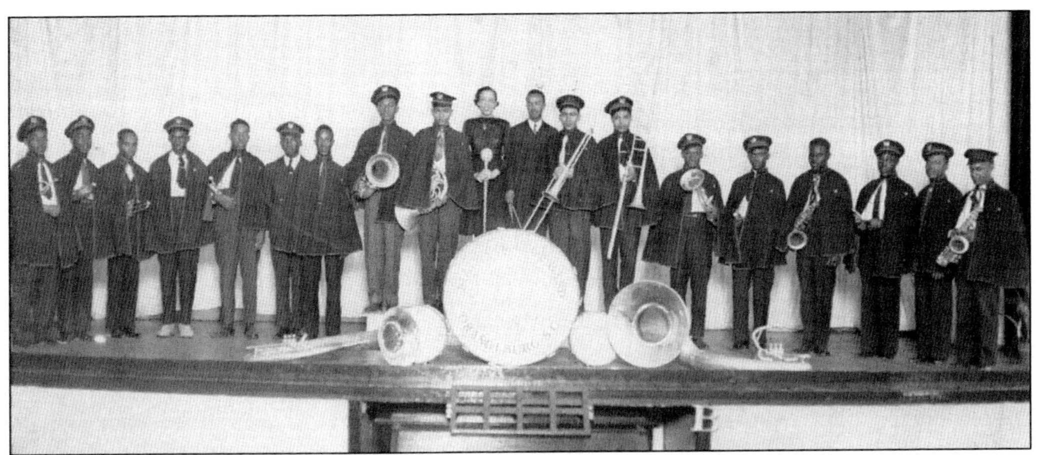

The College Band, 1939, gave concerts during the year and played for convocations and athletic events. Shown, from left to right, are as follows: Holland Daniels, Harry Gardin, Houston Richardson, Walter Stewart, Philip Gear, William Muldrow, Switzon Wigfall, Addison Bowman, Ranzy Weston, Helen Bright (drum majorette), Reginald Thomasson (director), Herman Ray, Nathaniel Singleton, John Motley, Robert Walker, John Lawson, Ernest Roper, Alpha Josie, and Phillip Letcher.

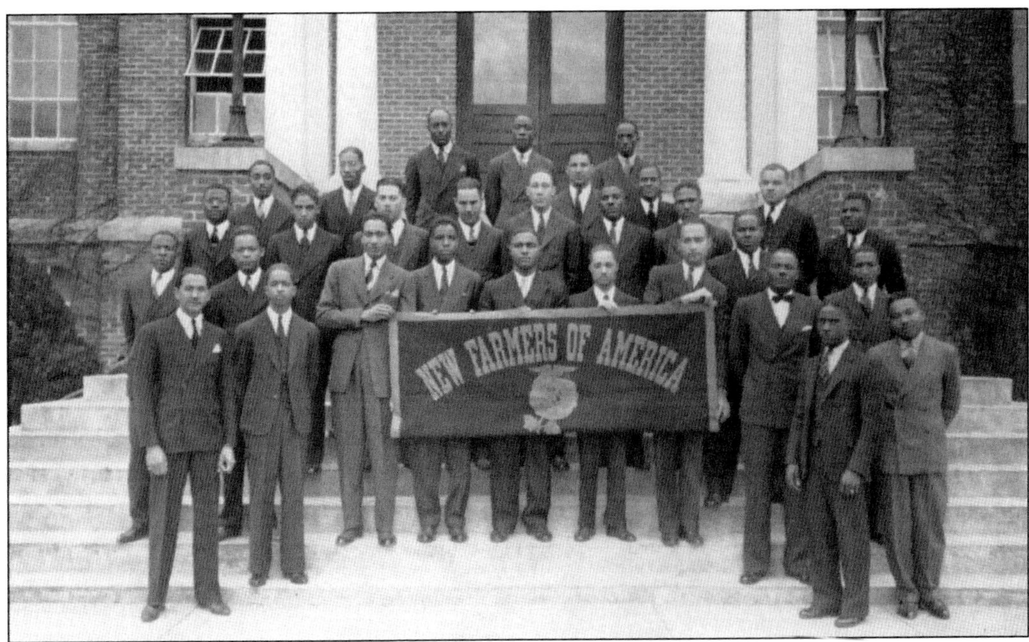

The New Farmers of America, 1939, was the national organization of Negro male students studying vocational agriculture in public schools throughout the United States. When it was organized in Virginia in 1926–1927, it had only a few chapters and very few members. It expanded and numbered some 800 chapters and over 20,000 active members.

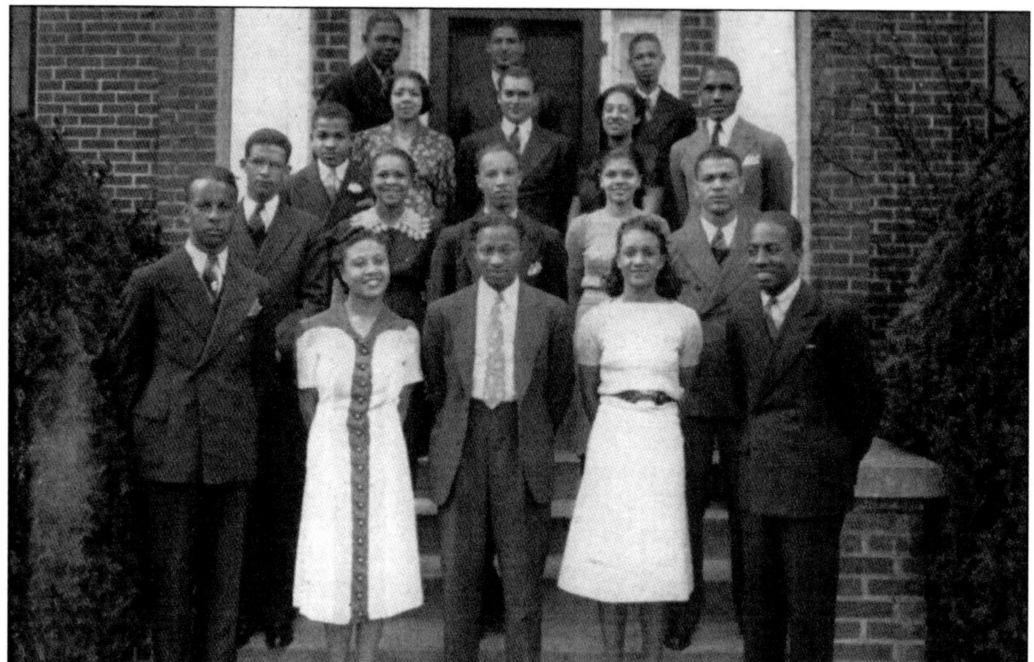

The Panhellenic Council, shown here in 1939, was composed of three representatives from each of the Greek letter organizations on the campus. Its purpose was to create a more cooperative spirit among these six fraternal groups. Included were representatives from Alpha Kappa Alpha and Delta Sigma Theta sororities, and Alpha Phi Alpha, Kappa Alpha Psi, Omega Psi Phi, and Phi Beta Sigma fraternities.

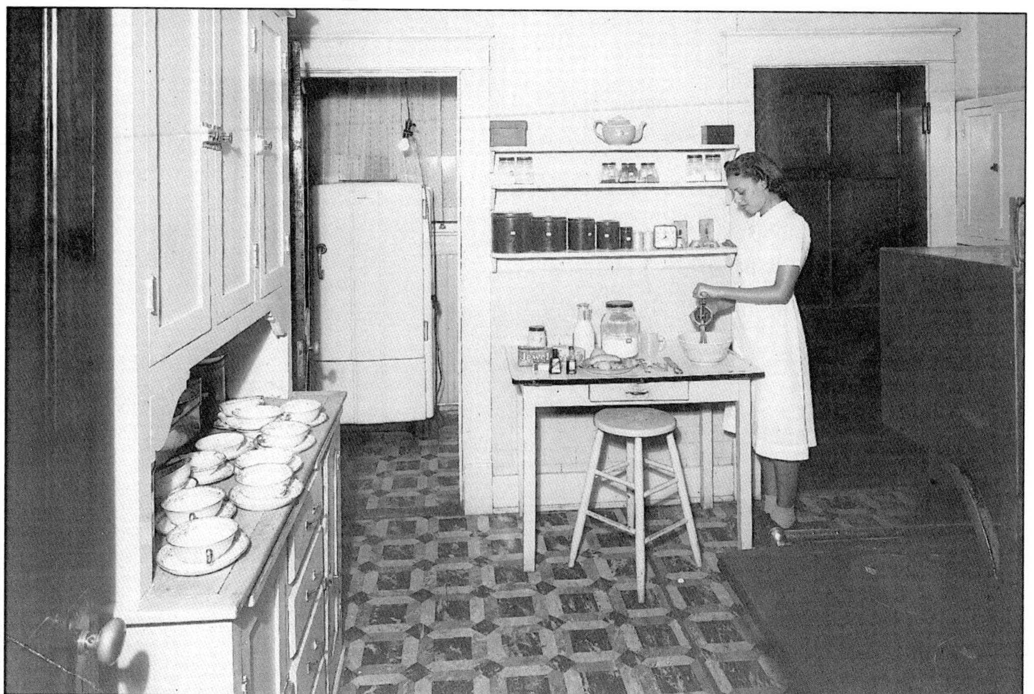

Student Nellie Hart is seen here in a home economics cooking class in 1942.

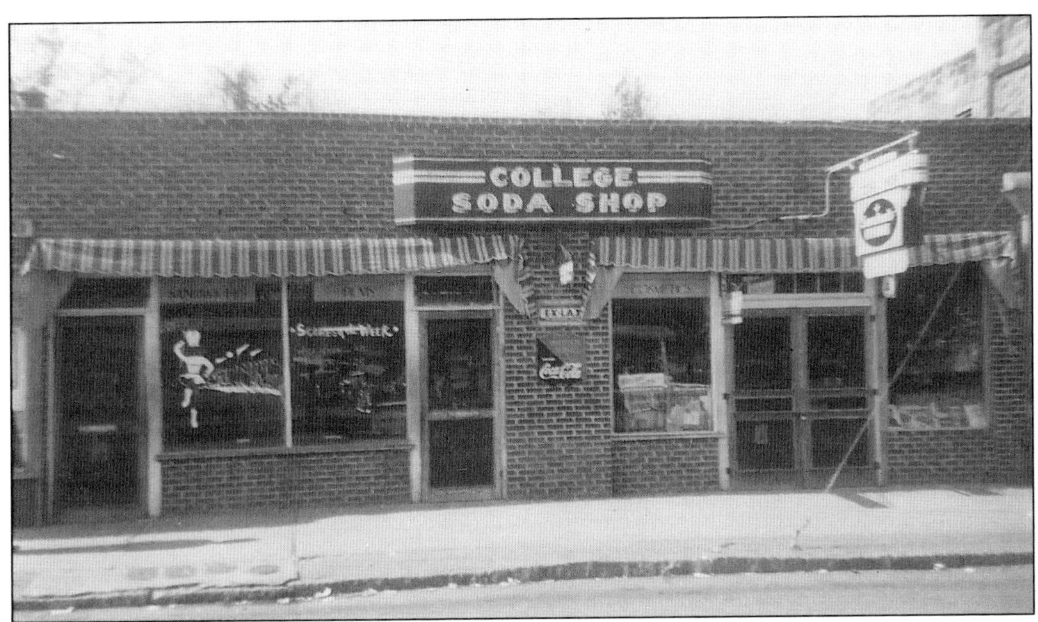

Dr. Clemmie E. Webber and her husband, Paul R. Webber Jr., owned and operated two soda shops near State's campus. The College Soda Shop, shown above, opened in 1941 and was closest to campus. The Webbers sold the shop in 1960. (Photo courtesy of Dr. Clemmie E. Webber.) The Riverside Soda Shop, shown below, opened in 1945 and later became the site of the first African American-owned pharmacy in Orangeburg County. Shown inside the Riverside Soda Shop are the following: Paul R. Webber Jr. (behind the counter); Albert Felder (left, seated on stool at counter); Earl Cummings (standing next to counter in front of door); Paul R. Webber, III (seated, in foreground); John Williams (seated, second from right); Theodore Curry (standing, far right); and two unidentified men. Not only did the soda shops provide a place for students to gather, but they also provided many students with employment.

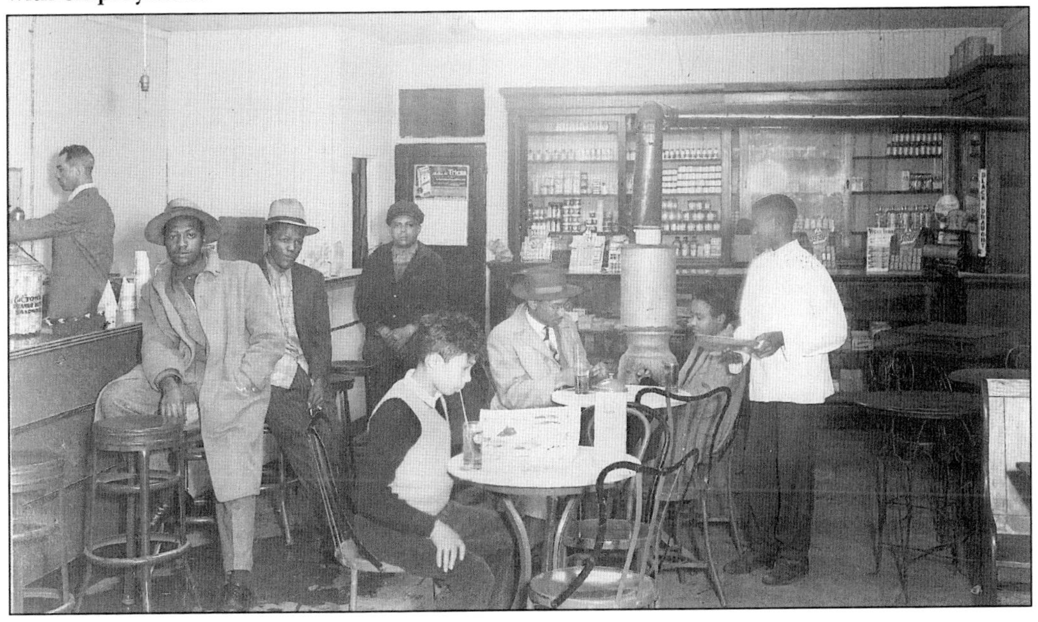

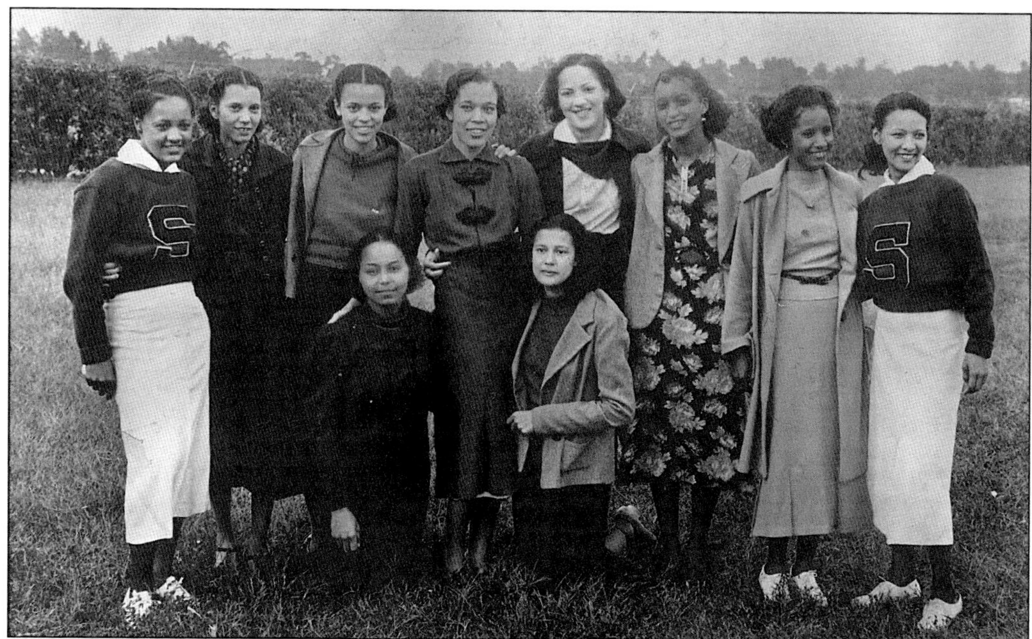

This group of young women, enrolled at the Colored Normal, Industrial, Agricultural and Mechanical College of South Carolina are, from left to right, as follows: (standing) ? Henderson, Louise Carter, Cecil Whittaker (niece of the college's third president), Helen Bright, Leana Martin, Lawrence Mills, Odessa Dixon, and Lillian Lum; (kneeling) Mabel Shelton and Rubye Smith.

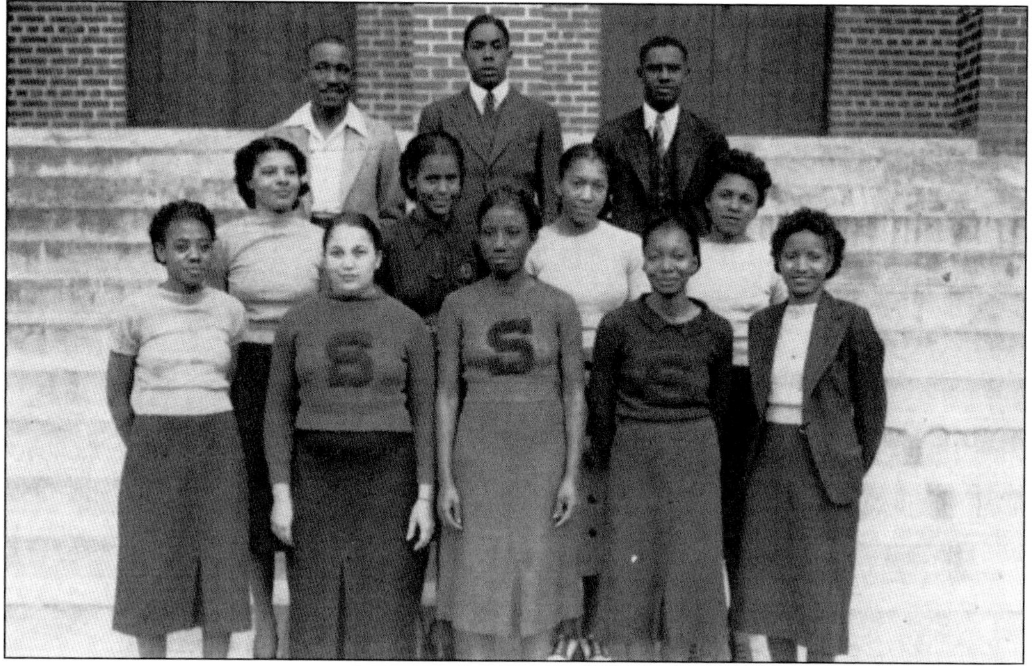

Shown here in 1939, the "S" Club was an organization founded upon the principles of good sportsmanship. It was composed of a group of young men and women who carried out through their fame as athletes their club's motto: "We Inculcate Good Sportsmanship."

Pictured is Miss Johnnie Mae Gilmore—May Queen, 1937, a junior from Rock Hill.

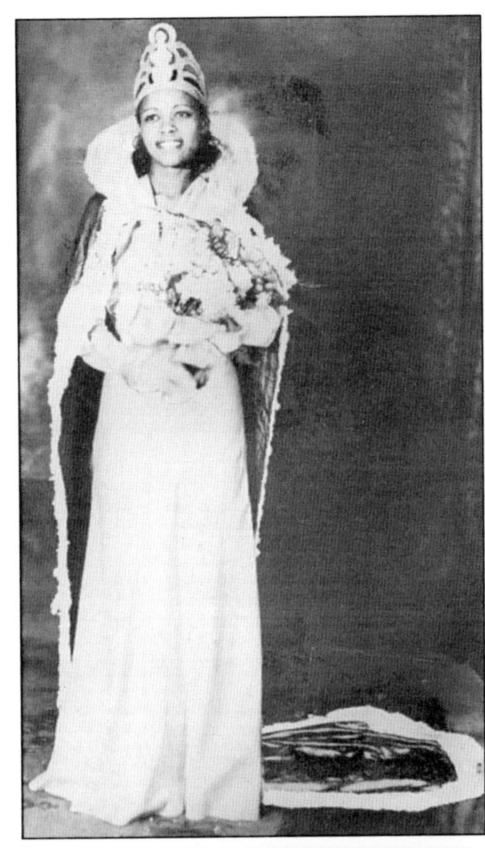

This photograph shows the May Queen of 1946, Miss Alba Myers (Lewis), a senior from Orangeburg, and her court.

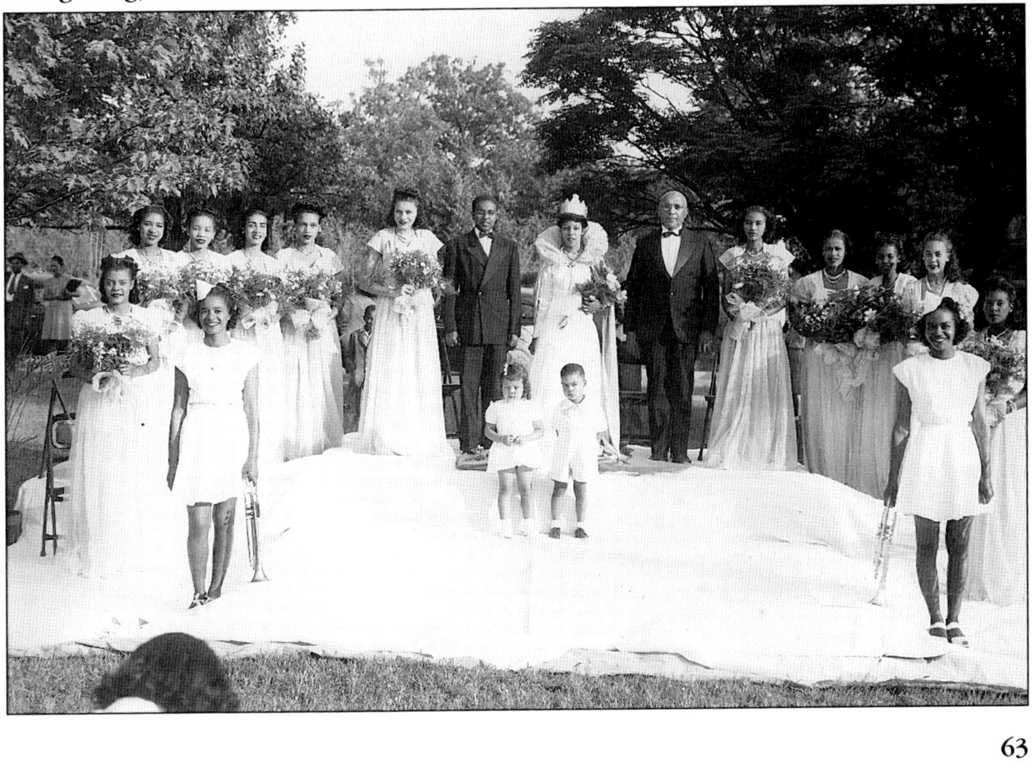

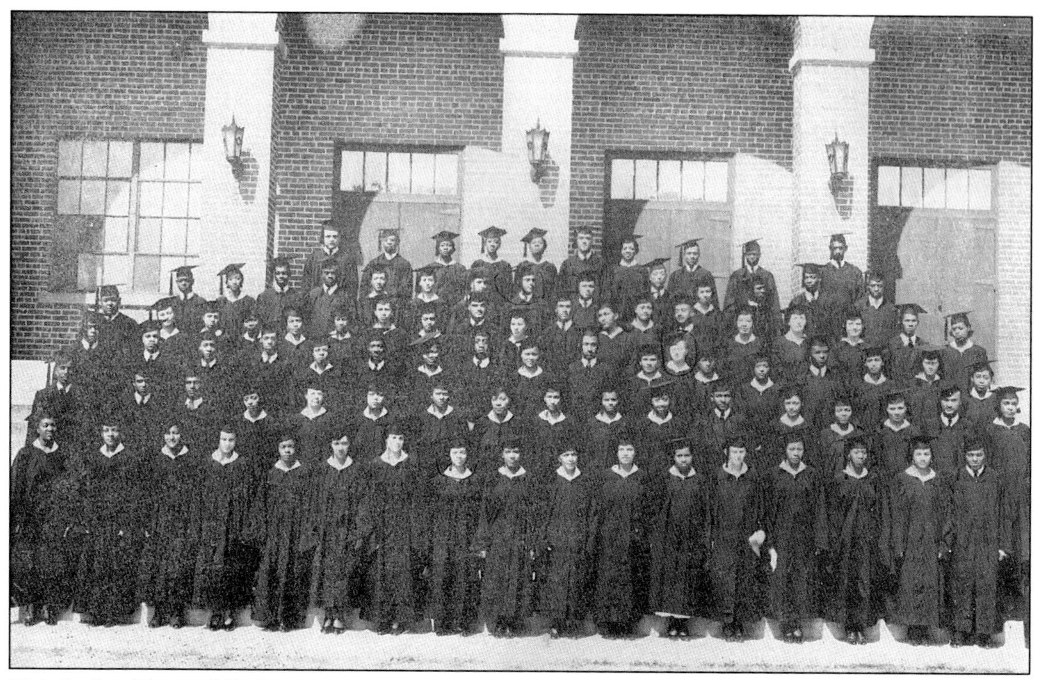

This is the Class of 1937.

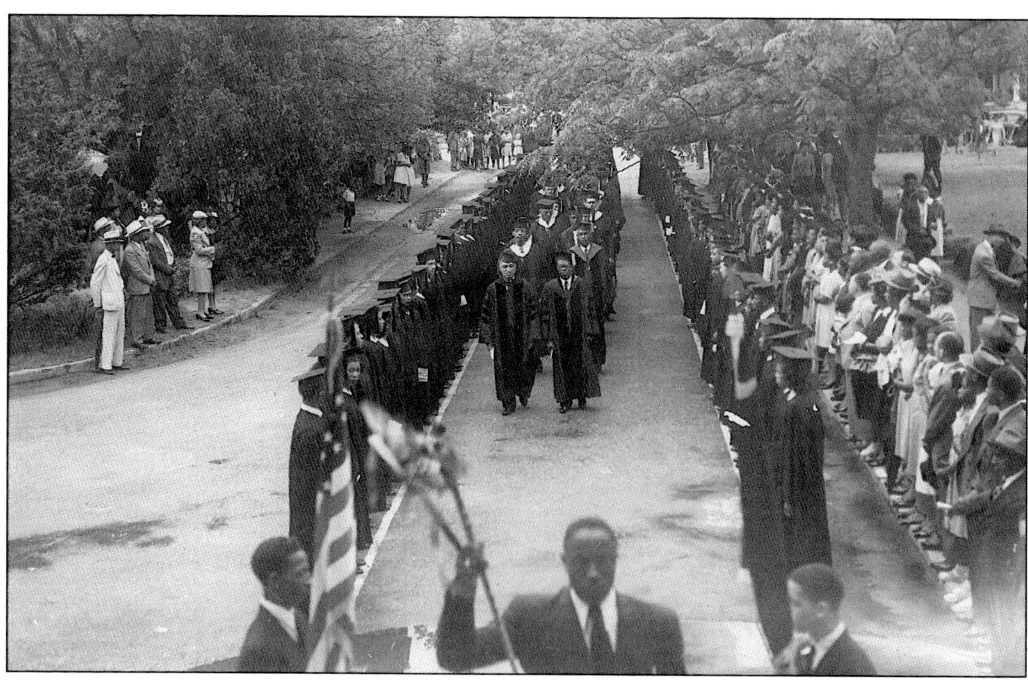

Shown here is the 50th Anniversary Commencement, 1946. The procession entering White Hall Auditorium includes, from left to right, the following: President Miller F. Whittaker (South Carolina State) and President J.J. Seabrook (Claflin College); (second row) Reverend James F. Thomas, chaplain, and President Benjamin E. Mays (Morehouse College).

This image shows Dr. Benjamin E. Mays, president of Morehouse College, Atlanta, standing on the steps of White Hall with President Miller F. Whittaker on the occasion of the 1948 Annual Easter Address, which Mays delivered to State College. Mays, a native of South Carolina and an educator of national significance, is known for his progressive work in race relations and as the mentor who helped shape the vision of Dr. Martin Luther King.

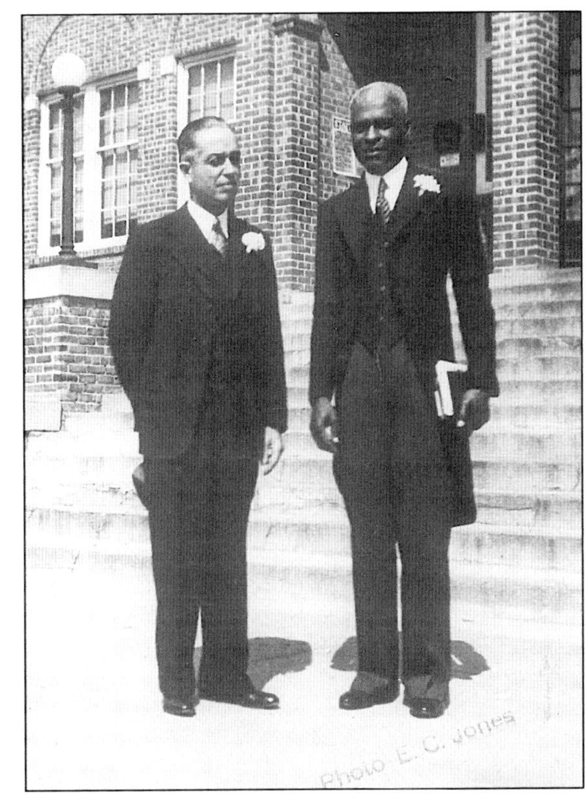

This retirement reception for members of the Industrial Education Department in the Y Hut includes, from left to right, the following: W.C. Lewis, Phillip Harris, W.T. Calhoun, Miller F. Whittaker (president), Squire Morgan, Willie White Williams, Charles Watermann, unidentified, and Marion Birnie Wilkinson (seated). (Photograph by Sharperson Studio.)

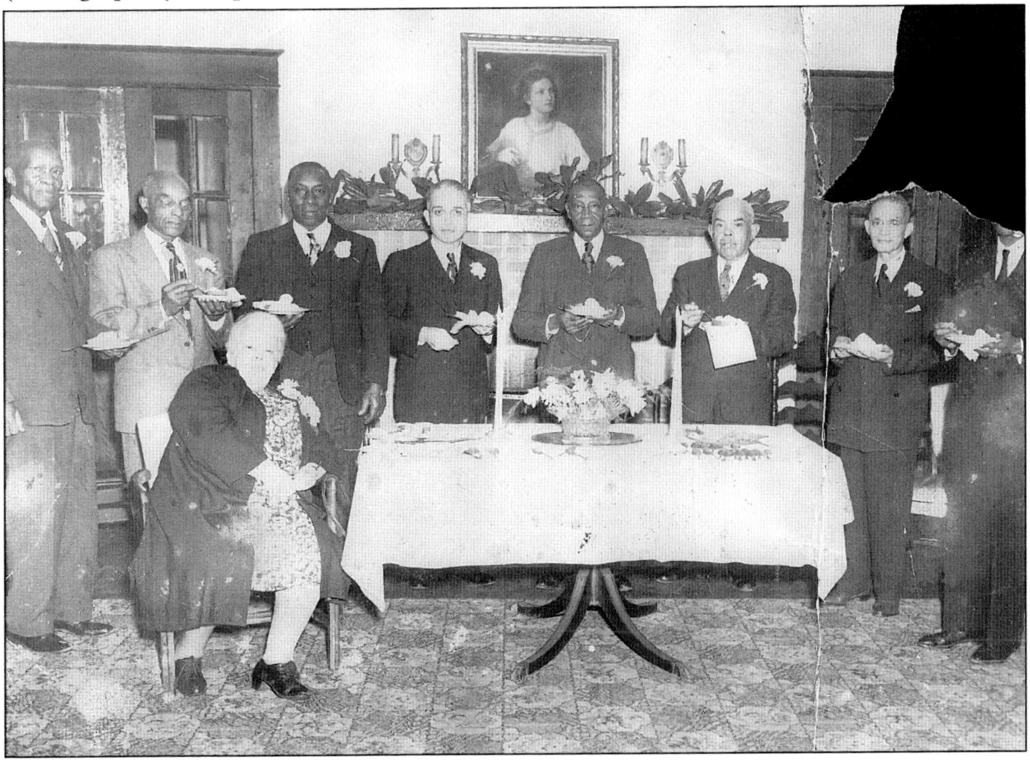

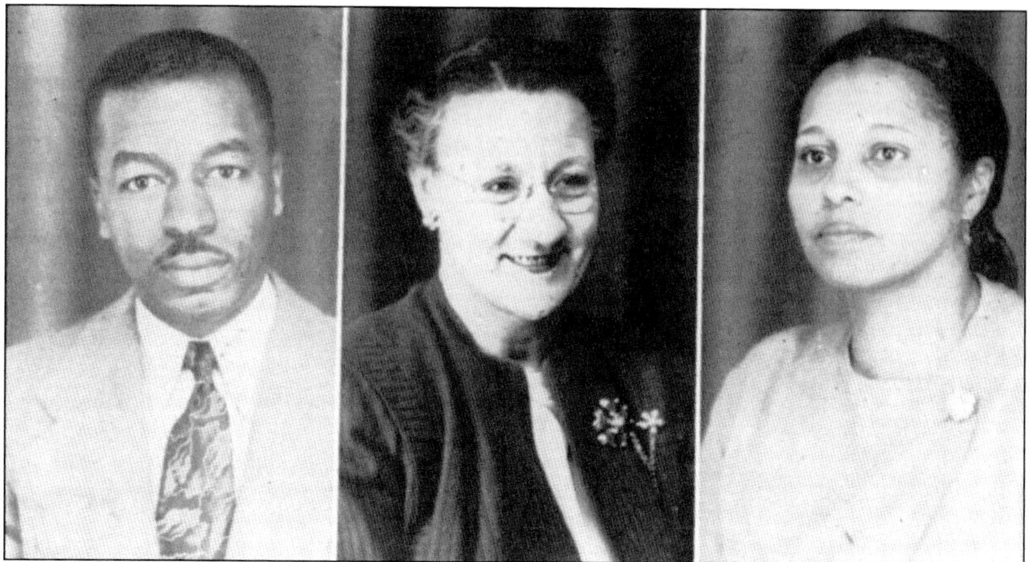

The first graduates of the master's degree program, from left to right, are Melvin Adams, Rosa D. Harris, and Geraldyne P. Zimmerman. The graduate program began in September 1946.

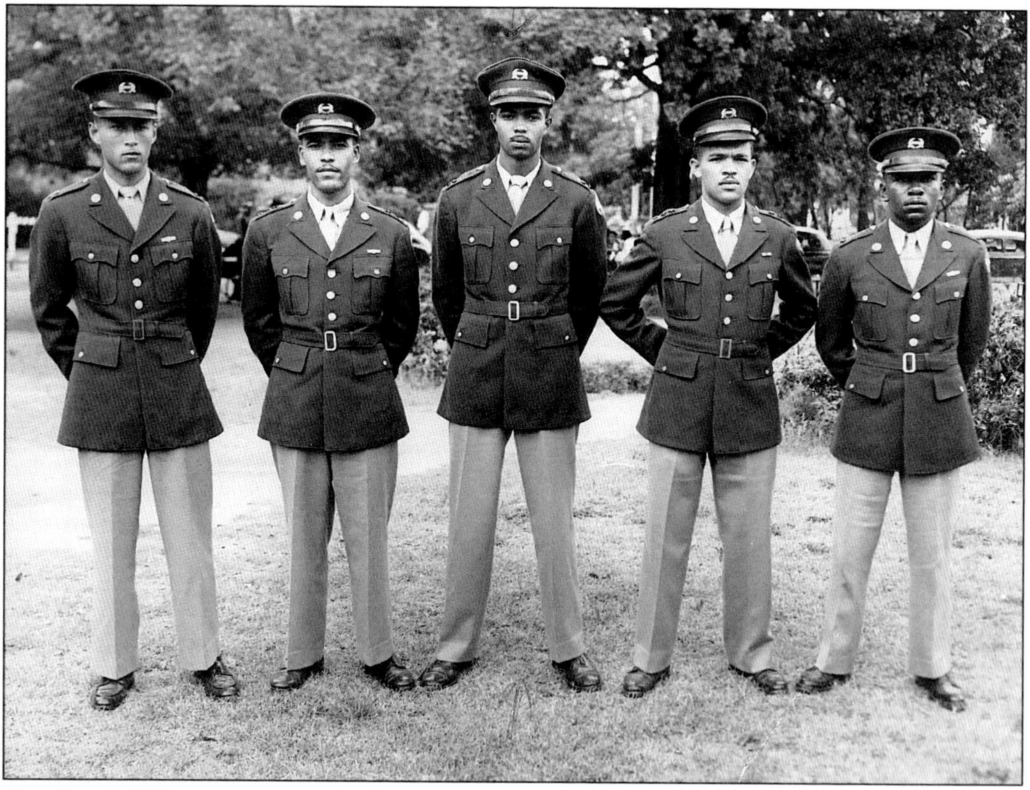

The first ROTC commissioned officers, 1949 are, from left to right, as follows: Richard A. Williams, William J. Nelson, Spencer Bracey, Fred Dowdy, and George Wright. (Photograph by Sharperson Studio, donated by William J. Nelson.)

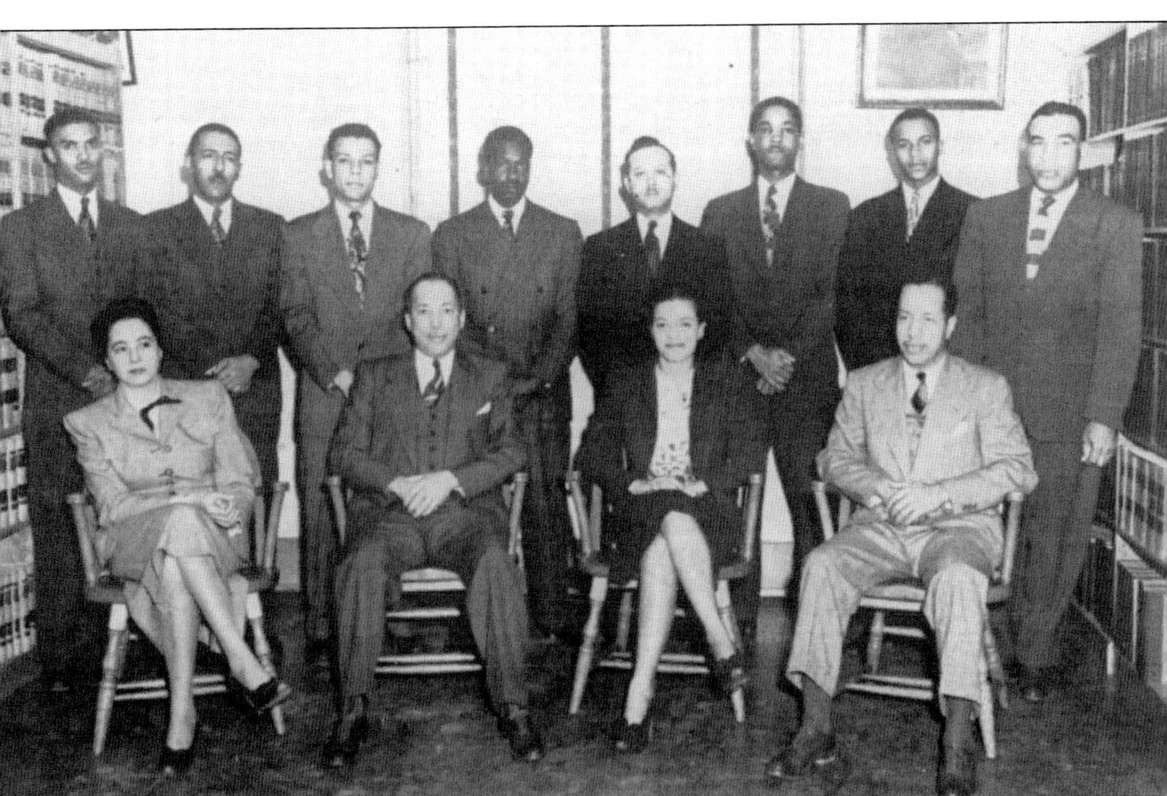

The Law School began operation at State College on September 17, 1947. Shown here are faculty and students, *c.* 1948. The Law School faculty consisted of, from left to right, the following: (seated) Cassandra E. Maxwell, associate professor and librarian; Benner C. Turner, professor; Eloise Vaughn, secretary; and Leo L. Kerford, associate professor. The first-year class consisted of eight students, and they are, from left to right, as follows: (standing) Alfred Pearson, three unidentified, Willie Smith, Matthew Perry, unidentified, and Ollie C. Dawson. The unidentified first-year students in this picture are Julius Williams, Albert Kennedy, Raymond White, and A.W. Brown.

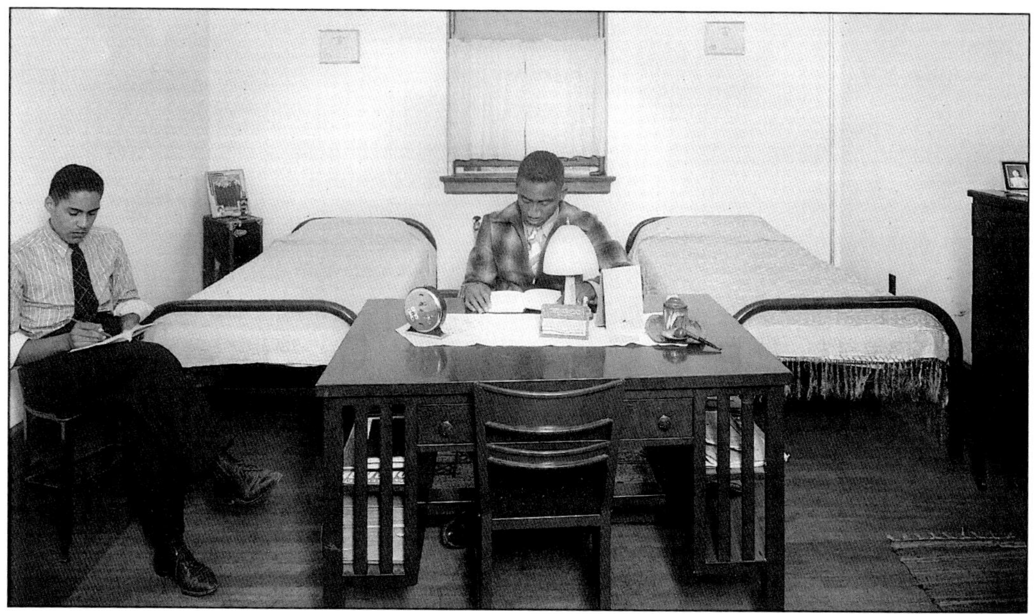
Male students are seen here studying in a dormitory room.

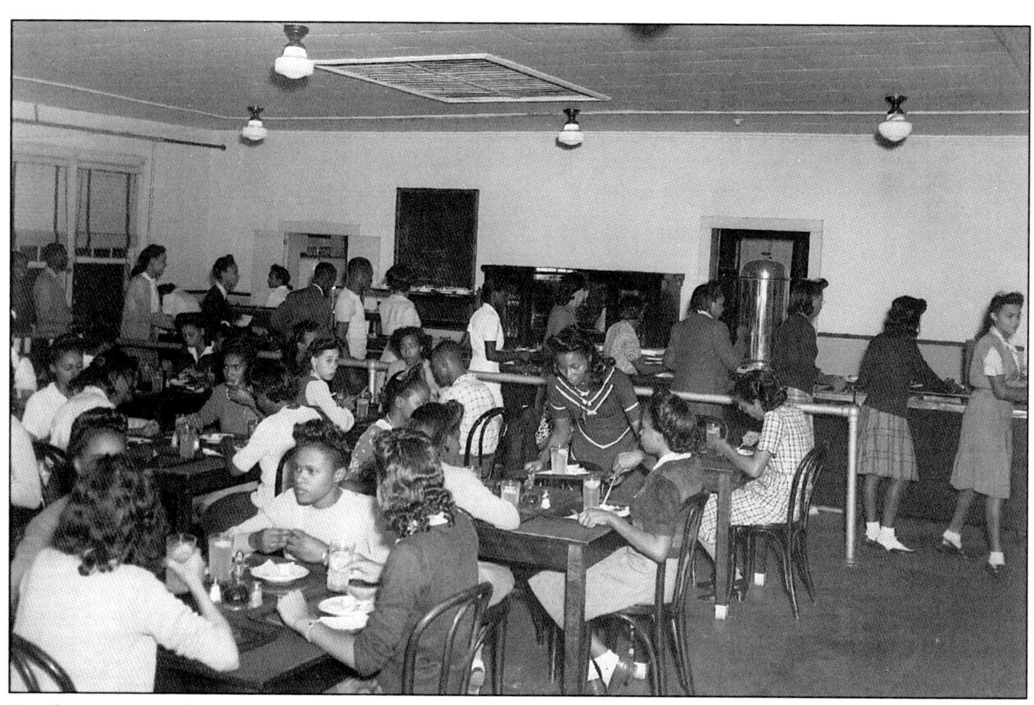
Students eat and socialize in Floyd Cafeteria.

Four

Benner C. Turner 1950–1967

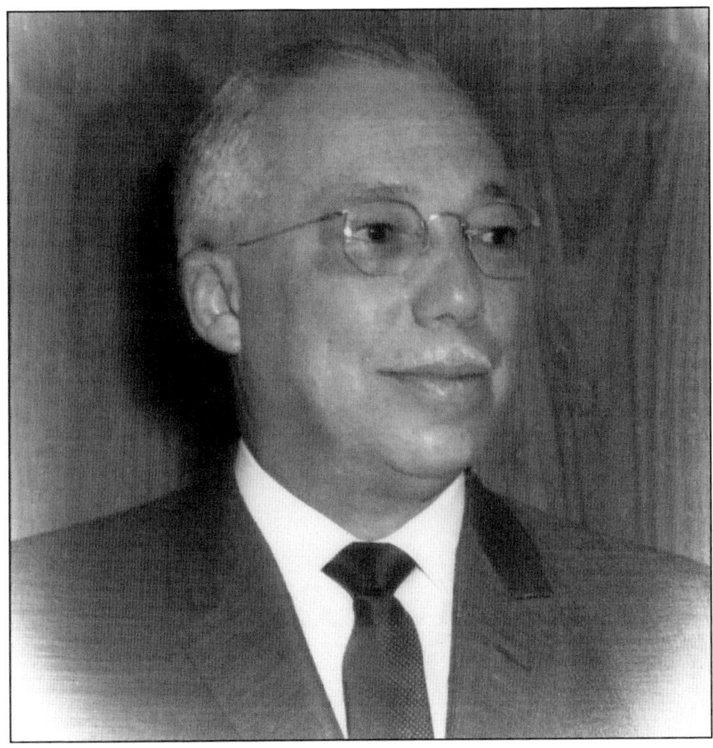

A native of Columbus, Georgia, Benner Creswill Turner attended the public schools there until he was accepted at the prestigious Philips-Andover Academy, in Andover, Massachusetts, where he graduated *magna cum laude* in 1923. Upon graduation, he also received the Henry Van Duzen Scholarship, an award for the student with the highest average among those who planned to attend Harvard University. He completed Harvard College and Harvard University, obtaining the Bachelor of Laws degree in 1930. He served as professor of law at North Carolina College, Durham, North Carolina, and in 1947 was appointed dean of the school of law at The Colored Normal, Industrial, Agricultural and Mechanical College of South Carolina in Orangeburg. After the death of President Miller F. Whittaker in 1949, Turner was appointed president of the college in 1950, during which year he also received a doctor of laws degree from Allen University in Columbia.

Under Turner's administration, the college made many strides. The Colored Normal, Industrial, Agricultural and Mechanical College of South Carolina became South Carolina State College in 1954. The college received full accreditation by the Southern Association of Colleges and Secondary Schools in December of 1960. Turner also expanded the physical plant with the construction of many buildings, including the Staley Agricultural and Home Economics Building (1954), the Student Center (1954), Bulldog Stadium (1955), the president's residence (1961), the post office and Washington Dining Hall (1962), and Felton Laboratory School (1964). Despite the strides made by the college during Turner's tenure as president, his administration was not without troubles. Many felt that Turner was too conservative on civil rights issues, insisting that students should focus on their education rather than on political activities. Despite these troubles, Turner guided the college into a period of intellectual and academic growth and progress.

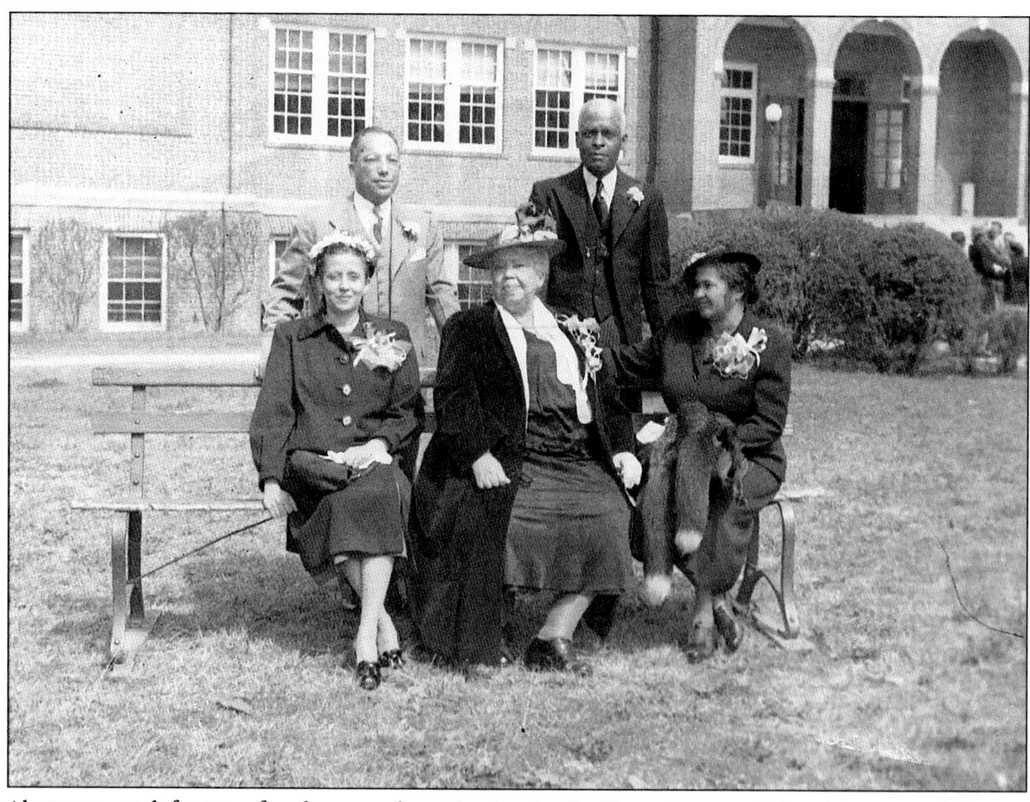

Alumnus and former faculty member Benjamin E. Mays began giving his annual Easter message in 1935. Shown here are, from left to right, (seated) Mrs. Julia Turner, Mrs. Marion B. Wilkinson, and Mrs. Benjamin E. Mays, (standing) President Benner C. Turner and Benjamin E. Mays on the occasion of the 16th annual Easter program in 1951, which was sponsored by the YMCA and the YWCA.

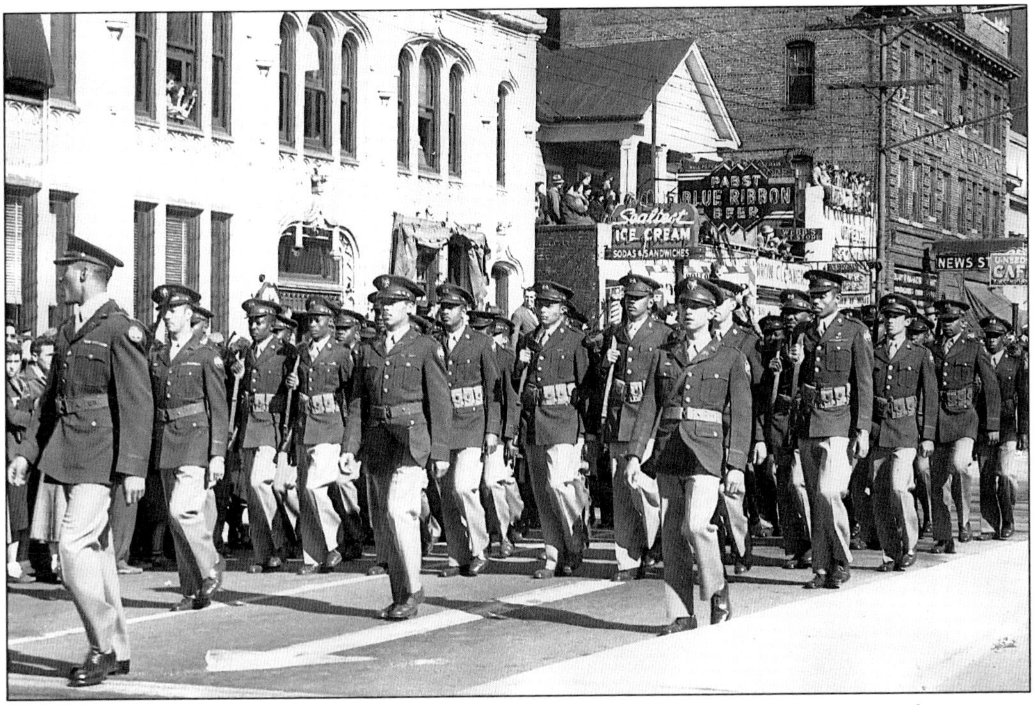

The college's ROTC marched in the January 1951 parade in Columbia, in honor of Governor James F. Byrne's inauguration. Included in the procession were Thomas Best, Watt McKeller, Jason Smith, Gonzales C. Pratt, Austelle Sherod, and Joseph C. Woodard.

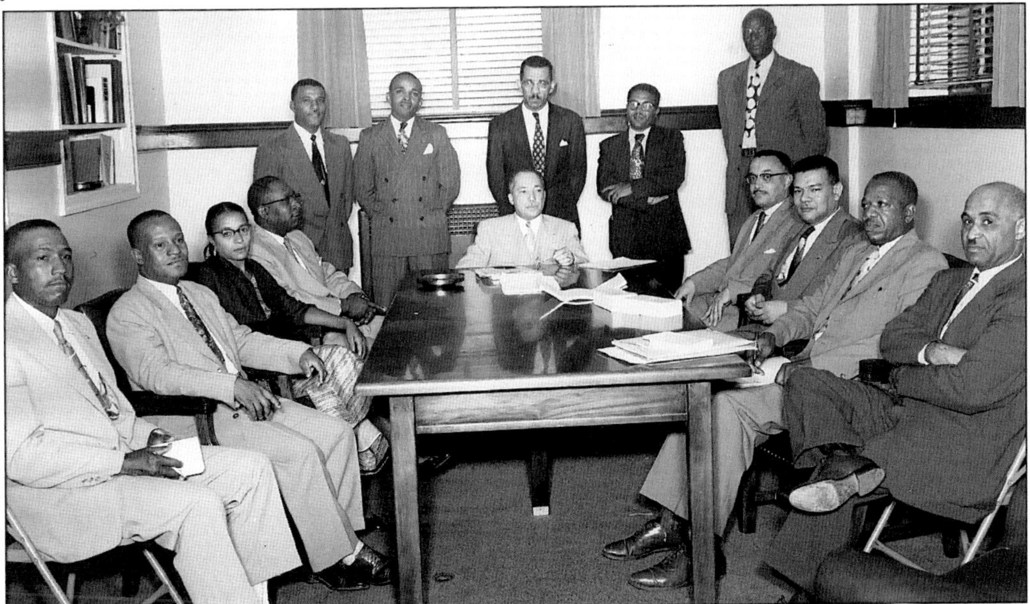

President Turner served as division chairman for the Boy Scouts of America. Shown here is the 1953 Boy Scout Campaign Committee, consisting of, from left to right, (seated) James Hall, unidentified, Mrs. Hilda Finney, Dr. J.C. Parler, President Benner C. Turner, Dr. George Hunter, Paul King, unidentified, and J.D. McGhee; (standing) Dr. Charles Thomas, unidentified, Dr. Ernest A. Finney, unidentified, and C.S. Ross. (Photo by Lackey's.)

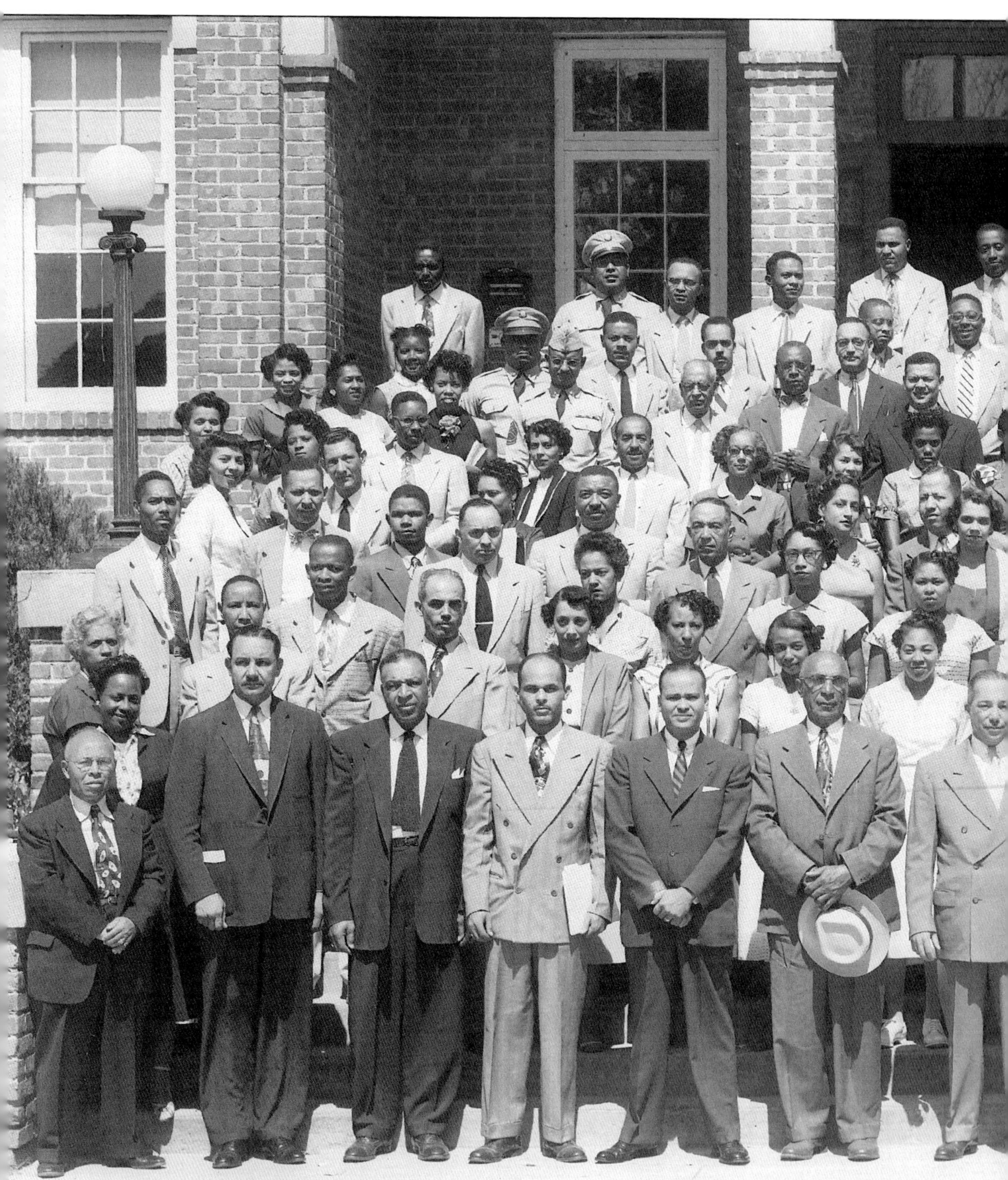

This photograph shows the college's faculty assembled on the steps of White Hall following an institute conducted in 1953. The chief executive and administrative personnel assembled in the front row and include names familiar to students of the modern campus by virtue of the fact that many structures utilized by contemporary students are named for the individuals shown in this image. The front row, from left to right, include the following: Dean Frank M. Staley (Staley Hall); Harold Crawford (Crawford Mechanical Arts and Industries Building);

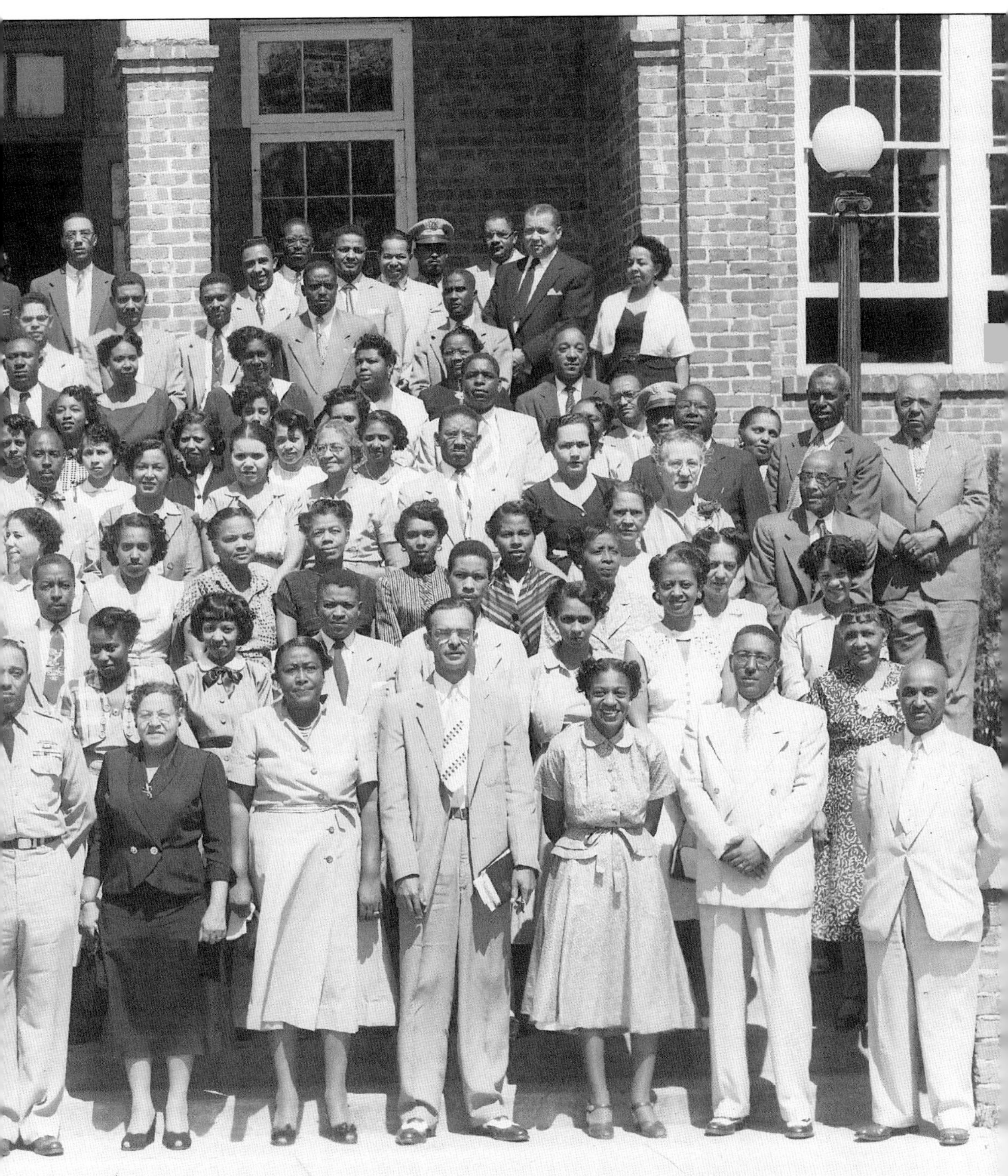

Oliver C. Dawson (Oliver Dawson Stadium); Peter Whittaker; Howard Jordan; Dean Kirkland W. Green (Kirkland Green Student Center); President Benner C. Turner (Turner Hall); Colonel Lofton; Dean Geraldine Penn; Mrs. Nix; Frank DeCosta, Dean of the Graduate School; Marie Vernon, Dean of Women; Archibald Brown; and Joseph McGee, Registrar. (Photo by Lackey's.)

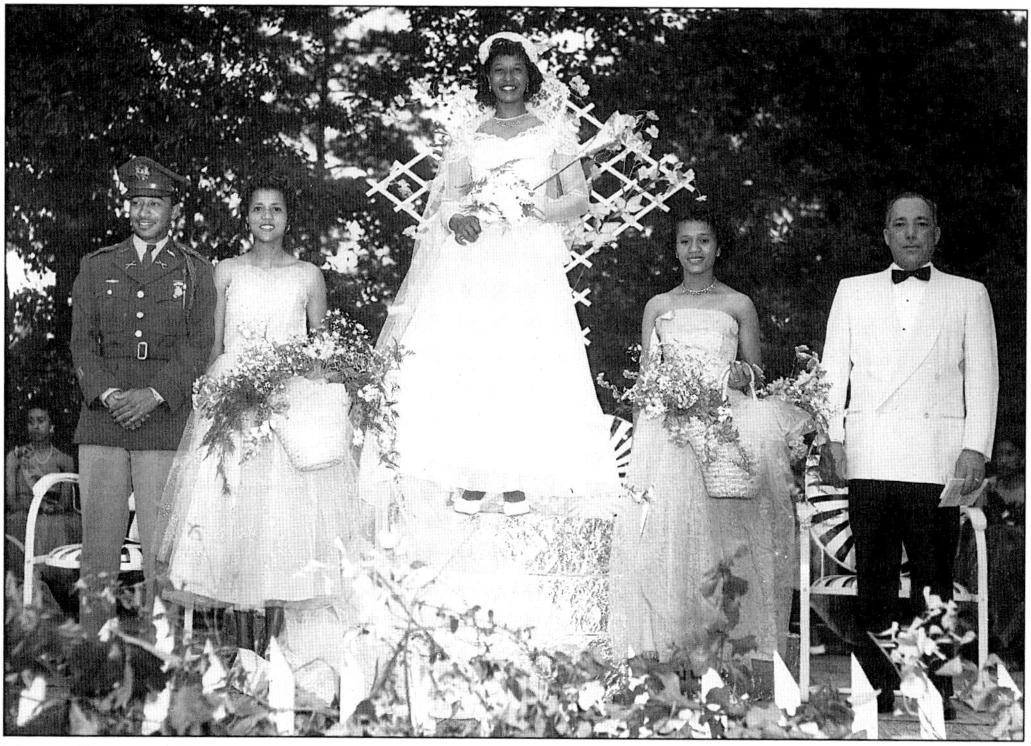

The college celebrated May Day with a variety of activities, including the crowning of a May Queen. This photo depicts, from left to right, an unidentified escort, Beatrice Singleton (Evans), May Queen Mary Loretta Burris, Betty Buck, and President Benner C. Turner during the 1954 May Day festivities. (Photo by E.C. Jones.)

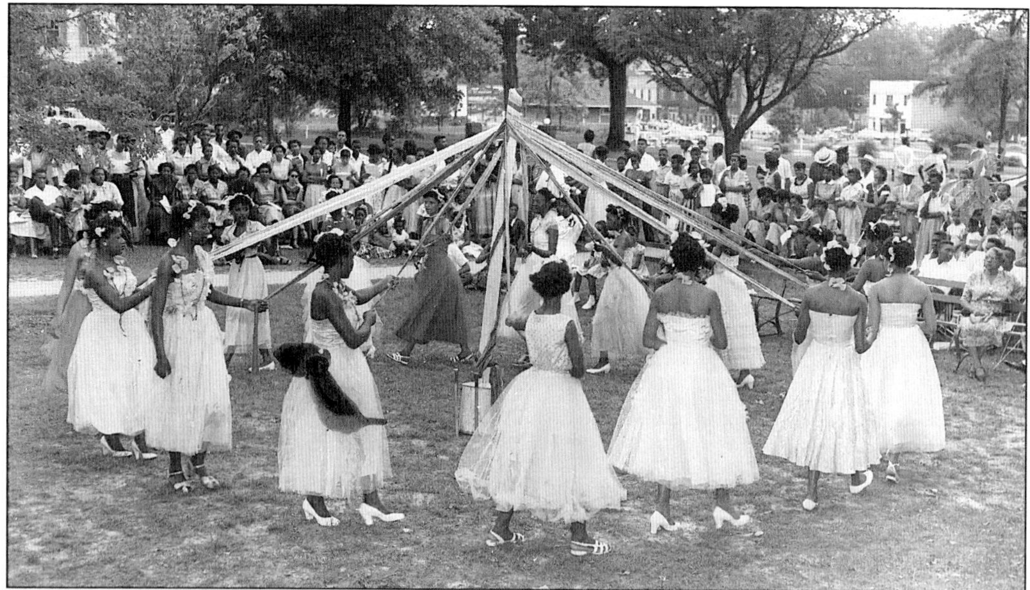

The traditional May Pole Dance was part of the college's May Day celebration, as depicted in this photo taken during the 1954 May Day festivities. May Day activities also included tumblers and characters from out-of-the-world fantasy. (Photo by E.C. Jones.)

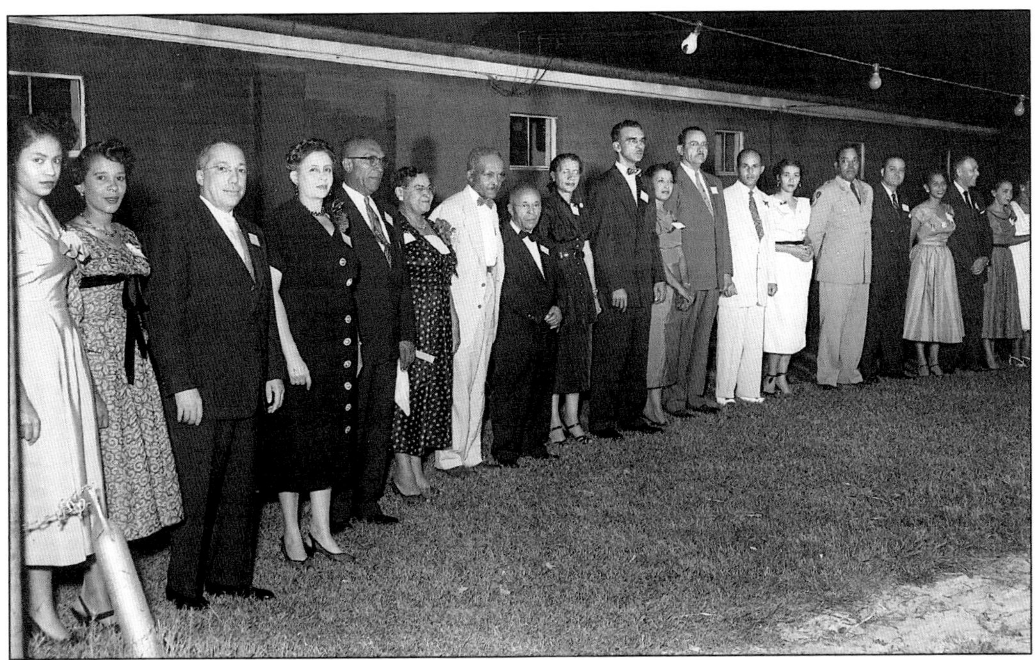

This image shows the receiving line at the 1954 Presidential Reception for freshmen, during which incoming students met the college community. Standing, from left to right, are the following: Emma Saylor, Rubye Grayson, President Benner C. Turner, Mrs. Julia Turner, Dean K.W. Green, Mrs. Geraldine J. and Mr. Penn, Dean and Mrs. F. Marcellus Staley, Dr. and Mrs. Frank DeCosta, Dr. Harold Crawford, Mr. and Mrs. Pete Whittaker, unidentified, Dr. and Mrs. Howard Jordan, Dean and Mrs. H.N. Vincent, and Dean Marie Vernon. (Photo by Lackey's.)

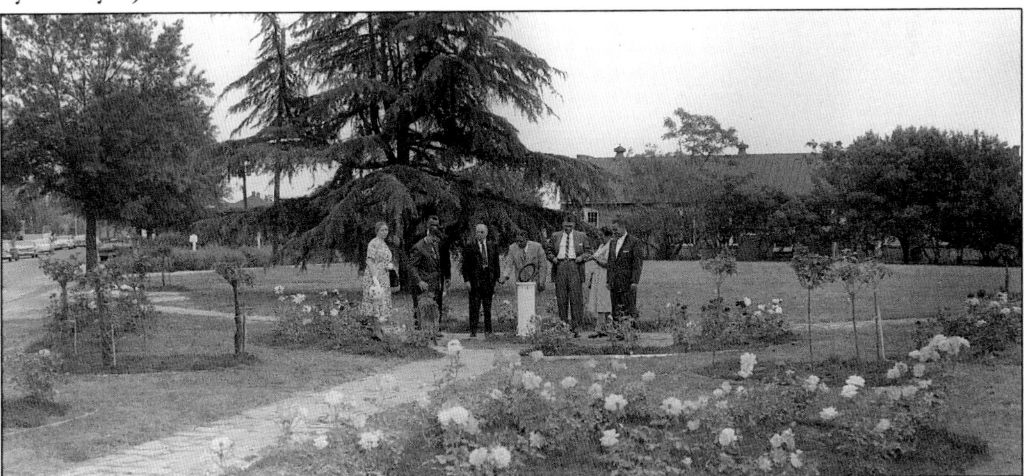

The first Board of Visitors was appointed by President Turner in 1960 to serve as a liaison between the college and the community. Members of this first board were Walker Solomon, Allard Allston, Benjamin Sanders, C.C. Woodson, Dr. Carl Green, Mrs. Ola D. Walker, and Reginald Barrett. This photo, taken during the board's 1961 campus visit, depicts from left to right, Mrs. Julia Turner, Reginald Barrett (petting "Sandy" the dog), C.C. Woodson, President Benner C. Turner, Benjamin Sanders, Allard Allston, Mrs. Ola D. Walker, and Walker E. Solomon on the campus's center court.

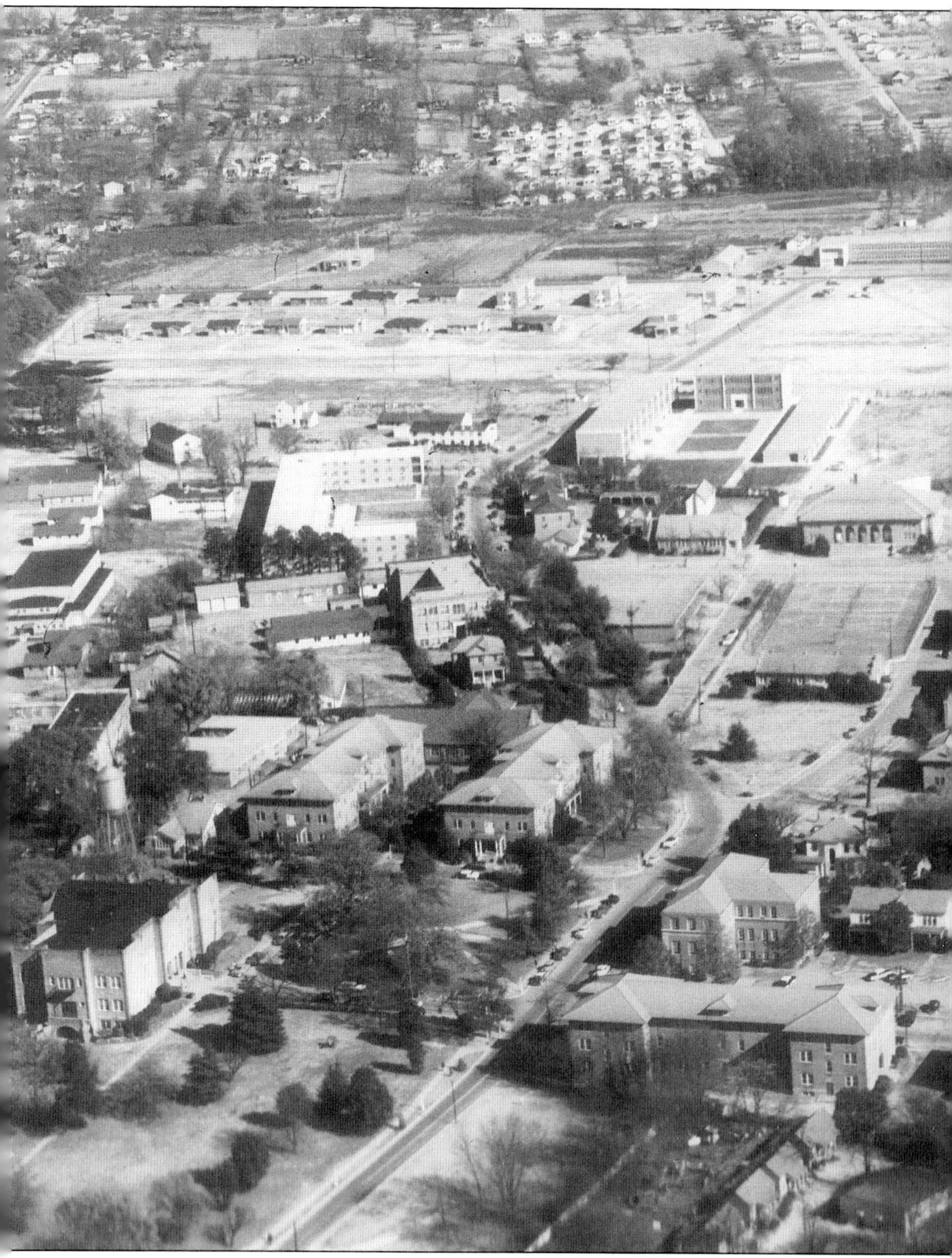

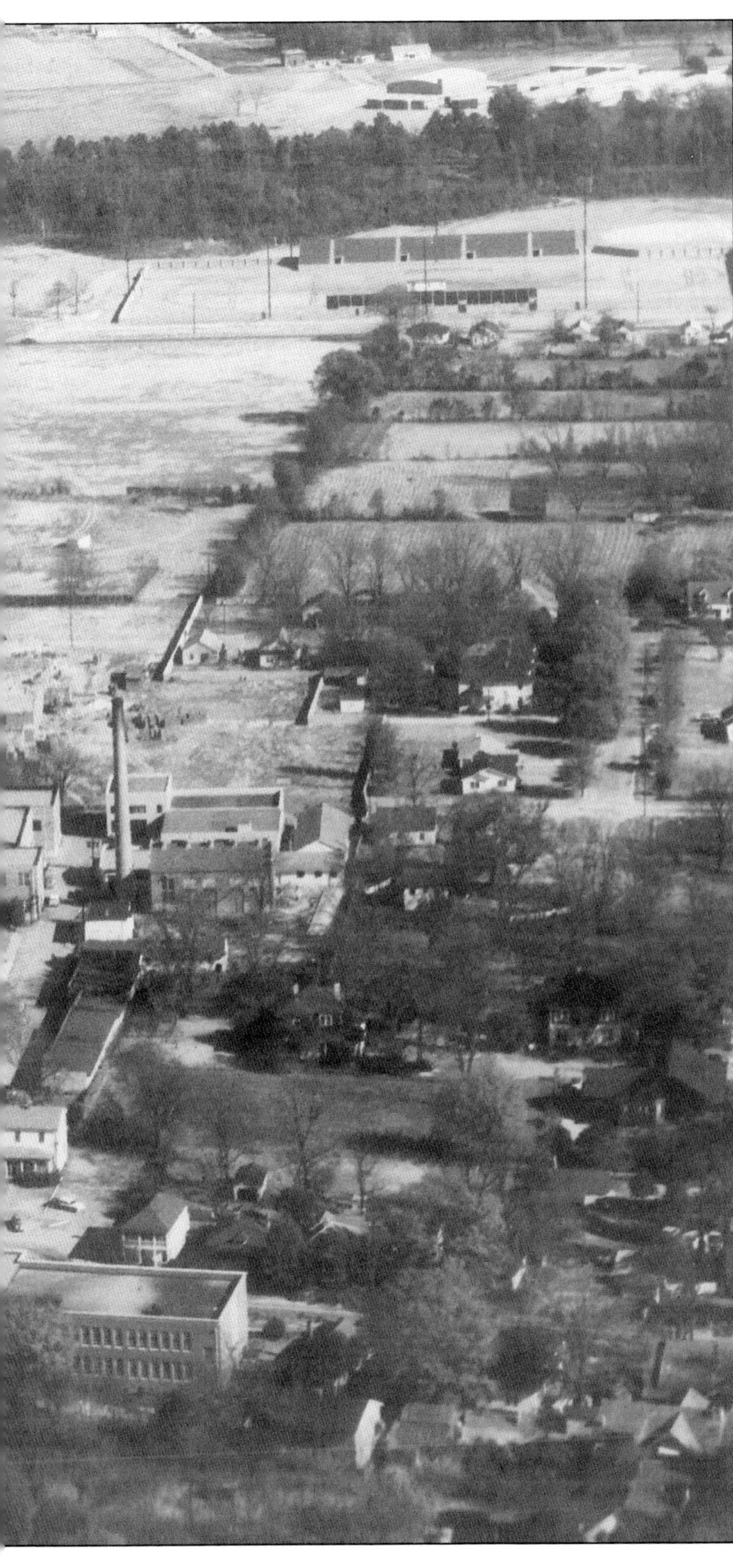

This aerial photo, taken *c.* 1956, depicts the campus during Turner's administration. (Photo by Cecil Williams.)

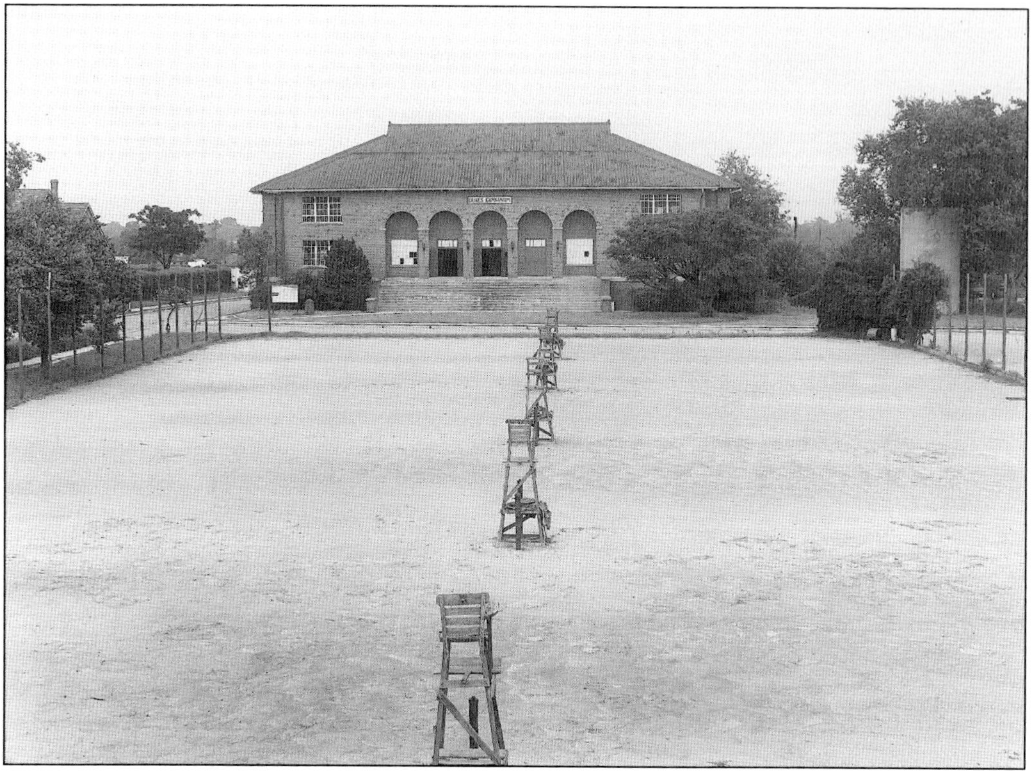

This photo, taken *c.* 1952, depicts the tennis courts in front of Dukes Gymnasium. (Photo by Lackey's.)

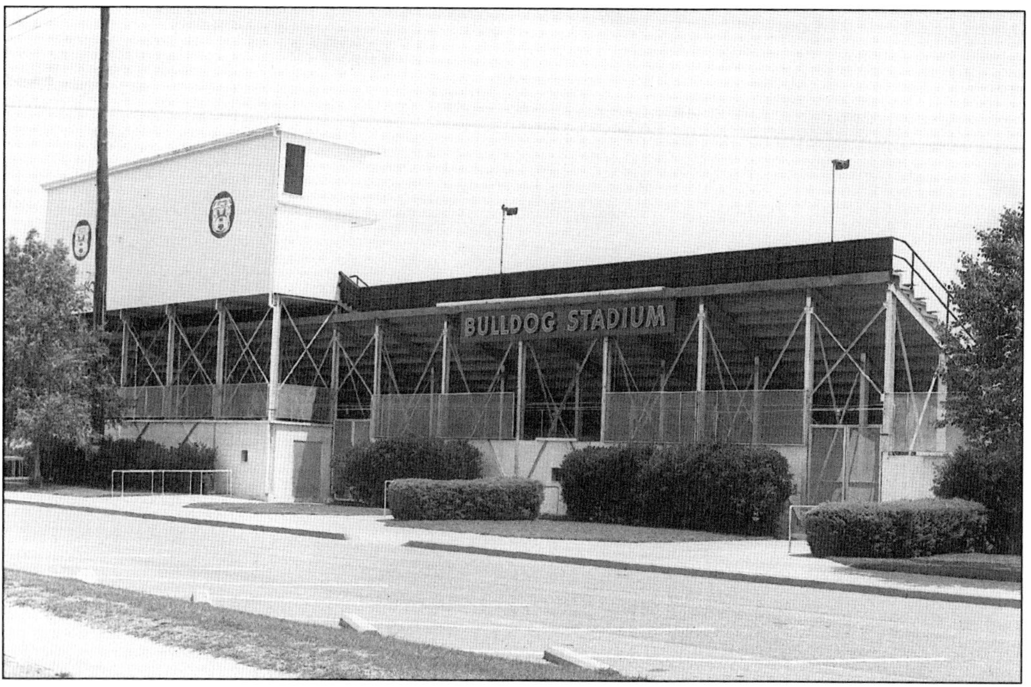

Bulldog Stadium was constructed in 1955 for use by the college and the community.

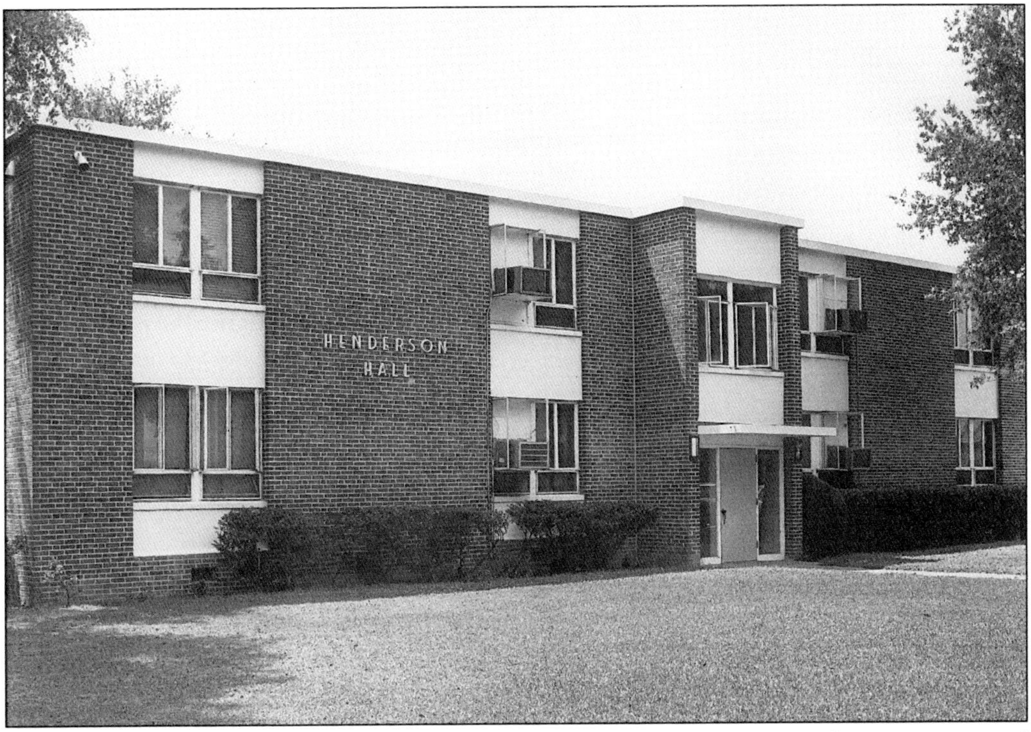

Named in honor of Mrs. Sara G. Henderson, an instructor, Henderson Hall was constructed in 1954 to serve as a faculty apartment building along with its likeness, Sheffield Hall, which was named in honor of Mrs. Helen Wilkinson Sheffield, chemistry teacher and dining hall manager. Both buildings were demolished in 1995, and the University's new Fine Arts Center now occupies the site. (Photo by Larry Mitchell.)

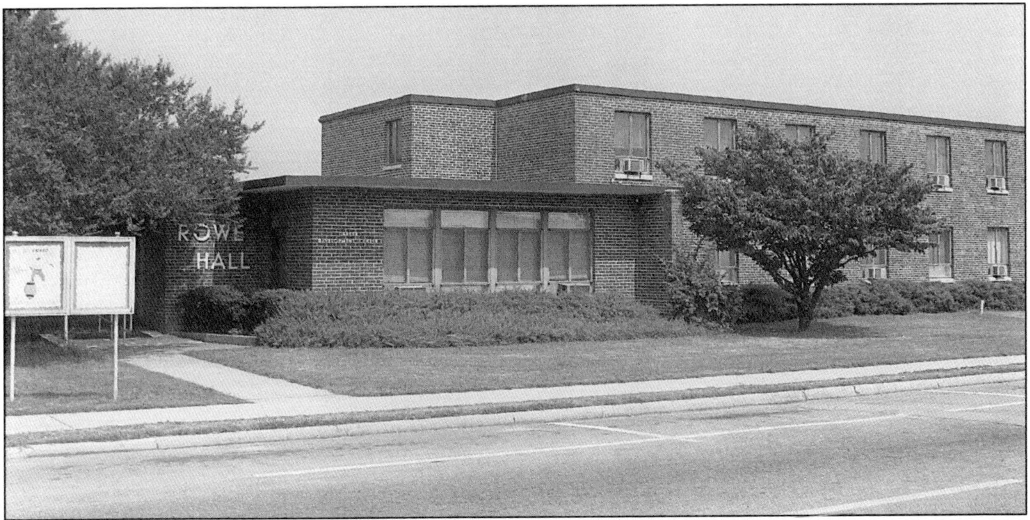

Rowe Hall, named in honor of Mrs. Etta Butler Rowe, education professor, was constructed in 1954 to serve as a dormitory for faculty women. It has also served as the college's Career Development Center. Rowe Hall also had a twin structure, Nix Hall, which was named in honor of Dean Nelson C. Nix. Nix Hall originally served as a dormitory for faculty men and has also served as the Speech-Language and Hearing Clinic.

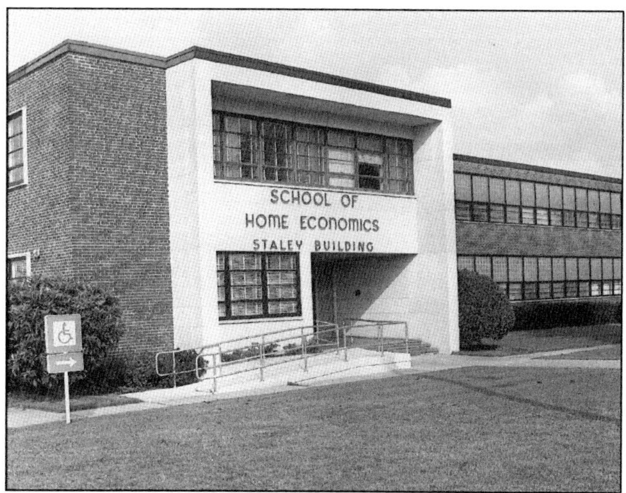

Named in honor of Frank Marcellus Staley, Dean of the School of Agriculture, Staley Hall was constructed in 1954 with funds donated by the General Education Board. The School of Agriculture and Home Economics, facilities for dairy processing, the School of Agriculture library, state offices of Agricultural Extension, Home Demonstration, and itinerant teachers of agriculture and home economics have all been housed in Staley Hall. (Photo by Larry Mitchell.)

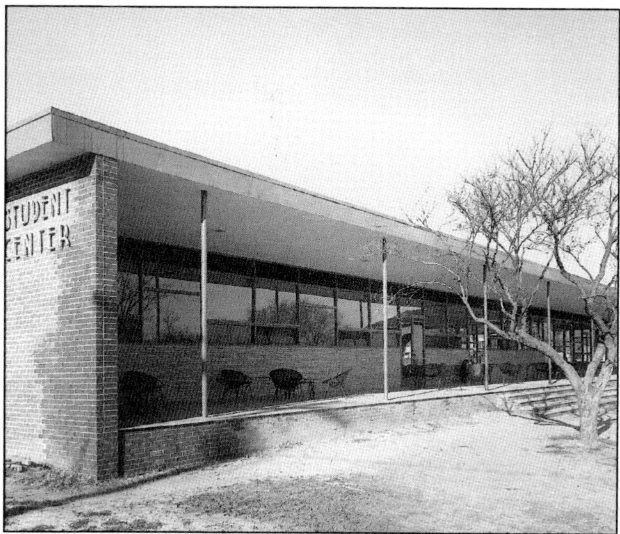

The Kirkland W. Green Student Center, named in honor of Dean Kirkland W. Green, was constructed in 1954 to house student activities, conferences, meeting rooms, and snack and game areas. (Photo by Larry Mitchell.)

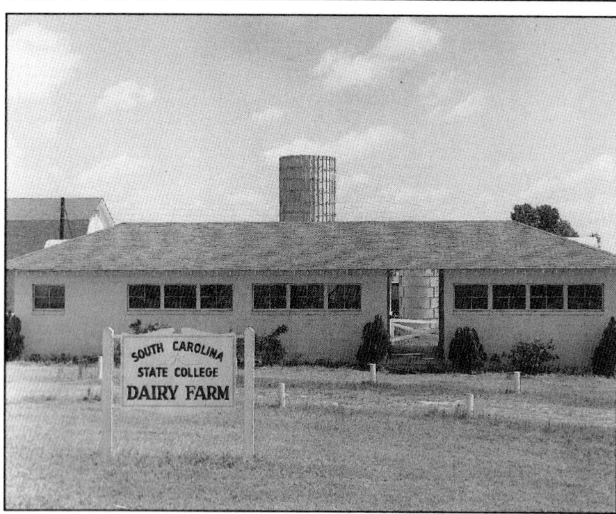

During Turner's administration, the college continued its commitment to agricultural education, as shown by improvements made to the dairy farm in 1954. The dairy farm was located 2 miles from the campus. It was transformed into the Hillcrest Recreational Center in the mid-1970s.

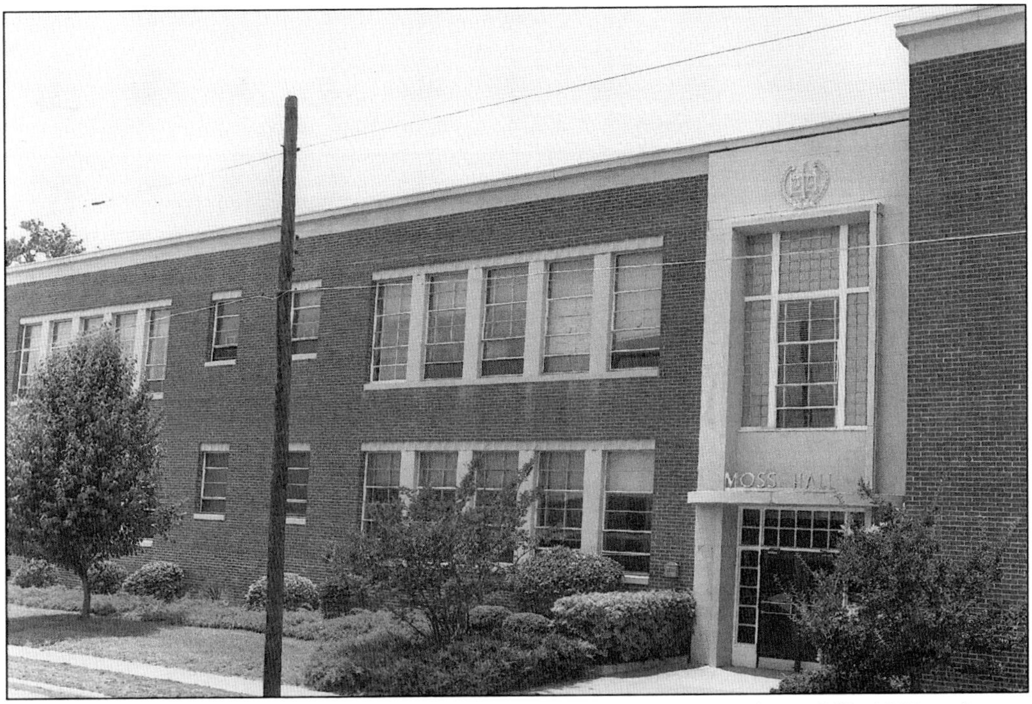

Named in honor of trustee Adam Moss, Moss Hall was constructed in 1949–1950 to house the college's law school. It has also housed the graduate school. The Freshman Programs office is presently housed in Moss Hall.

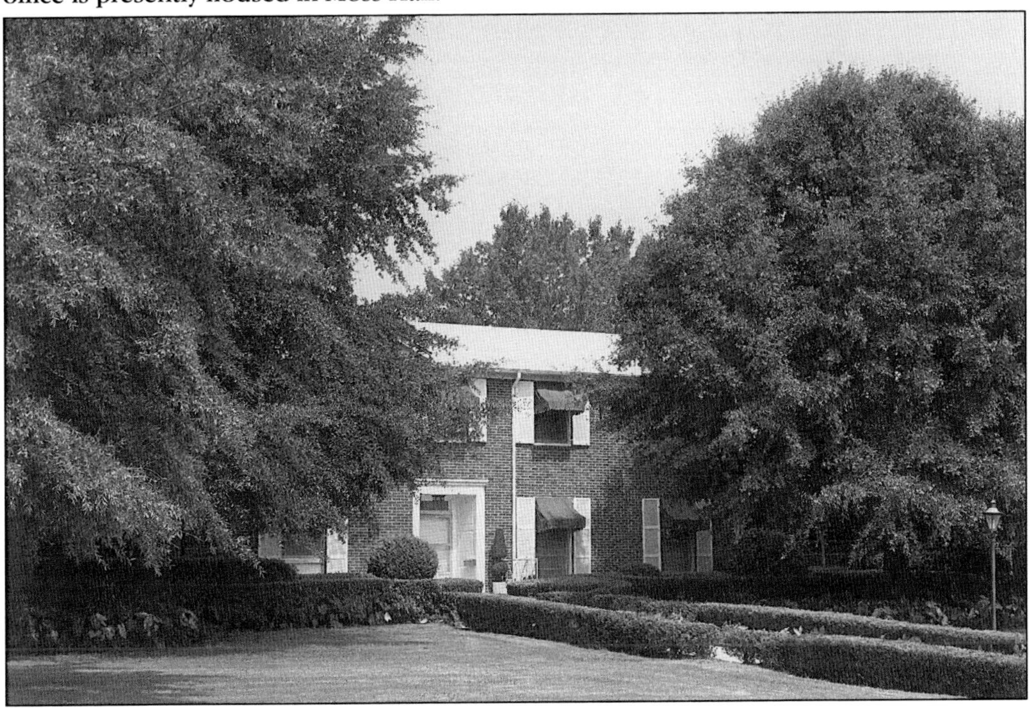

Constructed in 1961, this new brick structure replaced the college's original president's residence constructed during President Thomas E. Miller's administration.

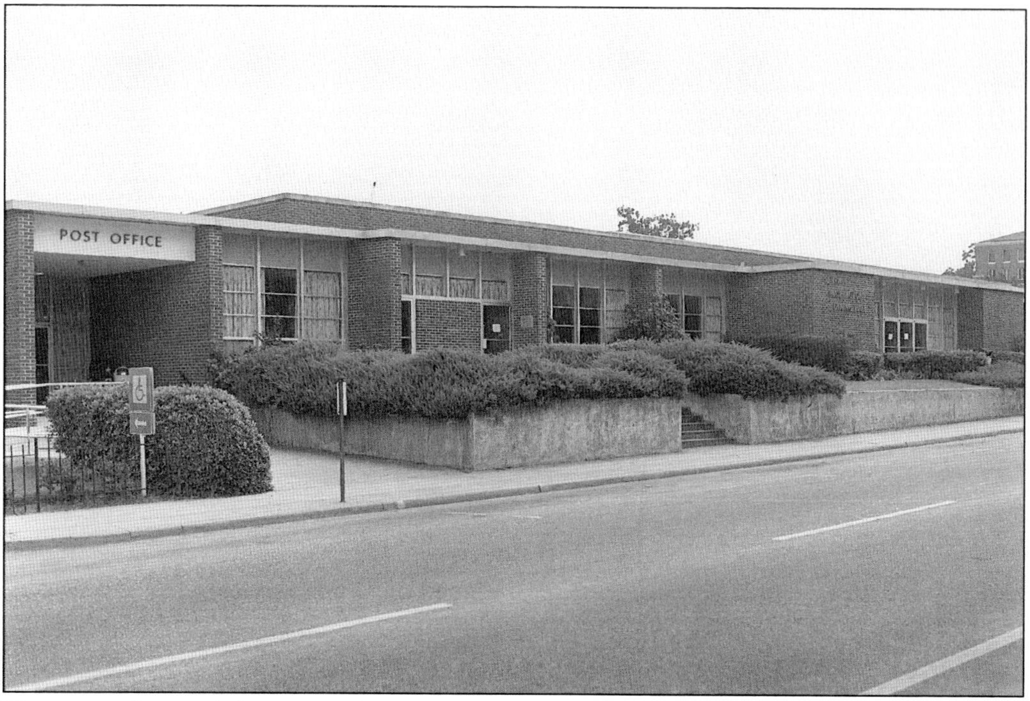

The post office and the J.I. Washington Dining Hall, named in honor of business manager J.I. Washington II, were constructed in 1962.

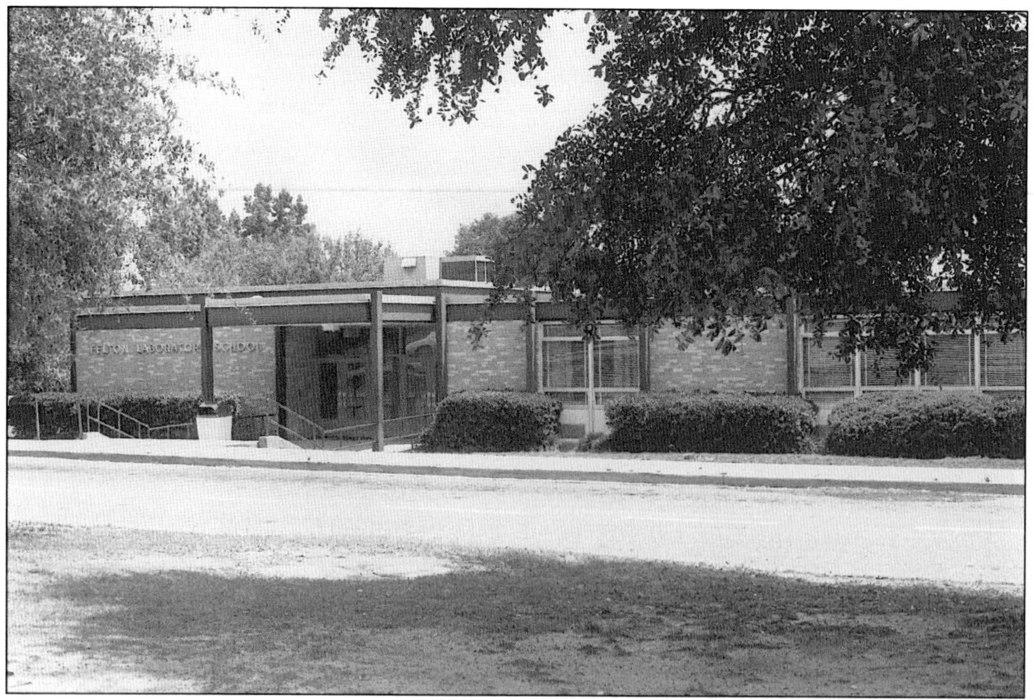

Named in honor of J.B. Felton, who was the supervisor of Negro schools, Felton Laboratory was constructed in 1964 to replace Felton Training School, which had been constructed in 1924.

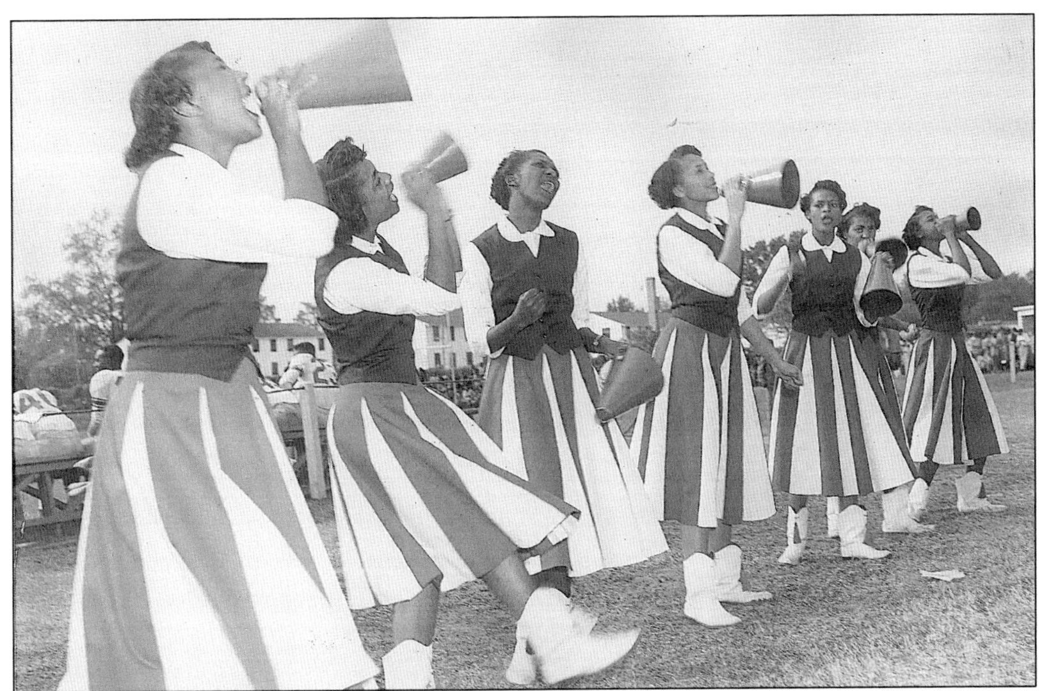

This image depicts some of the college's cheerleaders from the early 1950s. They are, from left to right, Shirley Richardson, Carrie Bodie, Edmonia Woolridge, Bobbie Mattison, and several unidentified cheerleaders.

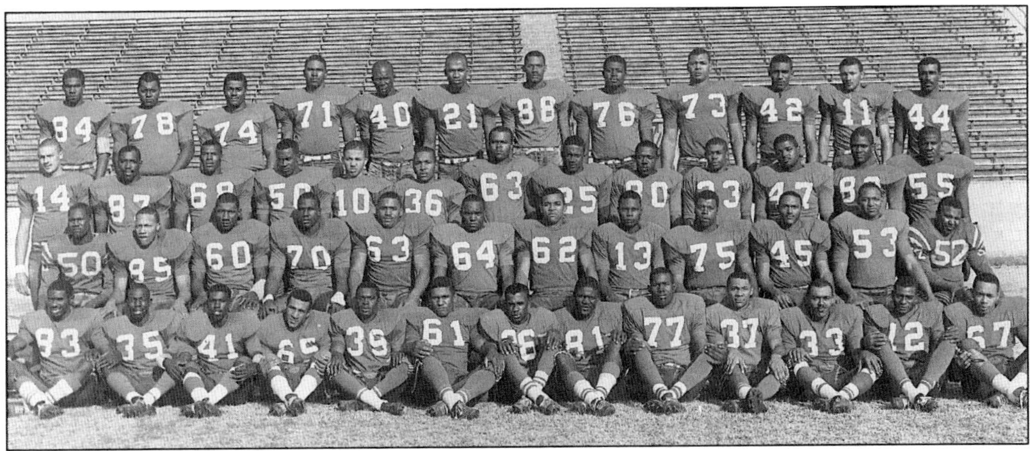

This photo shows the 1966 football team, consisting of, from left to right, the following: Josephy Wynns, William Stewart, Willis Ham, Antonio Harris, Johnny Wilson, Robert Reeves, Henry Cornish, Codell Sumter, Jimmy Bolding, Fellie Sweat, James Gordon, Milton Nicholson, and Robert Clardy; (second row) Harold Backmon, Virgil Sampson, Clifford McClain, Clarence Kegler, Robert Miller, John Ware, Joseph Pearson, Wallace Richardson, James Copeland, William Durham, Larry Wilson, and James Kelly; (third row) Robert Davis, Walter Mitchell, James Johnson, James Caldwell, Robert Scott, Jackie Epps, Adville Montgomery, Tracy Hodges, Fred Stephens, Samuel Leaphart, Lewis Mims, Odell Sumter, and John Brown; (back row) Thomas Kennerly, Philip Harrison, Joseph Hays, Tyrone Caldwell, Willie Grate, Bennie Blocker, James Sullivan, Benjamin Bryant, Jonathan Hardin, R.C. Gamble, Johnny Jones, and John Gilliam.

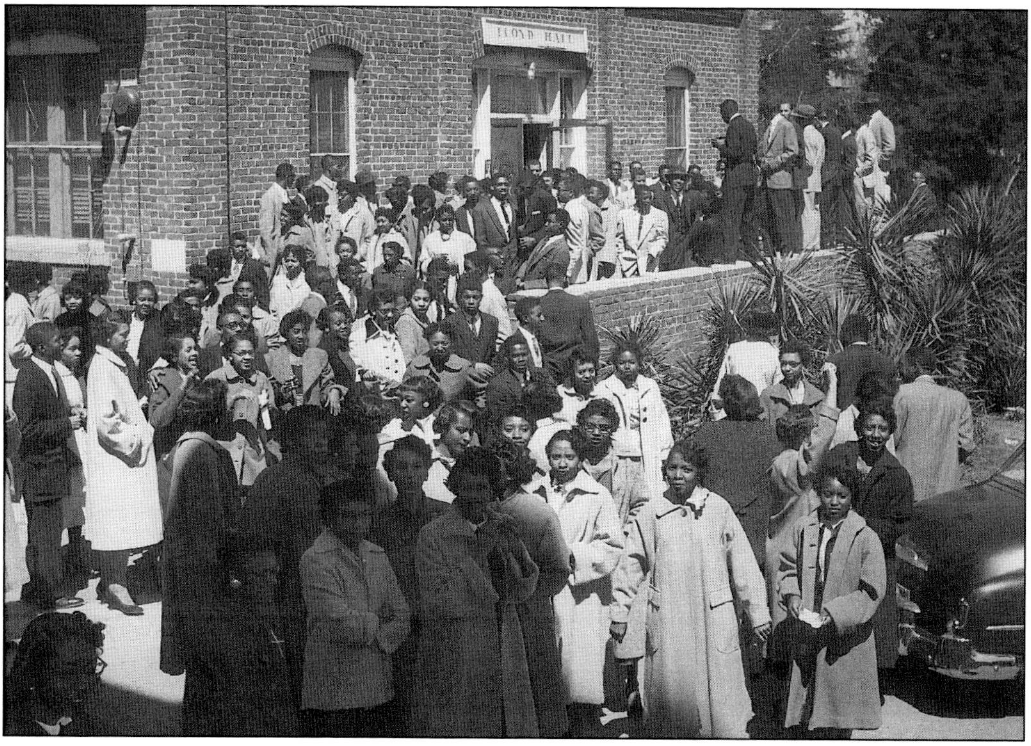

In 1955, 57 black residents of Orangeburg petitioned to have the local public schools integrated. When the local white community resisted, the NAACP began a selective buying campaign. Students at S.C. State supported the effort and refused to drink Coble milk or Sunbeam bread in the dining hall. Students subsequently began a boycott of the dining hall and of classes in 1956. The board of trustees promptly expelled Student Government Association President Fred H. Moore less than a month before he was to graduate. The photo above shows students walking out of Floyd Dining Hall, and the photo below shows students bidding farewell to Fred Moore. Fourteen other students were not permitted to return the following semester. (Photos by Cecil Williams.)

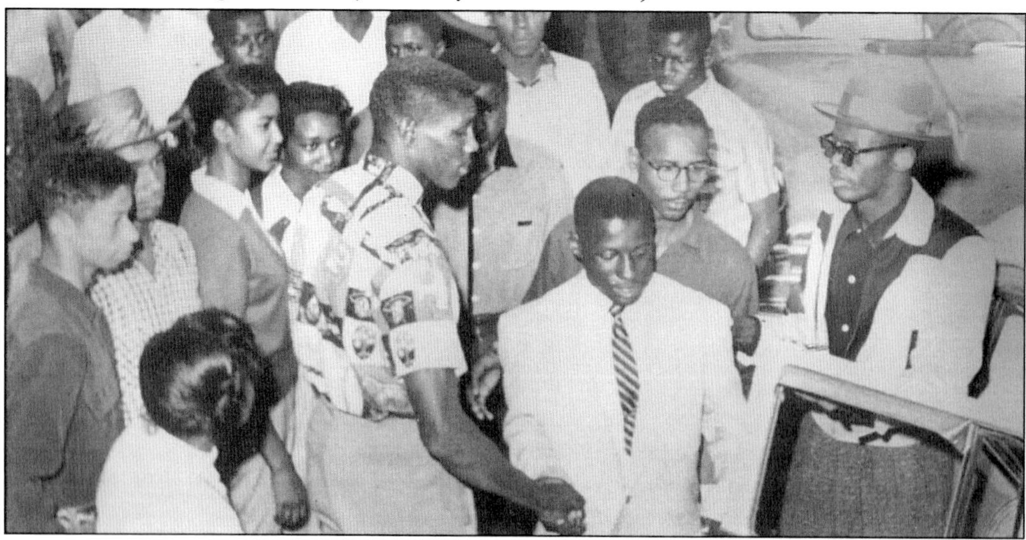

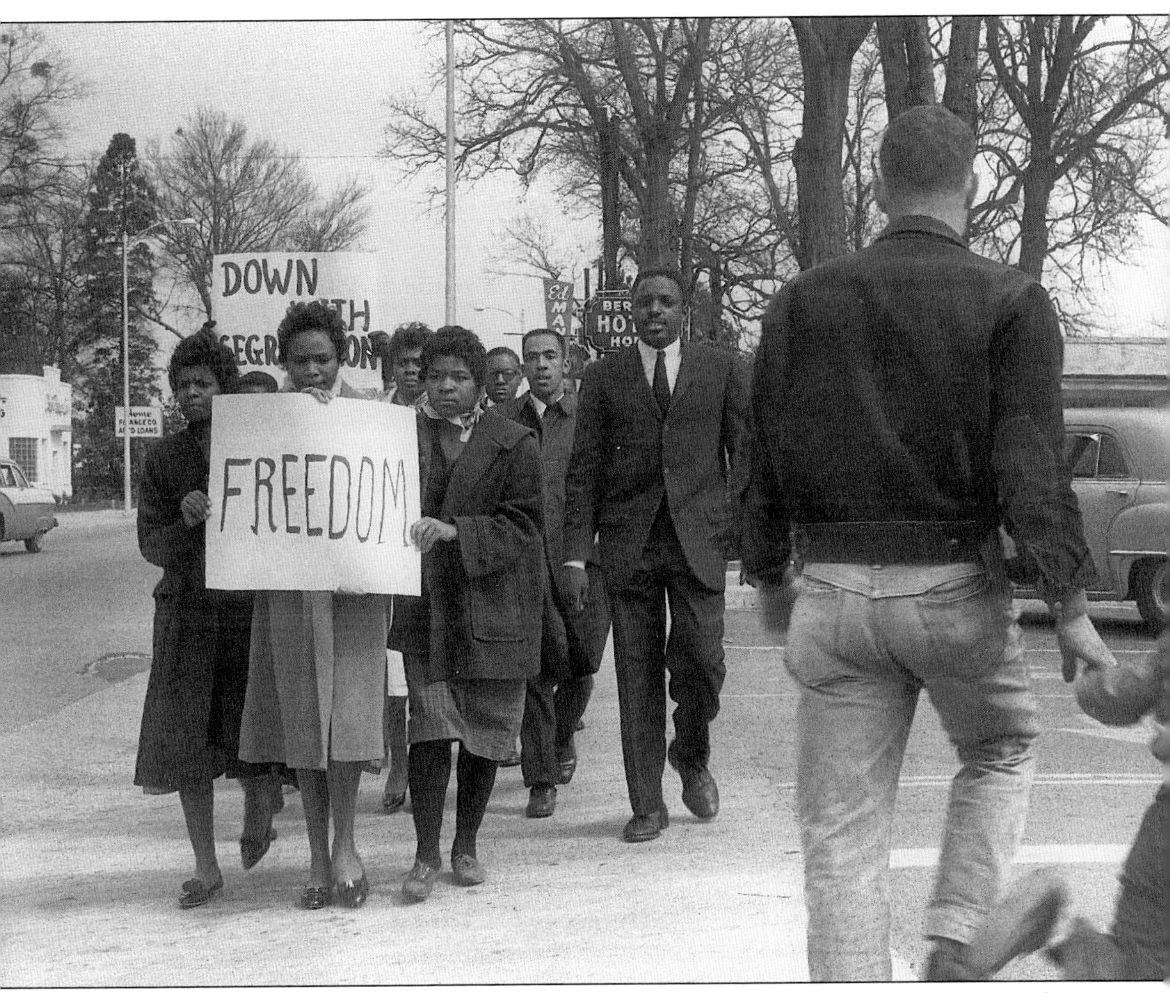

This image, taken March 15, 1960, shows the advent of the open demand and advocacy for freedom and equal protection under the law by blacks in the South and across the country. Beginning in Orangeburg in the mid-1950s, protest marches continued to be staged with regularity until 1968. Organization of protest activities by students of South Carolina State College and neighboring Claflin was crucial to the effectiveness of the freedom movement, since adults were often economically dependent upon approval by Caucasian entrepreneurs for their livelihood. Students, free from the constraints of making a living, could openly protest injustices in circumstances where their parents might have been forced into a survivalist conservatism. Included in the group are Juanita Starnes on the right and Herman Gaither (in partial view, also on the right). (Photo by Cecil Williams.)

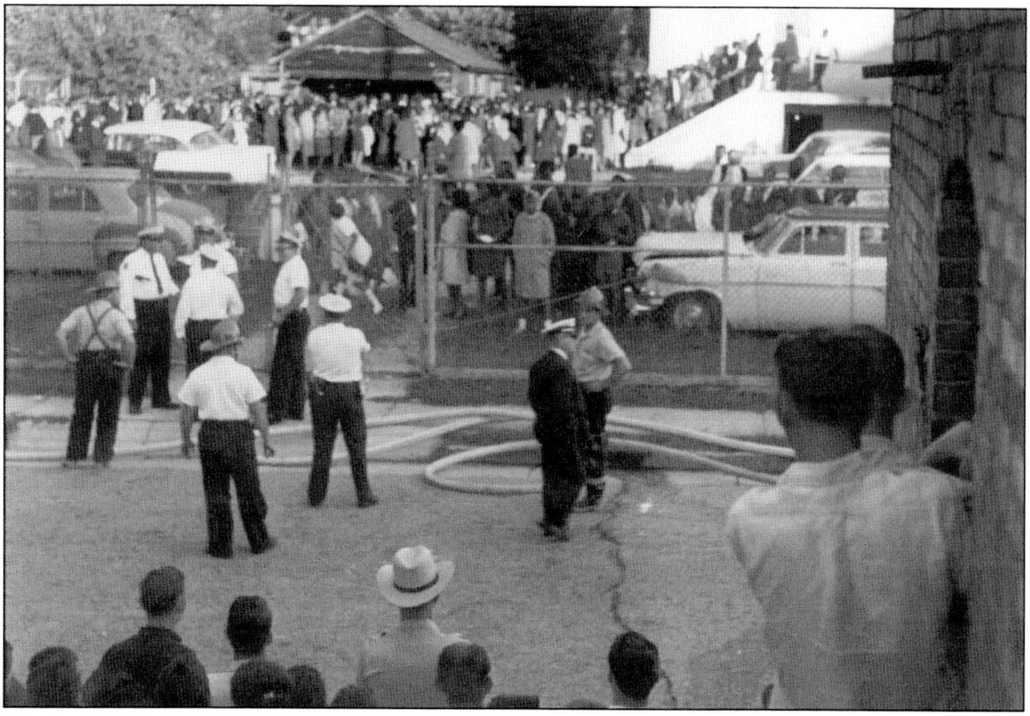

Nearly 400 students from S.C. State, Claflin, and Wilkinson High School were arrested on March 15, 1960, as they protested against segregation in Orangeburg. They were confined behind a stockade at the old county jail (affectionately referred to as the Pink Palace) until they were transferred to the Central Correctional Institution in Columbia. Many of them were soaked by fire hoses on that cold March day. (Photo by Cecil Williams.)

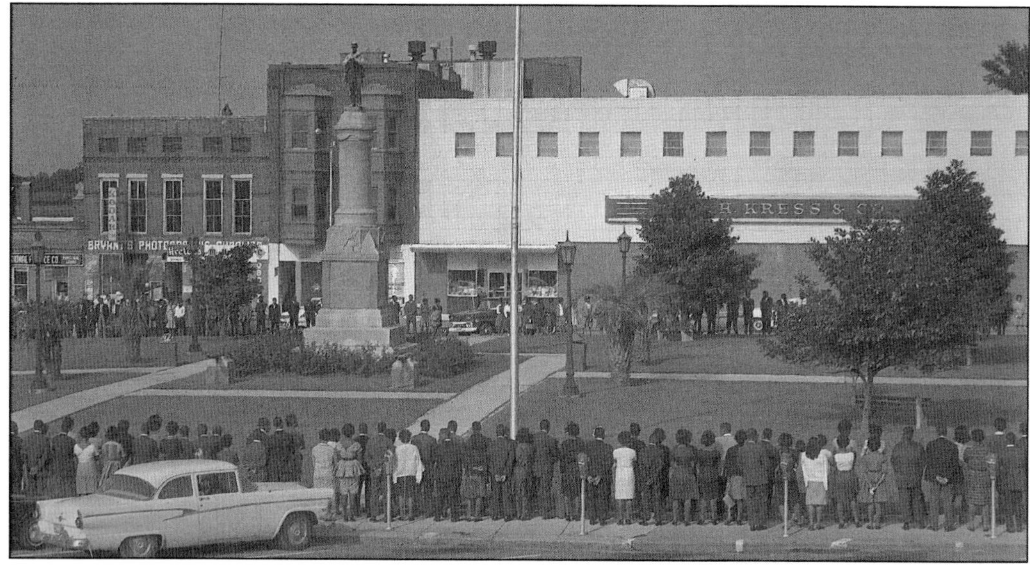

Protests by college and high school students against Jim Crow continued in Orangeburg. This photo shows well-dressed students accompanied by local clergymen gathered around the Confederate Memorial at the town square in Orangeburg in 1963. (Photo by Cecil Williams.)

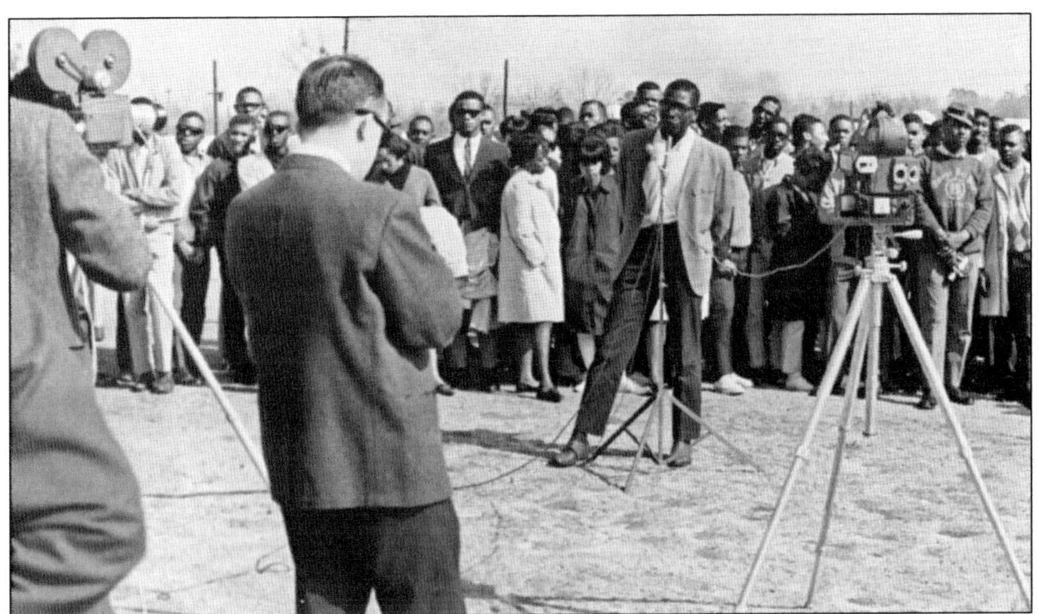

In "the cause" in the spring of 1967, students protested and boycotted classes in opposition to President Turner's autocratic leadership. Three students, Joseph Hammond, John Stroman, and Benjamin Bryant, had been summarily suspended without a disciplinary hearing. Led by Isaac "Ike" Williams, students threatened a march to Columbia as the crisis escalated. Governor Robert McNair intervened, and President Benner C. Turner was forced into early retirement.

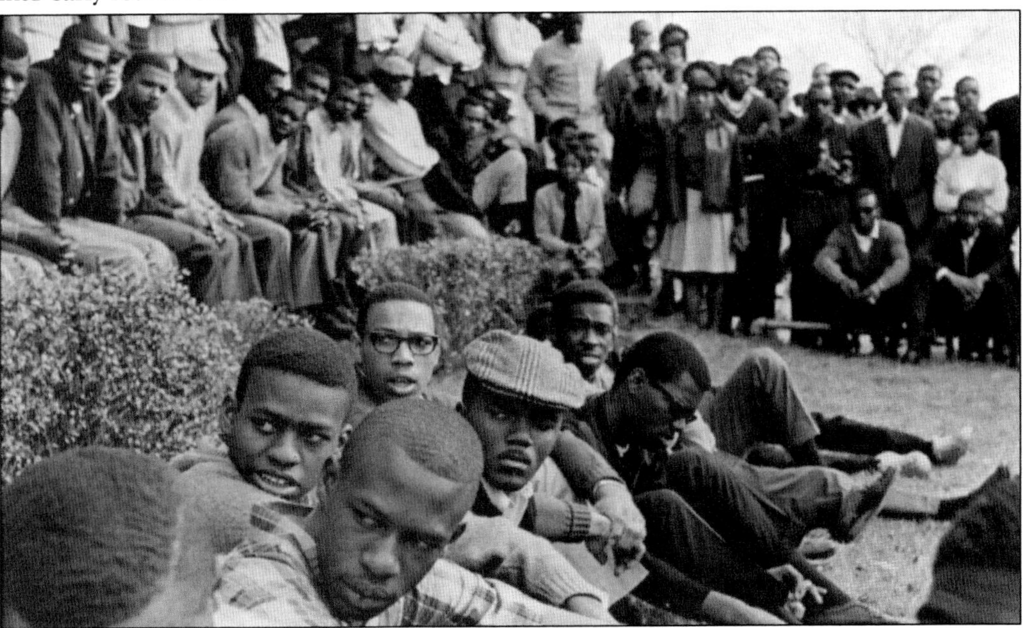

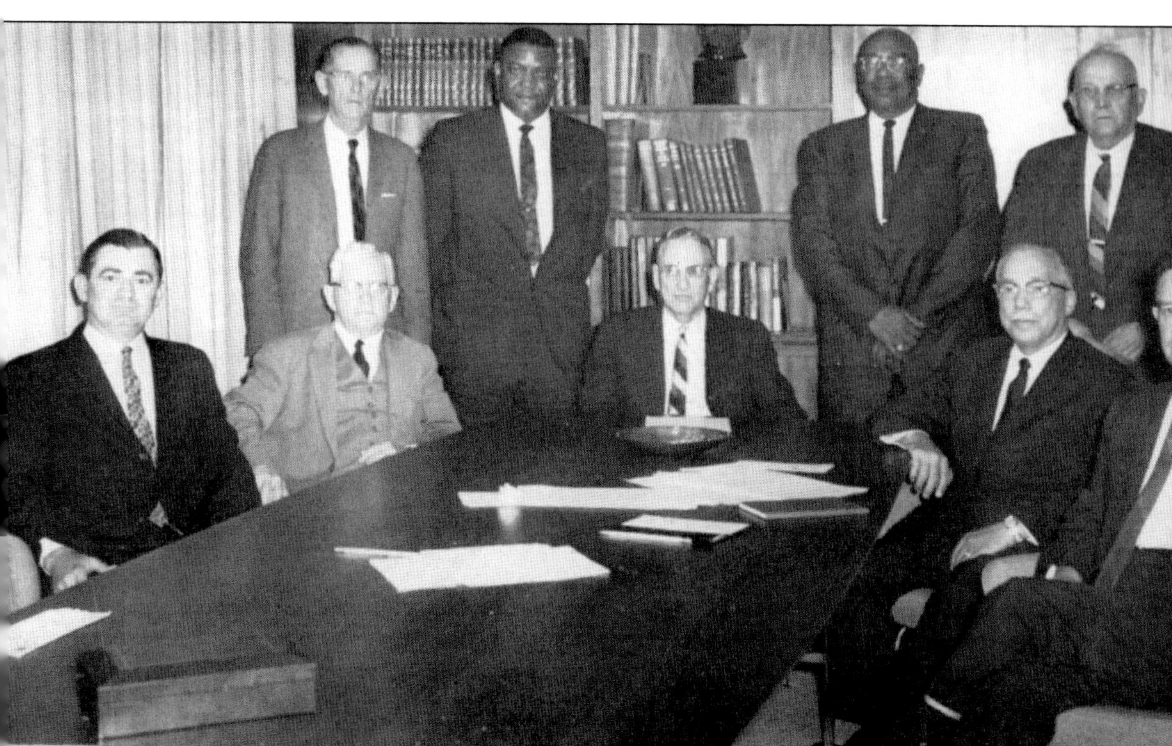

For its first seven decades, each member of the institution's board of trustees was white and male. In 1966, the general assembly elected the first two African-American men to serve on the board, I.P. Stanback and Dr. James Boykin. They are, from left to right, as follows: (seated) Elliott Elam; W.C. Bethea, secretary; Bruce W. White, chair; President Benner C. Turner; and James Moss; (standing) W. Felix Wheeler; Dr. James Boykin; I.P. Stanback; and Charles A. Jones. Dr. Howard Royal did not attend the meeting

Five

M. Maceo Nance Jr. 1968–1986

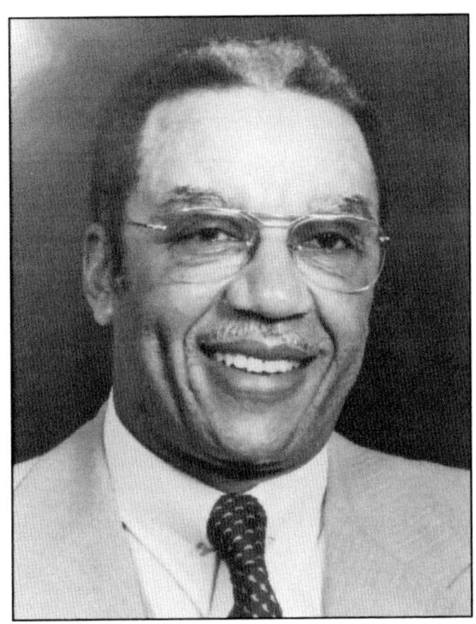

An individual whose name remains synonymous with South Carolina State University, M. Maceo Nance Jr. assumed leadership over the institution at a turbulent and tragic period in its evolution. A native of Columbia, Nance was the first graduate of the college who served as president, and he was the first president who was inaugurated.

The Nance years saw remarkable growth and expansion in the physical facilities, programs, and reputation of the college. The college seal, adopted at Nance's inauguration and designed by Leo F. Twiggs, professor of art, remains a lasting and indelible contribution. Under President Nance's supervision, and in keeping with significant changes in civil rights in the South and in the nation, the college's student body and faculty became more diverse while maintaining its historic commitment to providing educational opportunities to Americans of African descent. In his 19 years as president, Nance oversaw the addition of 20 degree programs, including the doctoral program in educational administration. The I.P. Stanback Museum and Planetarium was conceived, erected, and dedicated with the strong support of Nance. In 1971, the program in agriculture came to an end, closing a historic era in the college's history. The college farm was leased to the City of Orangeburg and became Hillcrest Recreational Center. The institution's legacy as a land-grant college dedicated to public service continued under the 1890 Extension and Research program in conjunction with the U.S. Department of Agriculture.

In his two decades of steady leadership, Nance created a stronger college and thus laid the foundation for it to become a university.

The Orangeburg Massacre, February 8, 1968, was the most tragic episode in the history of South Carolina State University, as well as in the history of the state of South Carolina during what had been a mostly nonviolent civil rights movement. Three young men were killed and 27 injured on the campus that painful night.

The spark that ignited the tragedy was an effort by a small group of students led by John Stroman to bowl at the all-white All-Star Bowling Lanes. Students attempted to bowl on Monday and Tuesday nights, February 5th and 6th, but they were turned back by the owner and forced to leave. On Tuesday night there was an angry confrontation outside the bowling alley. One law enforcement officer suffered an eye injury. Police clubbed and beat several women students. Enraged students broke windows and destroyed the property of a number of businesses on Russell Street between the campus and the bowling lanes.

Tensions increased and the crisis escalated as city, state, and federal authorities were unable to determine whether the All-Star Lanes was covered by provisions of the 1964 Civil Rights Act. The delay had fatal consequences. In a meeting with city officials, students identified other examples of racial discrimination in the community in job opportunities, at the local hospital, at drive-in theaters, and elsewhere.

Students were confined to the campus on Wednesday night, February 7th. By then, there was a large contingent of State Highway Patrolmen and National Guardsmen in Orangeburg. Young men gathered on the front of the campus and hurled stones, sticks, and obscenities at passing motorists on Highway 601, and the thoroughfare was subsequently closed.

On Thursday night, February 8, young men again assembled at the front of the campus. Molotov cocktails failed to ignite, but they did start a bonfire that was extinguished by city firemen. Highway patrolman David Shealy was hit by a banister that was taken from a nearby abandoned house. Several minutes later, at about 10:30 p.m. and after Shealy had been taken for medical treatment, nine highway patrolmen with no warning opened fire on the crowd of unarmed students. Most of the students who were hit were struck in the back as they attempted to flee. They were hit by lethal double-ought buckshot. Henry Smith, Samuel Hammond, and Delano Middleton died while 27 young men were injured. Smith and Hammond were students at South Carolina State while Middleton attended Wilkinson High School.

In the aftermath, the FBI made a thorough investigation to determine if the students had firearms, but they turned up no such evidence. (They did find that shots had been fired earlier from the Claflin campus). The Department of Justice sued the owner of the All-Star Bowling Lanes, and it was opened to black patrons. The Department of Justice tried but failed to persuade a federal grand jury to indict the nine highway patrolmen for depriving students of their civil rights. The Justice Department then brought lesser charges against the patrolmen in federal court in Florence in 1969. A jury of ten white people and two black people acquitted the patrolmen.

Cleveland Sellers was the only individual convicted in the events surrounding the massacre. A native of Denmark, Sellers was not a student. He had been very active in the freedom struggle led by the Student Nonviolent Coordinating Committee (SNCC) in Mississippi. Although he did not participate in the initial efforts to desegregate the All Star Bowling Lanes, he was on the campus the night of the massacre, and he was wounded in the shooting. He was tried, found guilty of inciting a riot, and sentenced to a year in prison. In 1993, the State of South Carolina pardoned him.

On February 8, 2000, South Carolina State University President Leroy Davis, Student Government Association President Mark Dudley, and Tracy Powers of the South Carolina Department of Archives and History dedicated a historical plaque to the Orangeburg Massacre, located on the front of the campus.

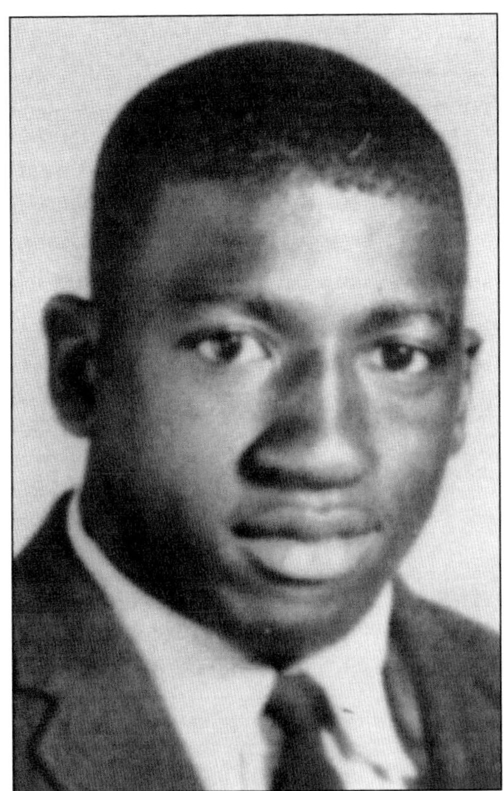

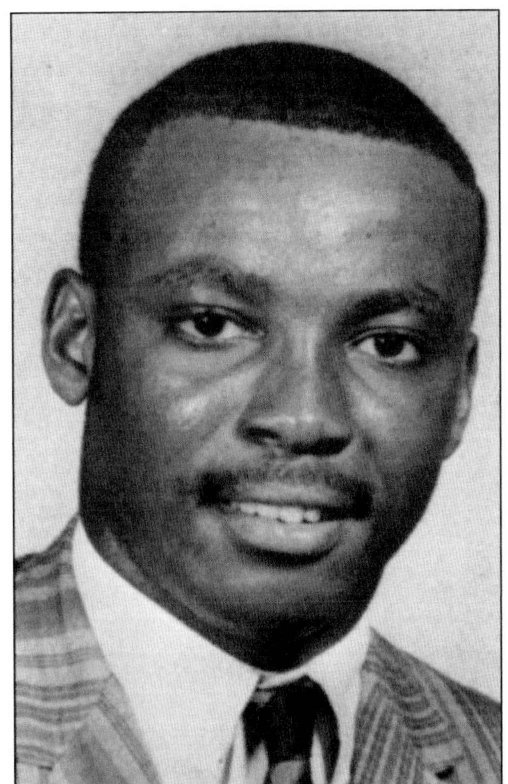

Photos of the three young men who were killed in the Orangeburg Massacre—Delano Middleton (above, left), Samuel Hammond (above, right), and Henry Smith (bottom, right).

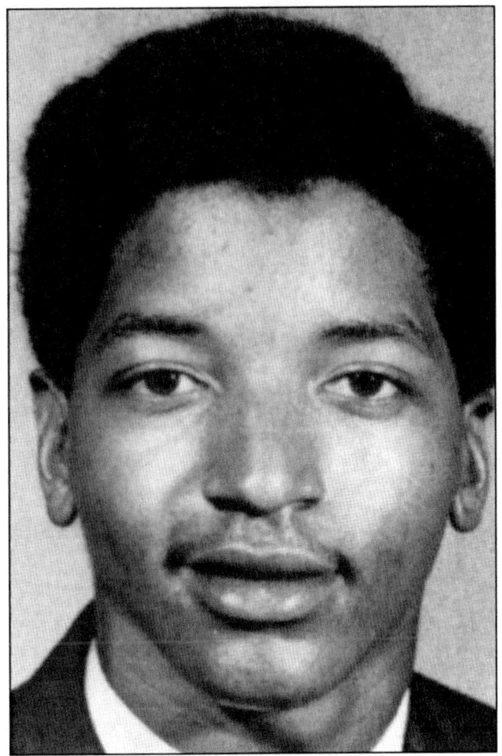

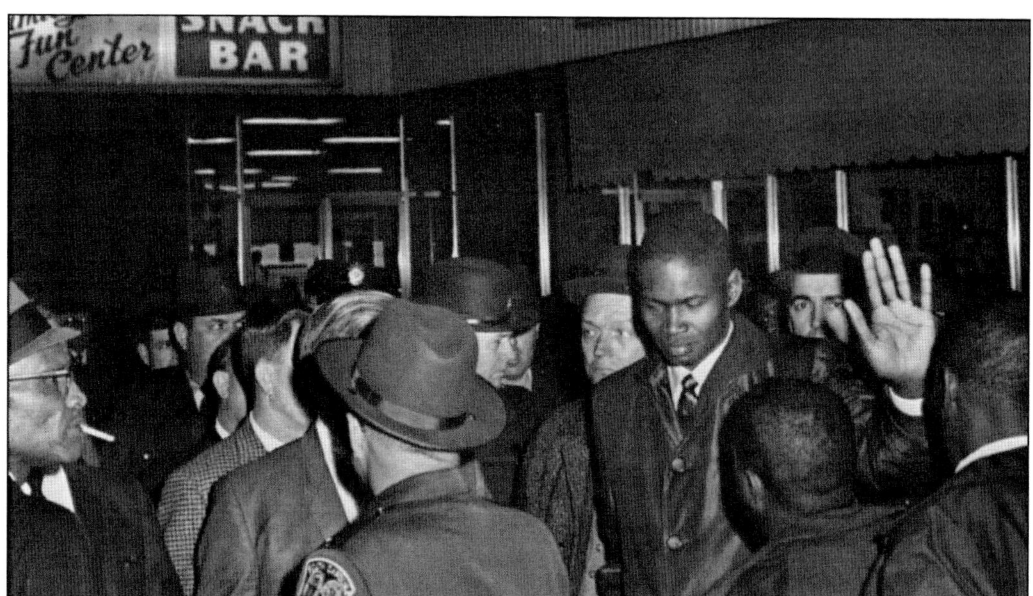

Oscar "Pete" Butler, Dean of Students, attempted to bring some calm and order to a tense confrontation in front of the All-Star Bowling Lanes on Tuesday night, February 6, 1968.

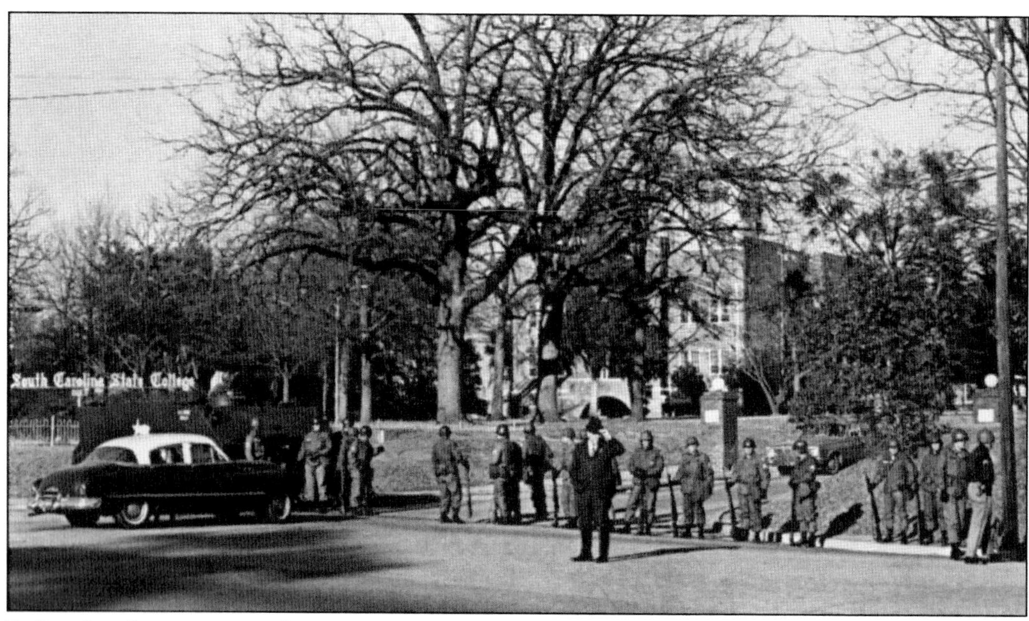

Following the massacre, the campus was closed for two weeks and students were sent home. The National Guard surrounded the campus. White Hall stands silently in the background.

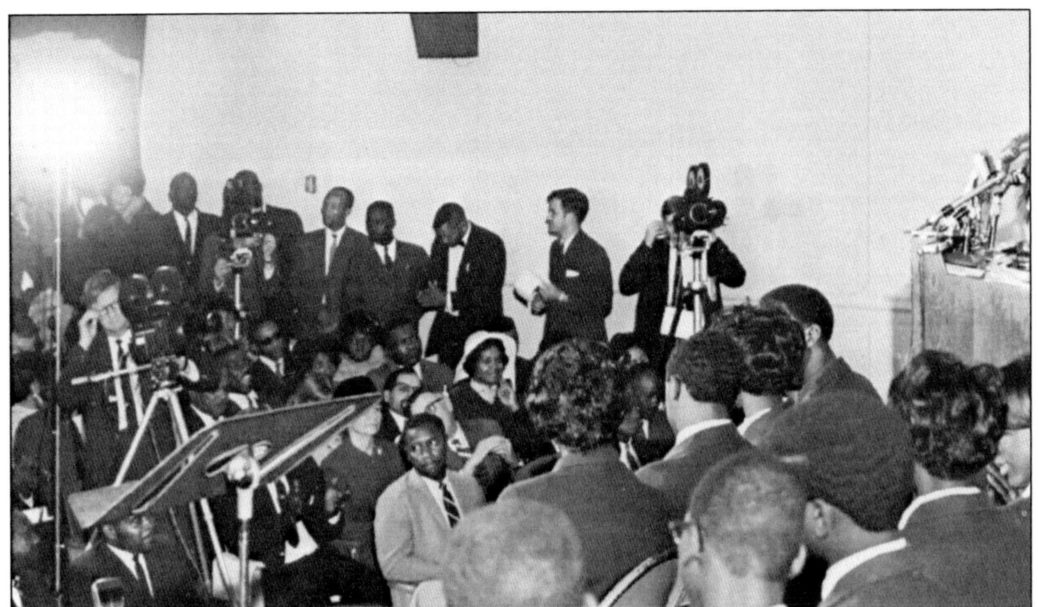

On February 25, 1968, Roy Wilkins, the executive director of the NAACP, appeared on campus to protest the Orangeburg Massacre. The collegiate chapter of the NAACP led by George Campbell helped host Mr. Wilkins.

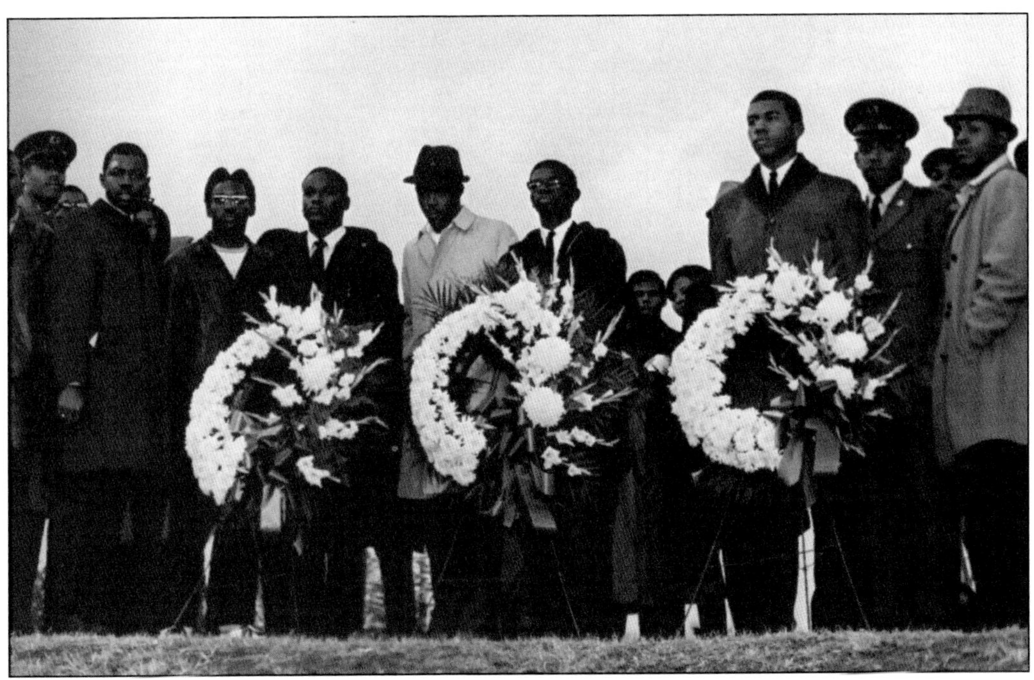

Three wreaths were placed on the front of the campus by students at a ceremony on February 29, 1968, to pay tribute to Henry Smith, Samuel Hammond, and Delano Middleton. Included in the photo are student government association president Robert Scott and wreath bearers Willie Fennel, Anthony Williams, and Samuel Abney.

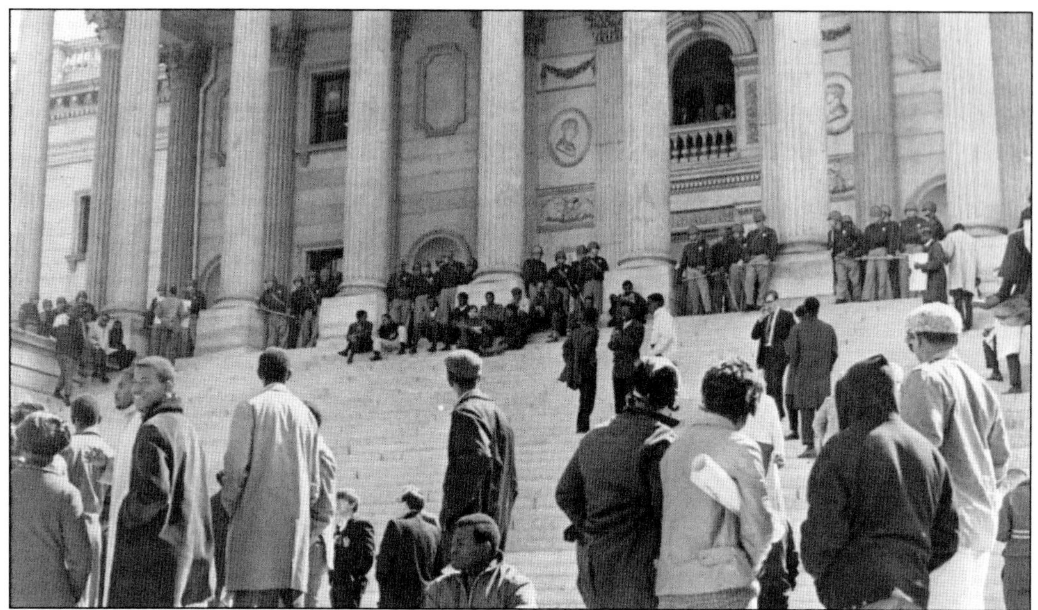

Most students and some faculty members participated in two marches in Columbia to protest the Orangeburg Massacre to Governor Robert McNair and the General Assembly. At the time, there were no black members in the legislature.

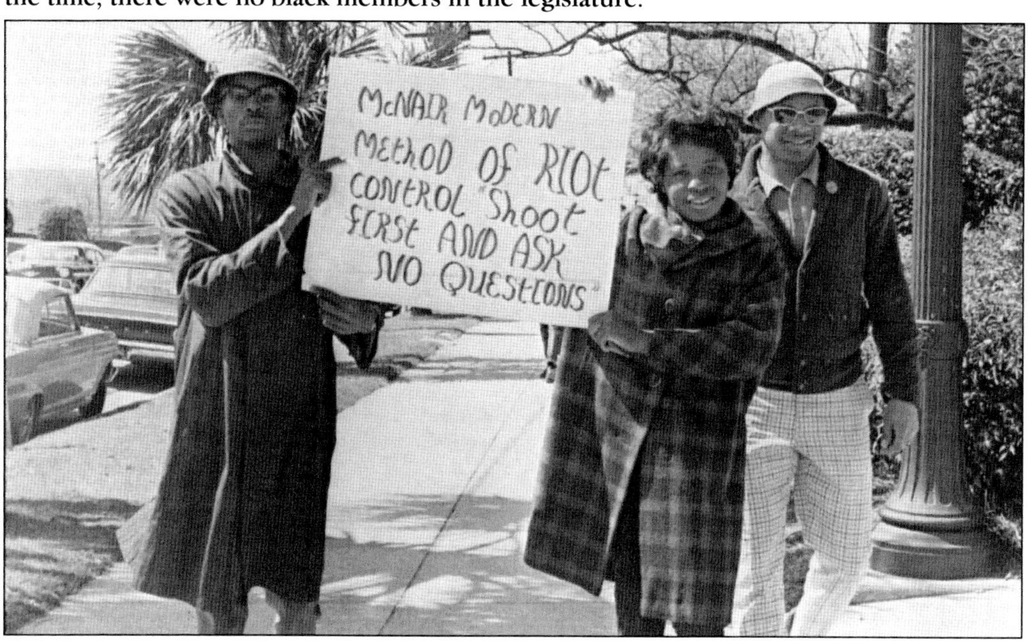

So when was this photograph taken? Could it have been the 1920s? Maybe it was the 1950s. Possibly the 1990s. Diligent detective work has determined that this seems to have been the 1970s. Note the 'fros and bellbottoms.

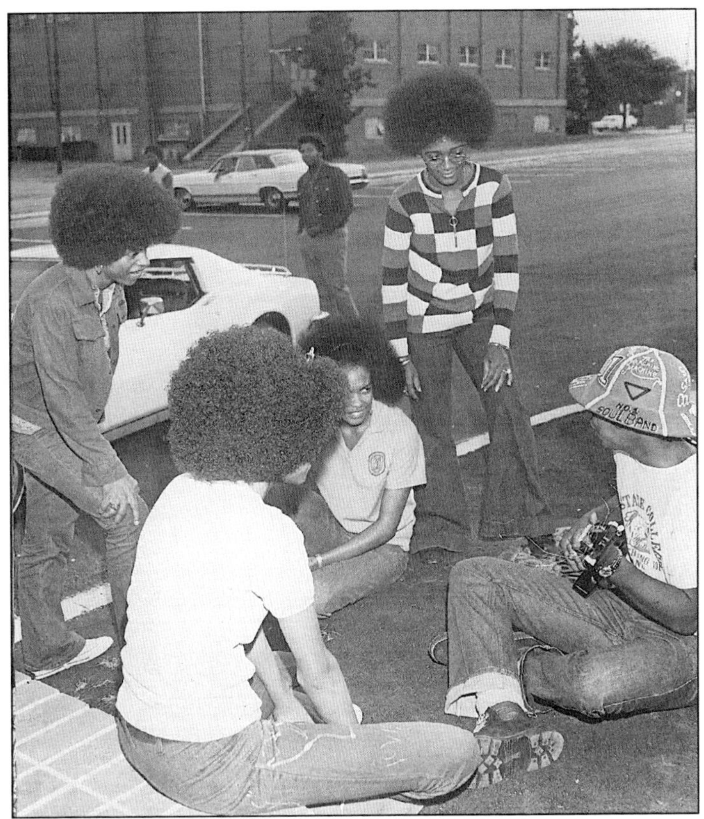

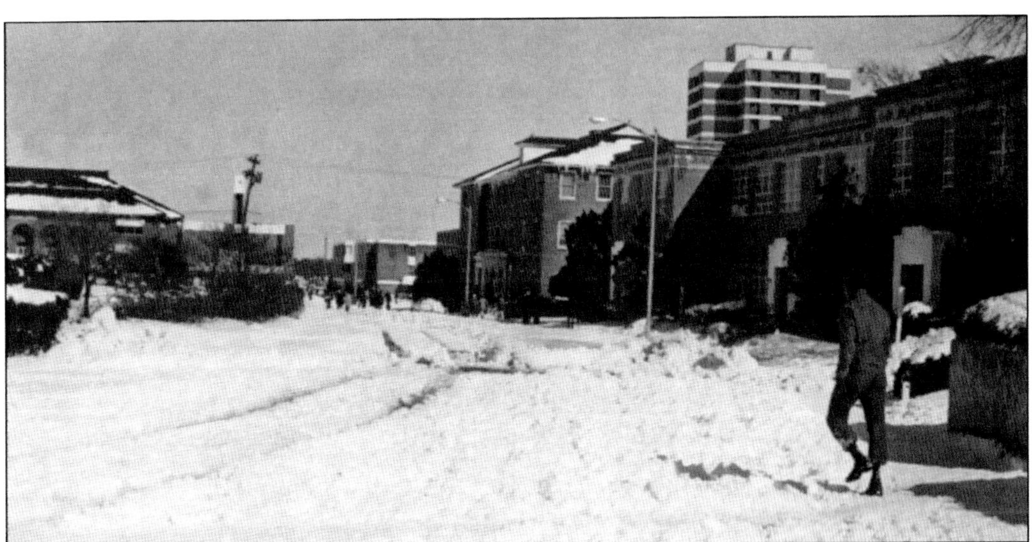

In February 1973, more than 20 inches of snow fell on South Carolina State and Orangeburg. The campus was shut down for a weekend, and three days of classes were canceled. As this photo shows, most students remained indoors studying to avoid the cold and white stuff.

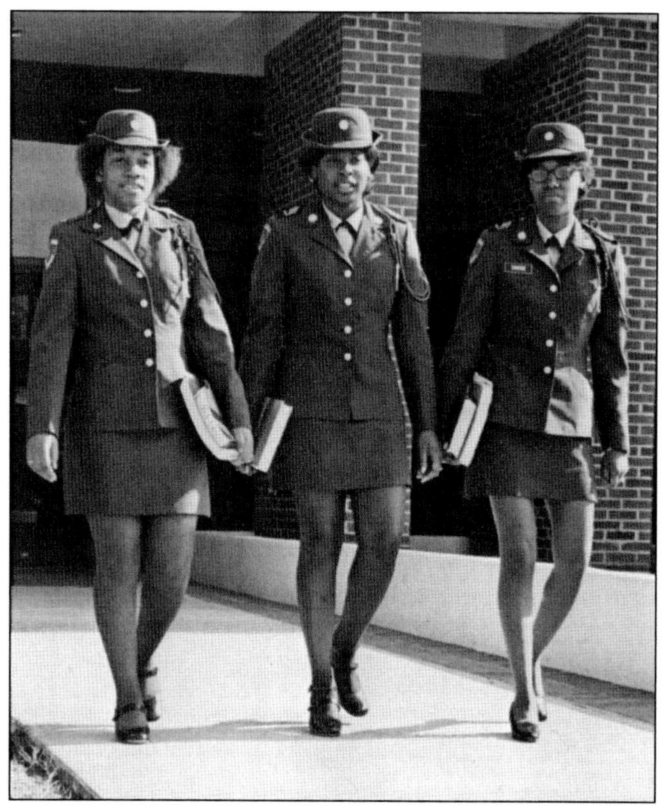

The military was a vital concern to college students nationwide in the 1960s and 1970s. At SC State, the military has represented a career opportunity for black men since the establishment of the ROTC program in 1947. South Carolina State has produced more black military officers than any other institution, and by 1972, women began to join the corps and earn commissions. In the 1973 photo to the left, cadets Mary Bridges, Joyce Leaks, and Patricia Simmons depart the Miller F. Whittaker Library at 13:15 hours.

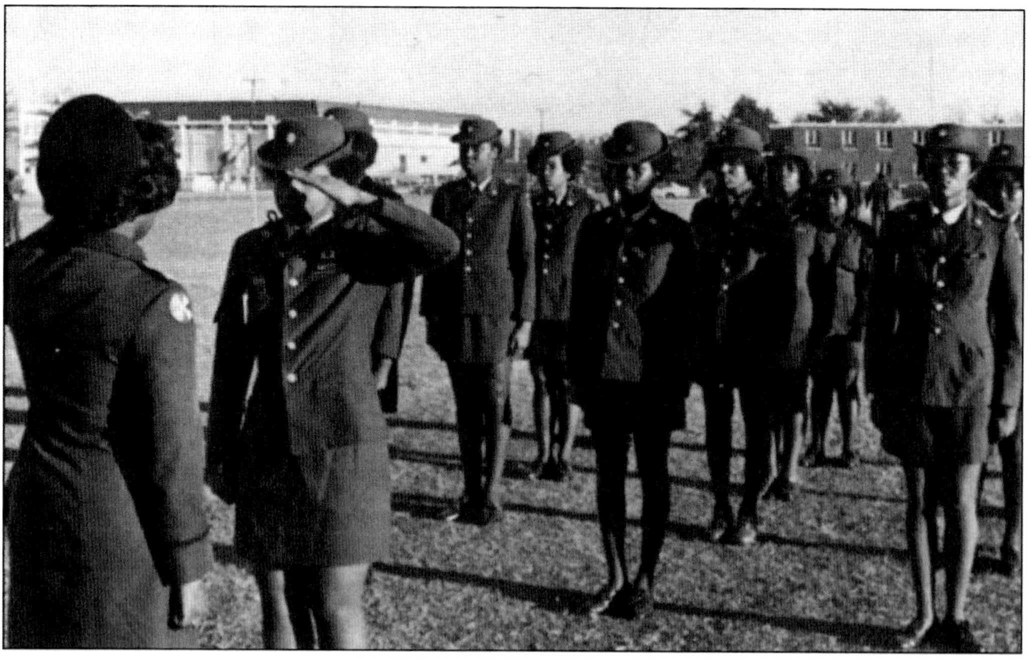

Under the direction of Horace D. Flowers II, the Henderson-Davis Players achieved national recognition by the 1970s, and the Henderson-Davis Theater was built to provide a state-of-the-art facility for the drama program. Here are Sandra Bowie and Samuel Wright, both of whom went on to become talented professionals in drama, film, and television.

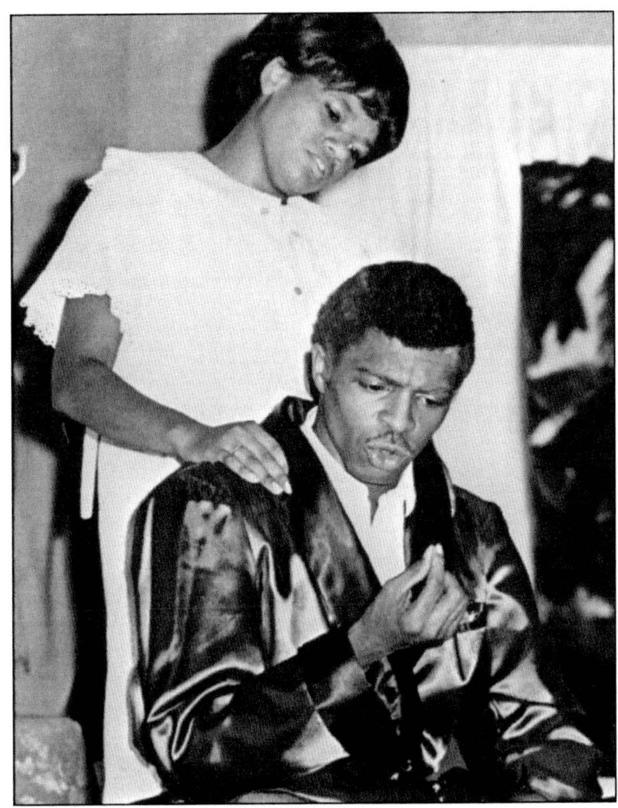

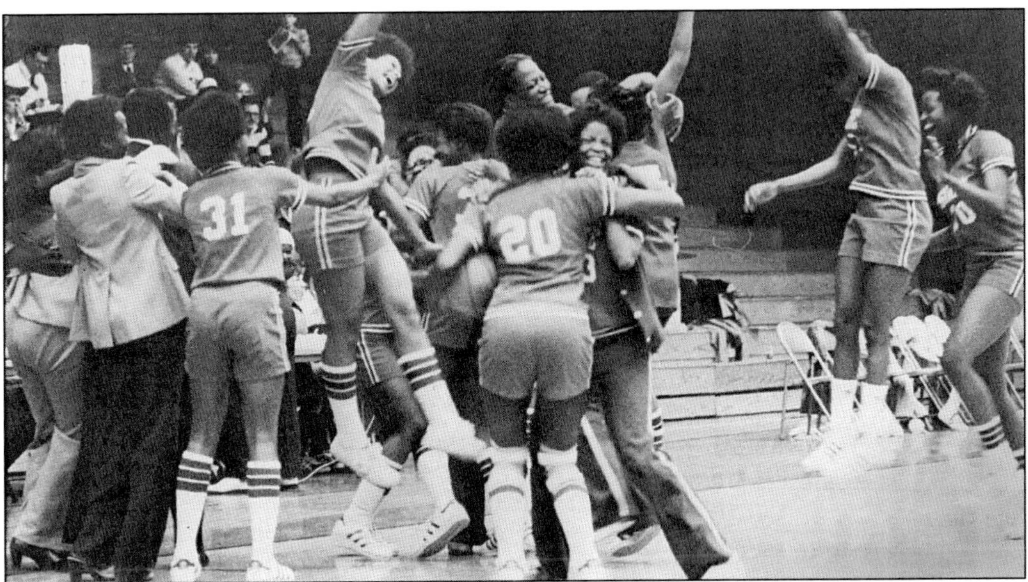

The women's basketball team won the AIAW national championship in 1979 under Coach Willie Simon. They defeated the University of Dayton 73-68 in the title game in Fargo, North Dakota. Roberta Williams and Margaret English were the co-captains.

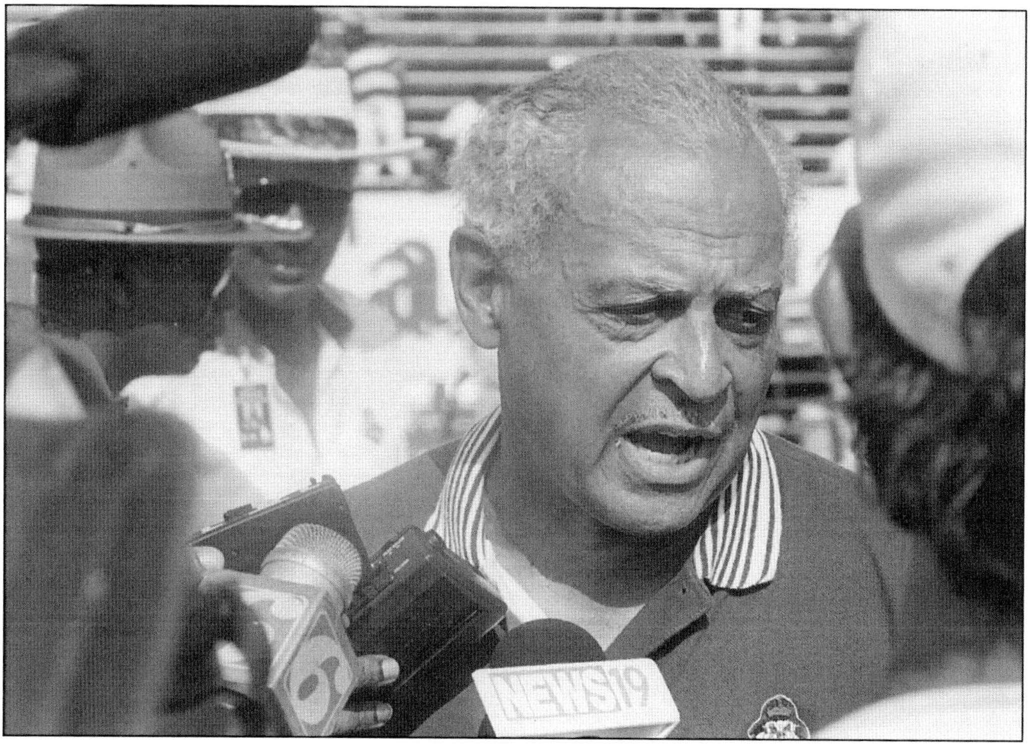

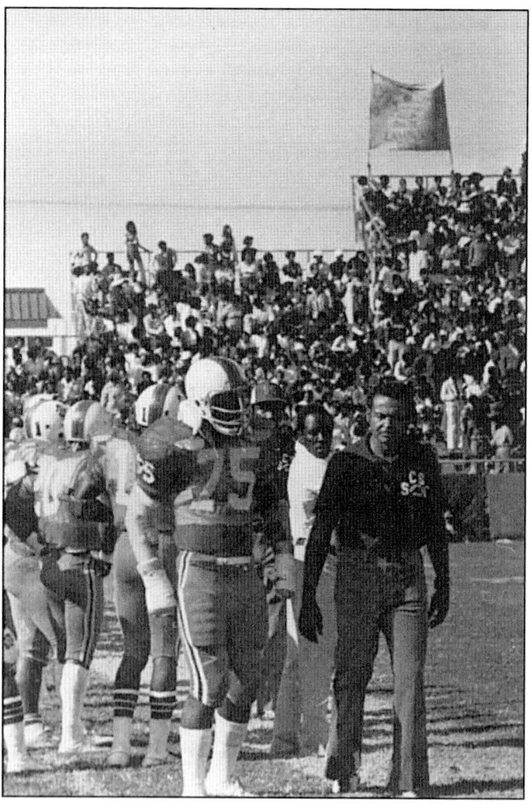

Under Coach Willie Jeffries, the Bulldog football team became a major I-AA power. The 1960 SC State graduate has served two stints as head coach, 1973–1978 and 1989 to the present. He has taken the squad to several bowl games, including three appearances at the Heritage Bowl in the 1990s. In the 1975 photo on the right, Jeffries is patrolling the sideline with Harry Carson, one of the finest players ever to wear the Bulldog uniform.

While Willie Jeffries was coaching at Wichita State and Howard in the 1980s, Bill Davis took charge of Bulldog football. In 1981, in I-AA playoffs, the Bulldogs defeated Tennessee State in overtime before losing to eventual national champ, Idaho State. In 1982, the Bulldogs defeated Furman before losing to Louisiana Tech.

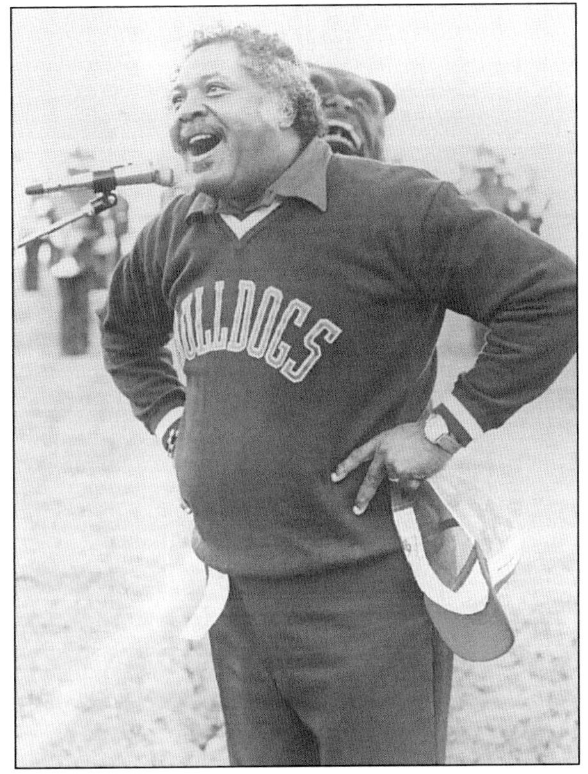

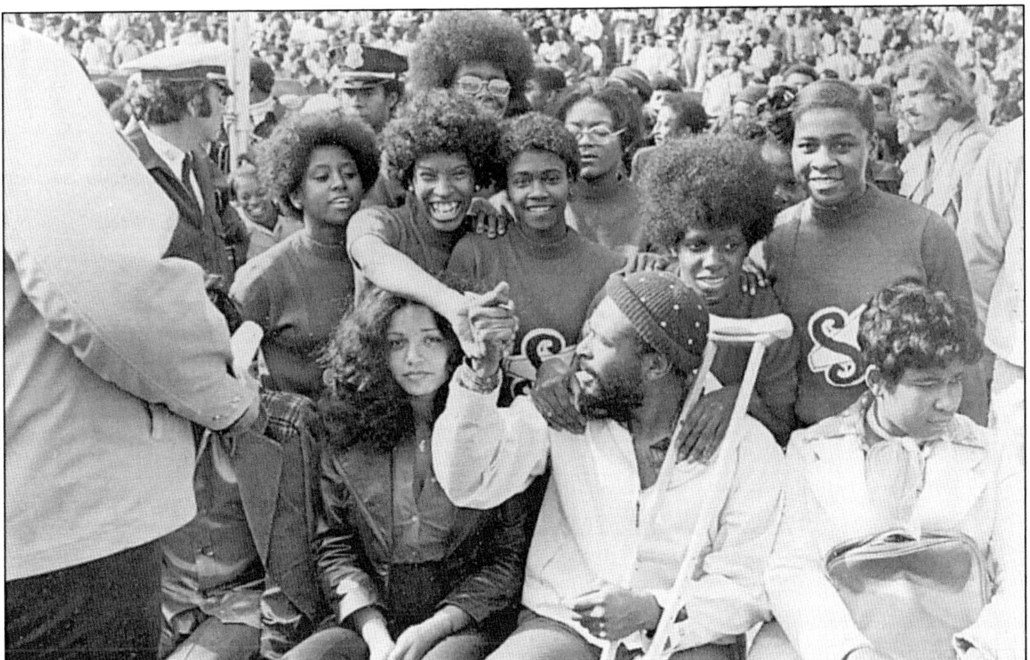

In 1974, the Bulldogs journeyed to New Orleans to play Grambling in the Pelican Bowl. They lost 28-7, but the cheerleaders had an opportunity to meet musical legend Marvin Gaye.

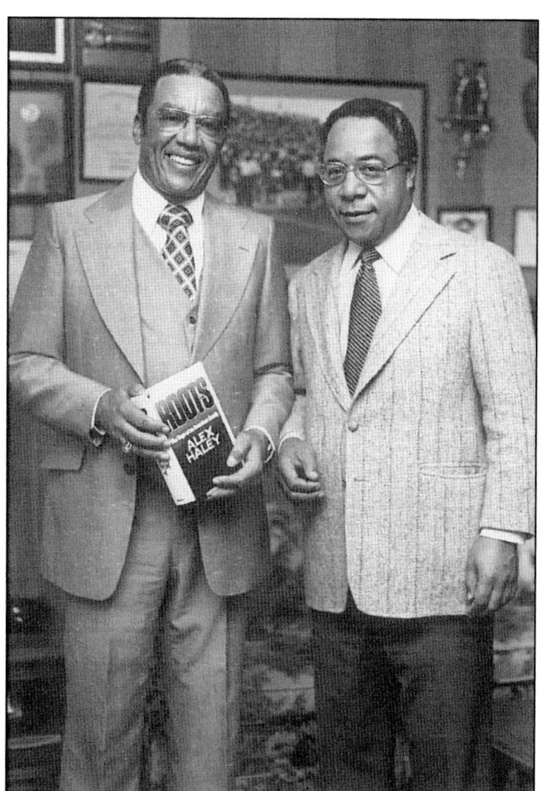

Alex Haley, the author of *Roots*, spoke to a Founders' Day gathering of nearly 5,000 people at Smith-Hammond-Middleton Memorial Center in 1977. Here, he presents a copy of that remarkable book to President Nance. The book was the basis for the highest-rated television series in history.

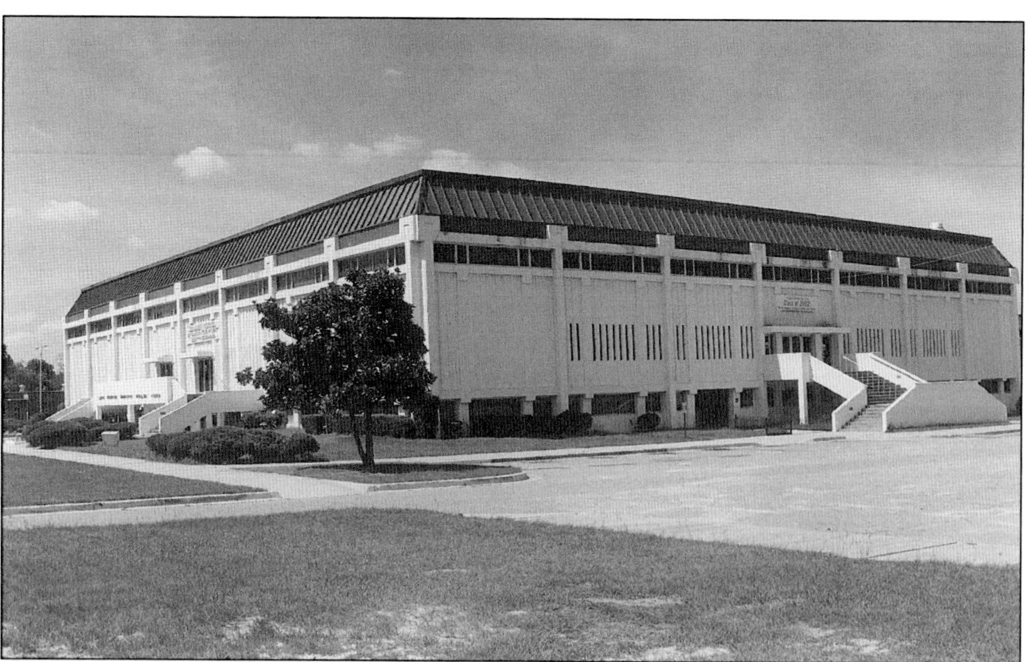

Constructed in 1968, the Smith-Hammond-Middleton Memorial Center, which provides gymnasium, auditorium, and swimming facilities, was named in honor of the Orangeburg Massacre victims.

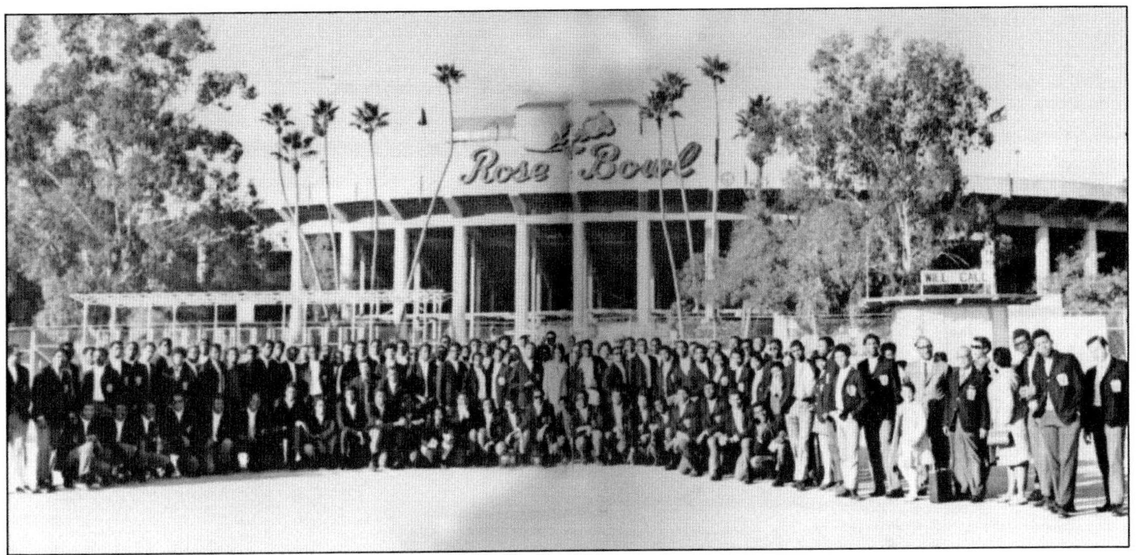

The Marching 101, the college's band, performed at the 1969 Tournament of Roses Parade in Pasadena, California.

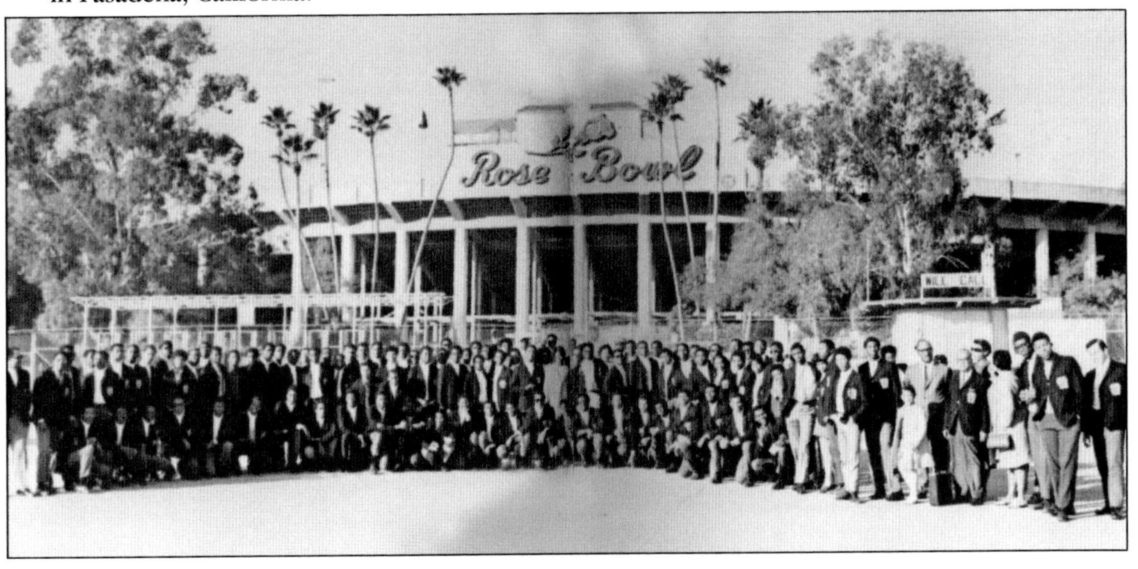

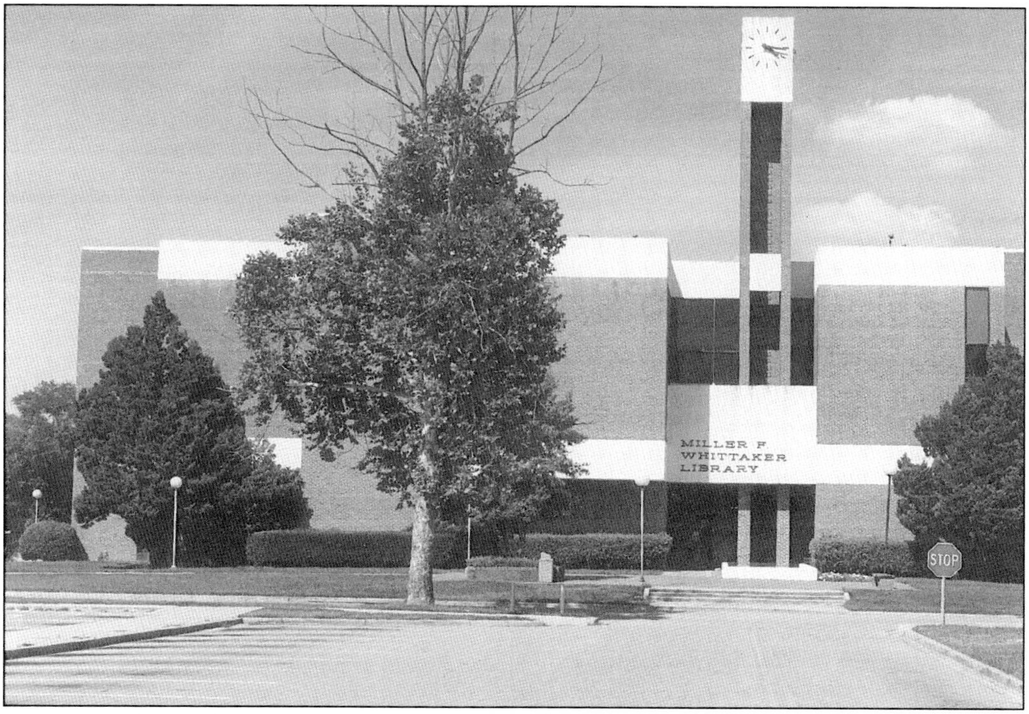

Constructed in 1968 and named after the college's third president, the Miller F. Whittaker Library became the first structure in the college's history completely dedicated to providing library services.

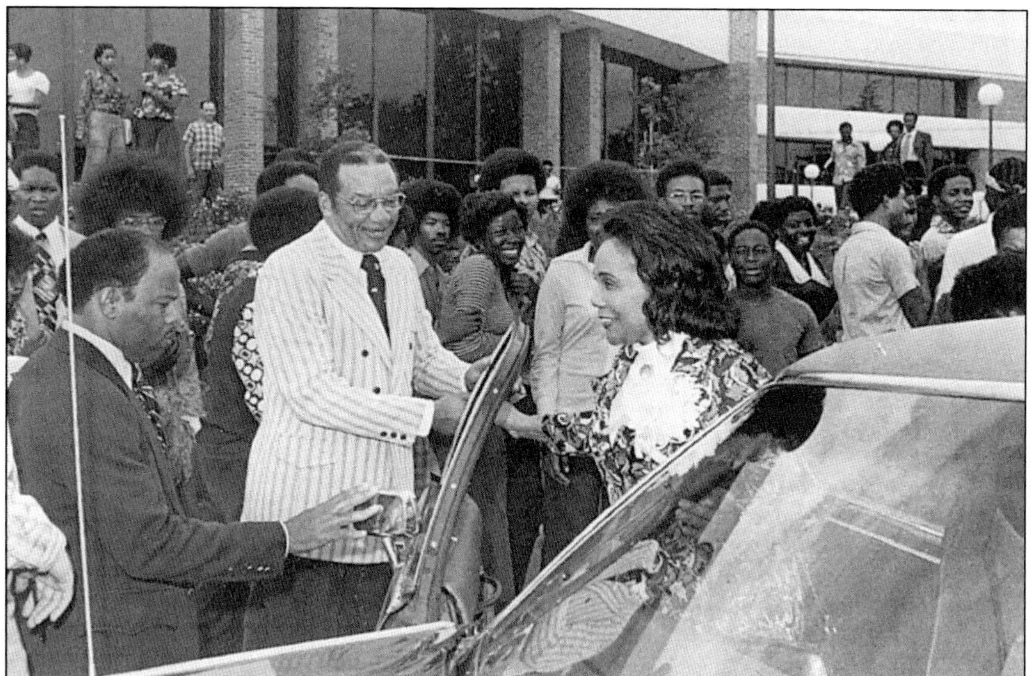

In 1975, Coretta Scott King visited South Carolina State to dedicate the Martin Luther King, Jr. Auditorium.

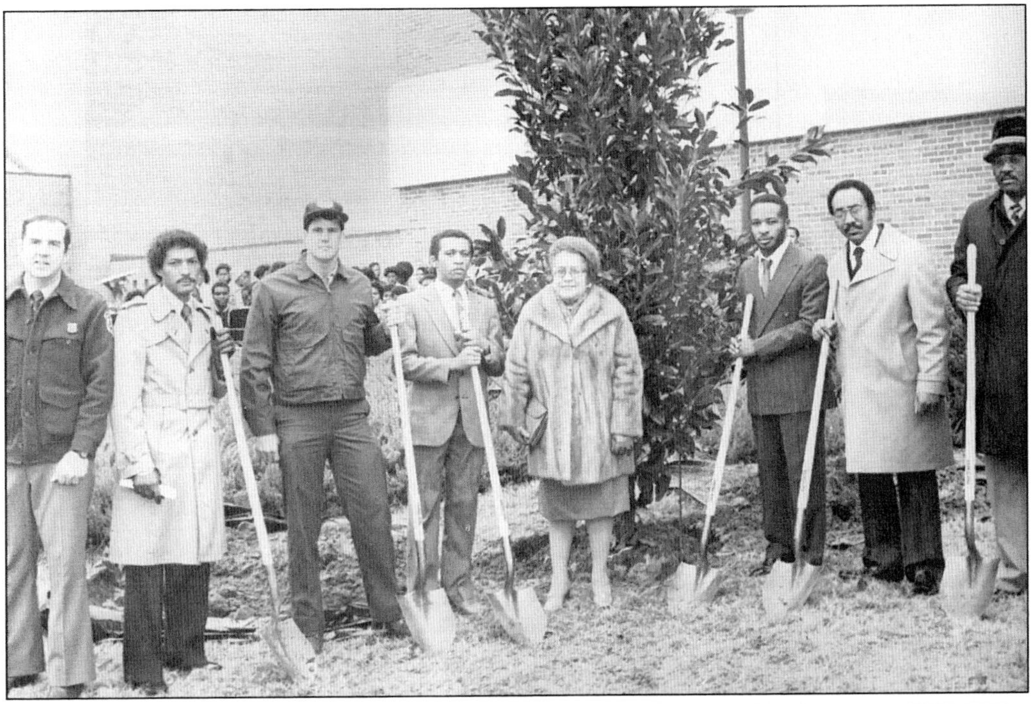

In 1984, the National Forest Service donated a magnolia tree that was planted in front of Nance Hall to honor Dr. Martin Luther King Jr. Participating in the dedication were Bill Craig of the forest service; Dr. Edward Jackson, chair of political science and history; Mack Erwin of the forest service; Terry Booth of the collegiate chapter of the NAACP; Mrs. Marguerite Howie, a sociology professor and member of the Association for the Study of Afro American Life and History; Maurice Washington, president of the student government association; Dr. Carl A. Carpenter, vice president for academic affairs; and J.C. Woodward of the forest service.

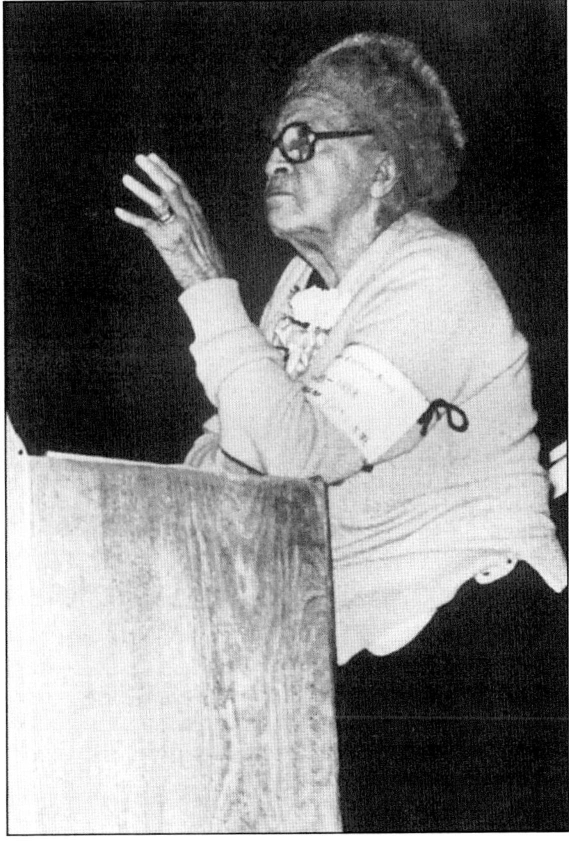

On January 15, 1986, Modjeska Simkins, one of the foremost civil rights leaders in South Carolina, spoke at the campus ceremony to commemorate slain civil rights leader Dr. Martin Luther King Jr.

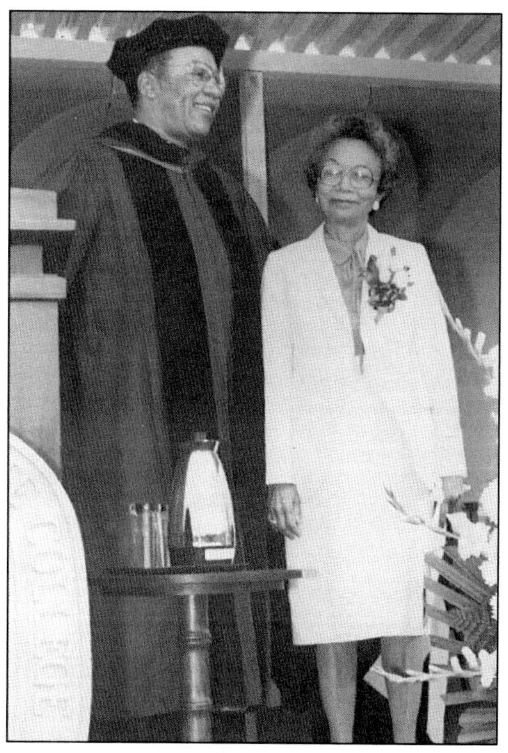

Retired chemistry professor Dr. Clemmie Webber was the 1983 National Mother of the Year. Dr. Webber and her husband, Paul, contributed immensely to South Carolina State both academically and socially. For many years, they operated a soda shop near the campus. Their son Paul, who is a superior court judge in the District of Columbia, was the Founders' Day speaker at the centennial of the university in 1996.

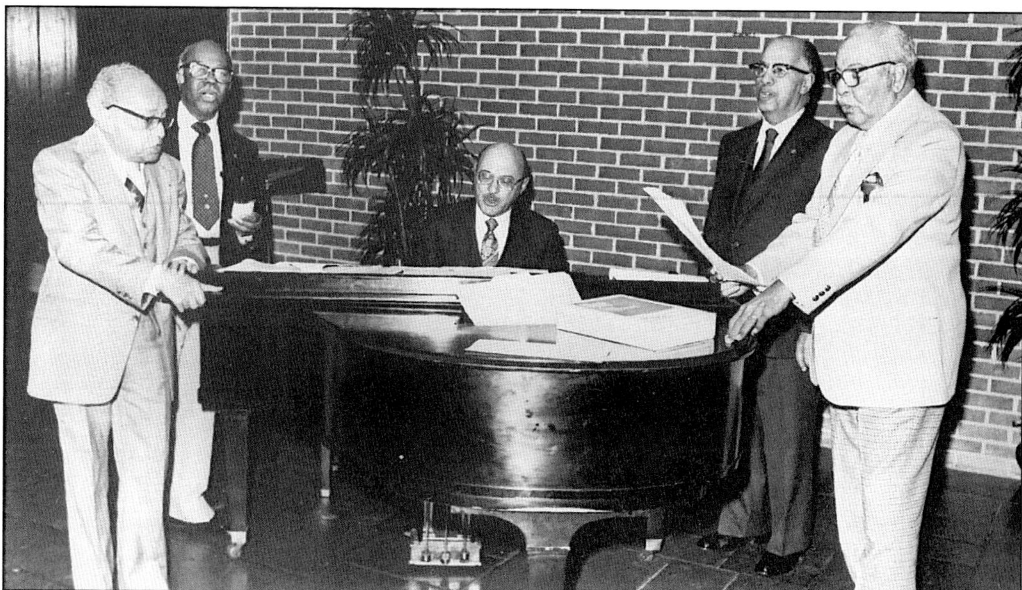

In 1982, five men intimately involved in the history of South Carolina State gathered around a piano to provide a musical lesson or two at the quarter-century club luncheon. From left to right are Mr. Reginald R. Thomasson, Mr. Alpha O. Josey, Mr. Eugene Pinson, Mr. Leo L Kerford, and Mr. Harleston Fleming. Mr. Thomasson was a professor of music and director of the marching band. Mr. Josey taught history and served as director of personnel. Mr. Pinson taught music to generations of students. Mr. Kerford was a law professor, and Mr. Fleming was a music professor.

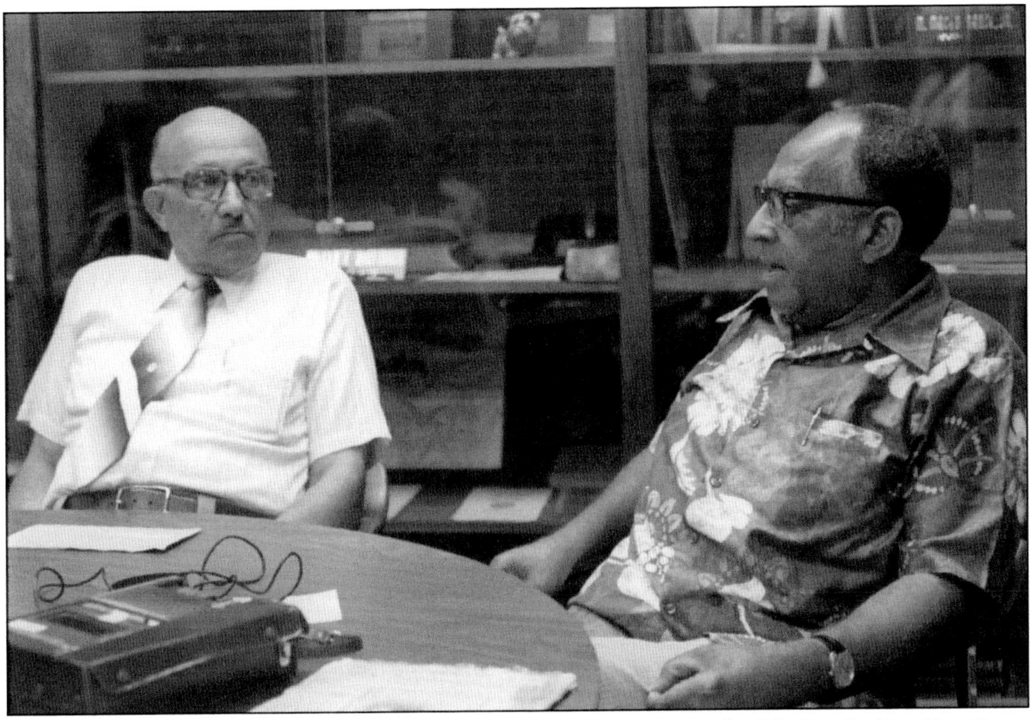

There are probably not two other men more closely associated with South Carolina State for a longer period of time than Mr. Dudley M. Zimmerman (left) and Mr. T.J. Crawford (right). Each was connected to the college for more than half a century. In fact, Mr. Crawford chaired the 50th anniversary celebration of the college in 1946 and was honorary chair of the centennial in 1996. Mr. Zimmerman served as director of facilities management. Mr. Crawford taught chemistry, directed public relations, and was the voice of Bulldog football for many years.

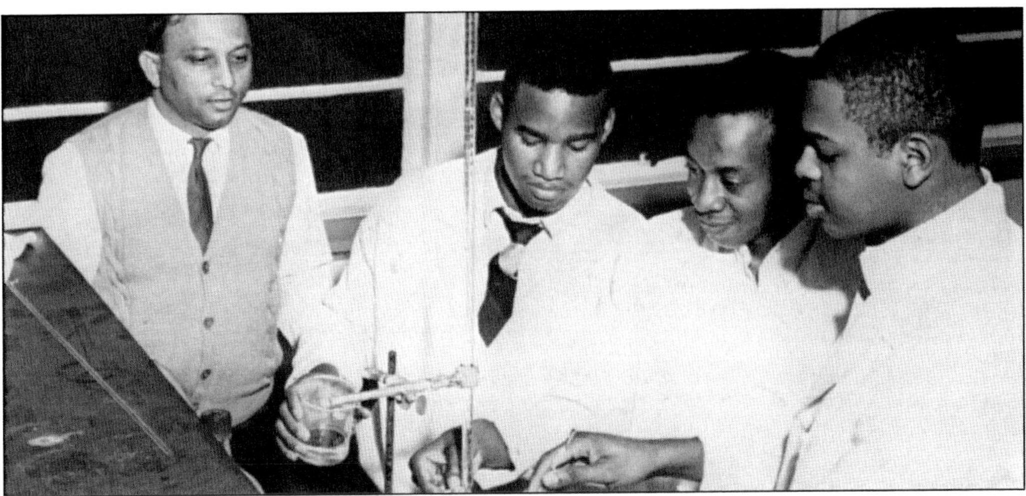

There have been constant changes in the academic programs at the university for more than 100 years. In the 1967 photo above, students under the direction of Dr. Kailash Mathur experiment to determine the acidity in milk. The program in dairy science was an important part of the institution's history for three-quarters of a century.

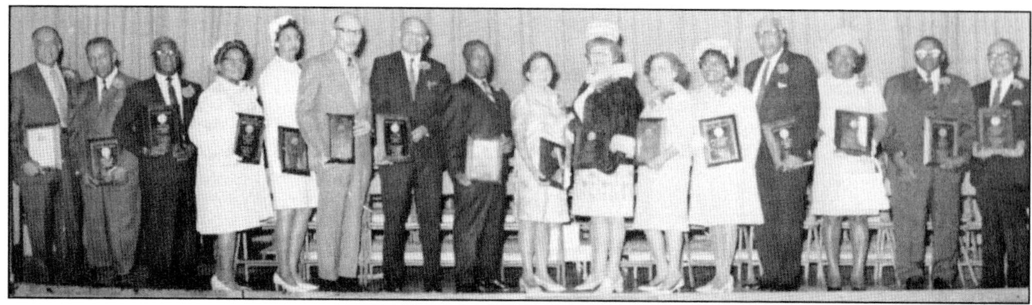

Charter members of the quarter-century club, *c.* 1970, shown from left to right, are as follows: T.J. Crawford, H. Holmes, Dr. G. Buckman, Mrs. L.M. White, Miss M. Thompson, D.M. Zimmerman, N. Austin, E.M. Adams, Miss O. Williams, Dr. N.P. Parler, Mrs. E. Vaughn, Miss T. Wimbush, O.C. Dawson, Mrs. E. Grant, H. Cain, and R.R. Thomasson. Two members—Charlese Sheffield and Mattie Pegues Jackson—were not present.

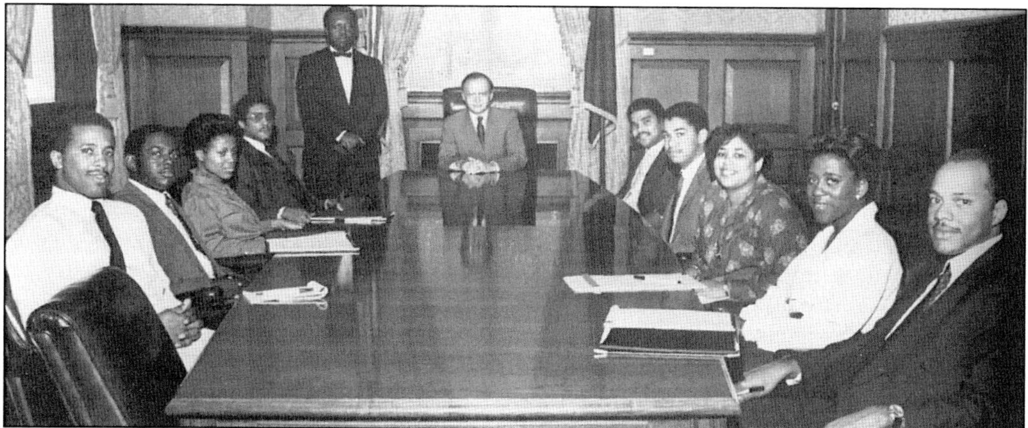

In 1986, student legislative interns met with Governor Richard Riley, who has maintained a close relationship with the university while serving as secretary of education since 1993. He delivered the commencement address in December 1998.

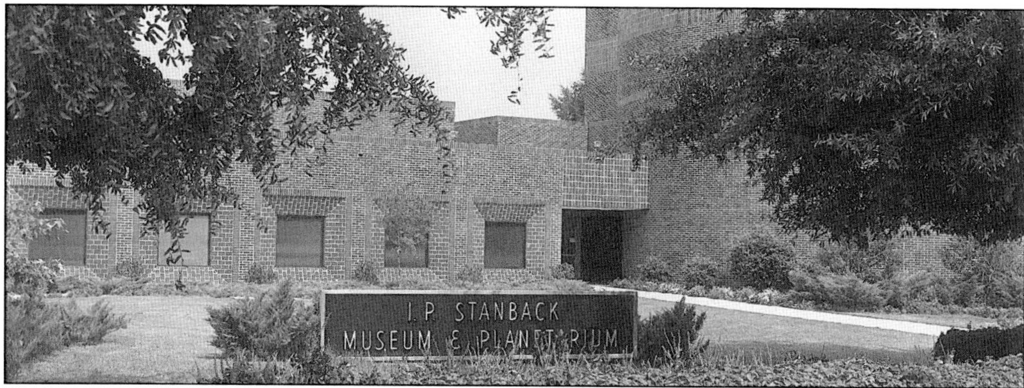

The I.P. Stanback Museum and Planetarium is one of the jewels on the campus of South Carolina State University. President Nance urged the development of the museum, and Dr. Clemmie Webber suggested that a planetarium be included in the project. The handsome building contains 3,750 square feet of exhibit space and an 82-seat planetarium with a 40-foot projection dome. It is named after I.P. Stanback, who served on the board of trustees from 1966 to 1982 and was its first African-American chair.

Six

Albert E. Smith
1986–1992

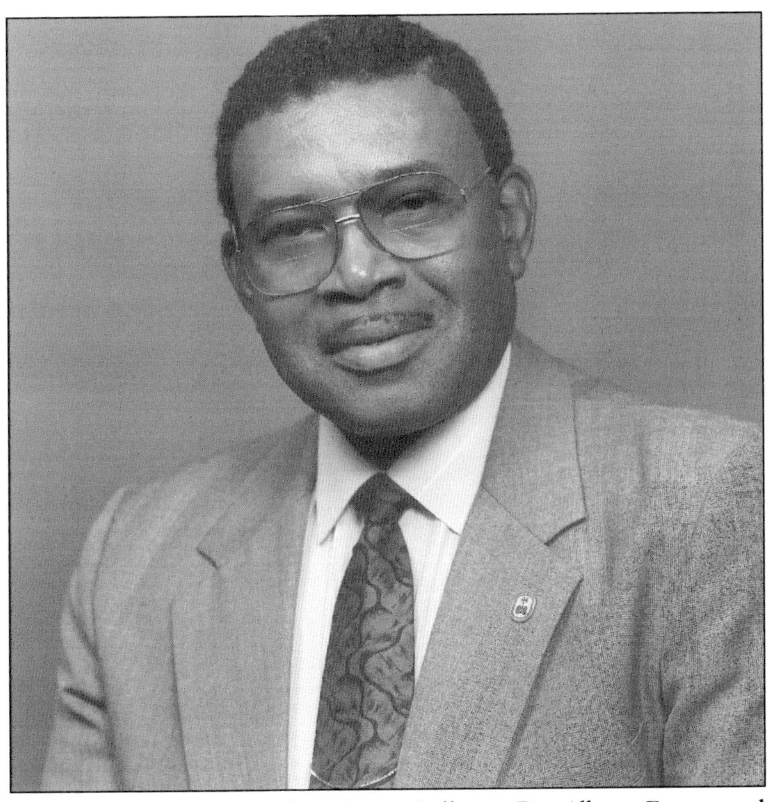

The sixth president of South Carolina State College, Dr. Albert Emmanuel Smith was appointed by the board of trustees on July 1, 1986. Dr. Smith established a theme of "New Directions" and implemented a long-range plan for the institution, emphasizing renewed dedication to academic concerns, improvement of student life, strengthening enrollment, and improving community relations. Under Dr. Smith's leadership, the college experienced extraordinary increases in enrollment, a restructuring of academic divisions, and an increased focus on faculty research. Non-traditional student programs were expanded and an attempt to reach under-served constituencies was made. Dr. Smith's association with the college concluded in 1992, and he currently serves as president of Florida Memorial College in Miami.

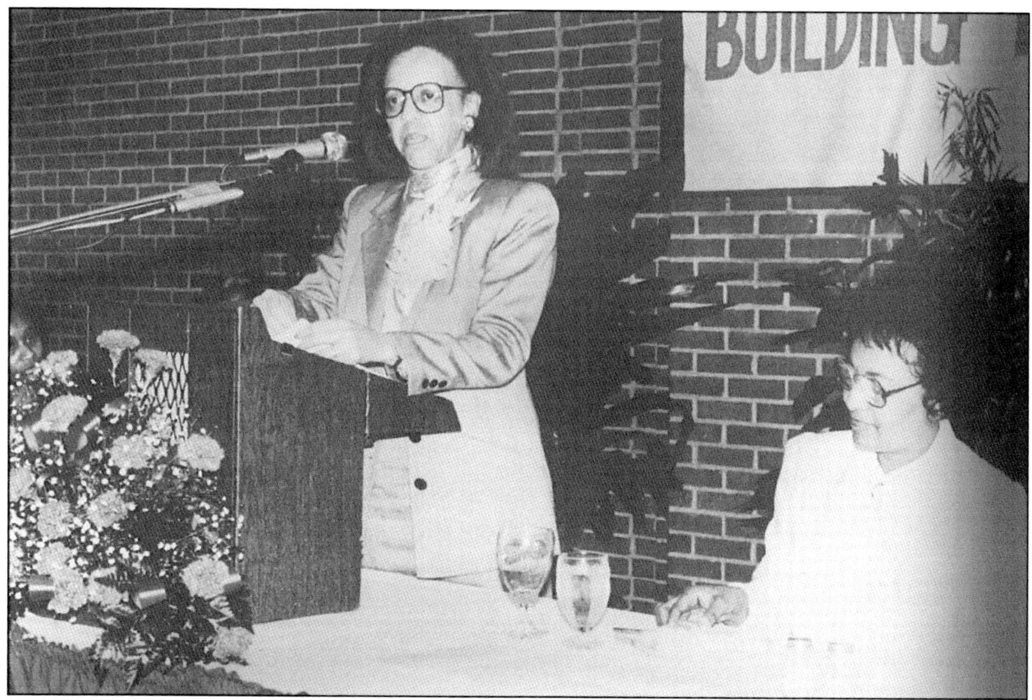

Begun in 1987 to honor First Lady Sadie Burris Smith (shown above, at right), First Lady's Day provided the college with an opportunity to focus on women's issues in the workplace, family, and society. Dr. N. Joyce Payne (above, at the podium) was director of the office for the Advancement of Public Black Colleges of the National Association of State Universities and Land-Grant Colleges in cooperation with the American Association of State Colleges and Universities, and was the guest speaker at the 1988 First Lady's Day program. Mrs. Smith (below, at podium) described First Lady's Day as an opportunity to "develop a sense of unity at the institution, to foster a positive sense of self-worth and self-esteem as individual women, to develop effective communication techniques that will improve family, social, and work relationships, and to develop coping skills that will aid in the effective management of home and career responsibilities."

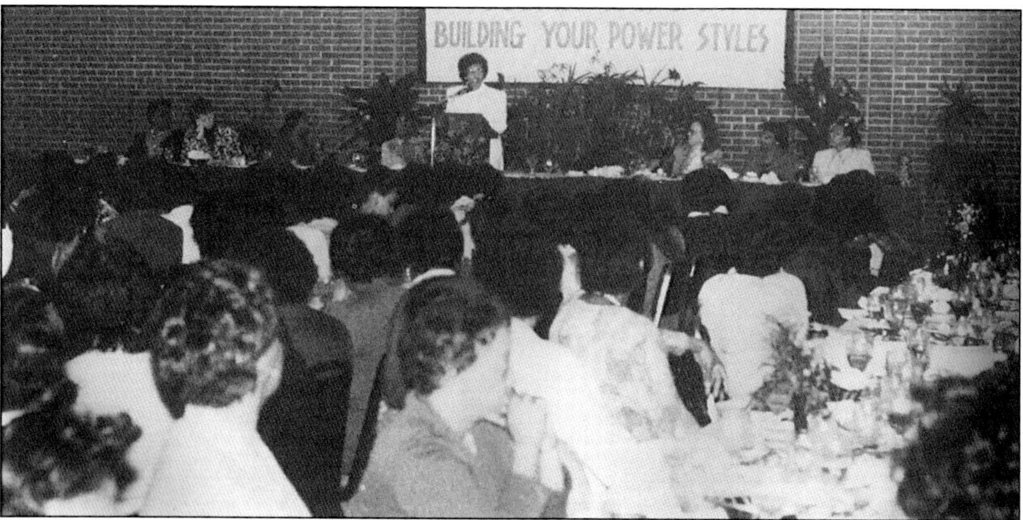

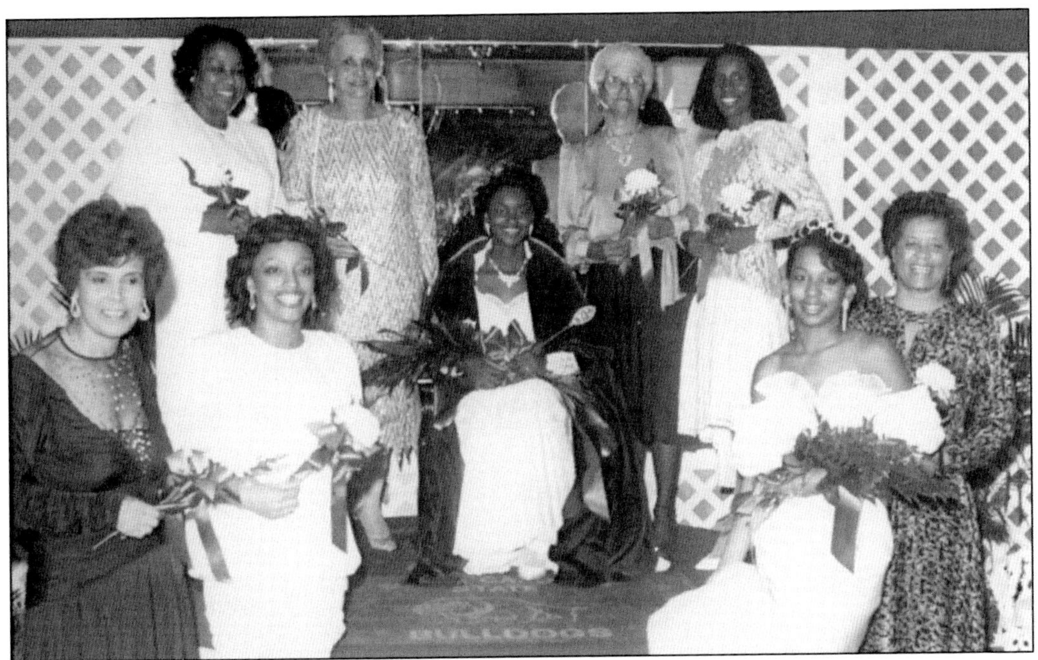

During the 1989 Coronation, Miss Marissa P. Manning, an English major from Dublin, Georgia, and the daughter of Mr. and Mrs. Charles W. Manning Sr., is surrounded by Miss SCSC queens from past years.

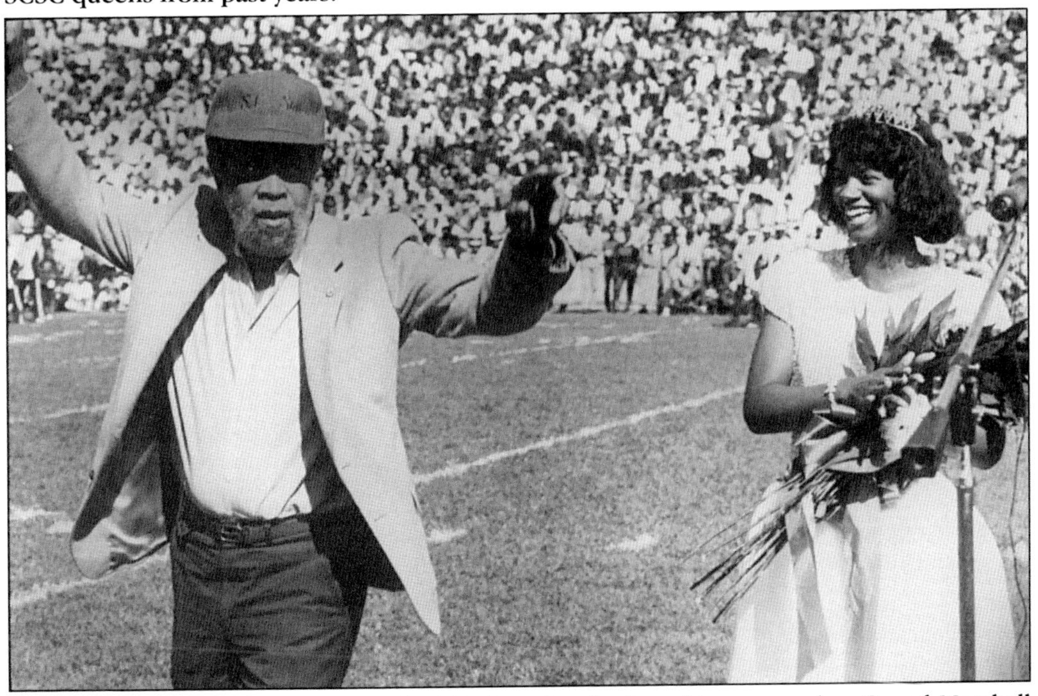

Whitman Mayo, a.k.a. "Grady" on the TV show *Sanford and Son*, served as Grand Marshall for the 1988 Homecoming parade. The theme was "Salute to the Stars." Marlene M. Capehart, a senior general home economics major from Newark, New Jersey, was crowned Miss Homecoming.

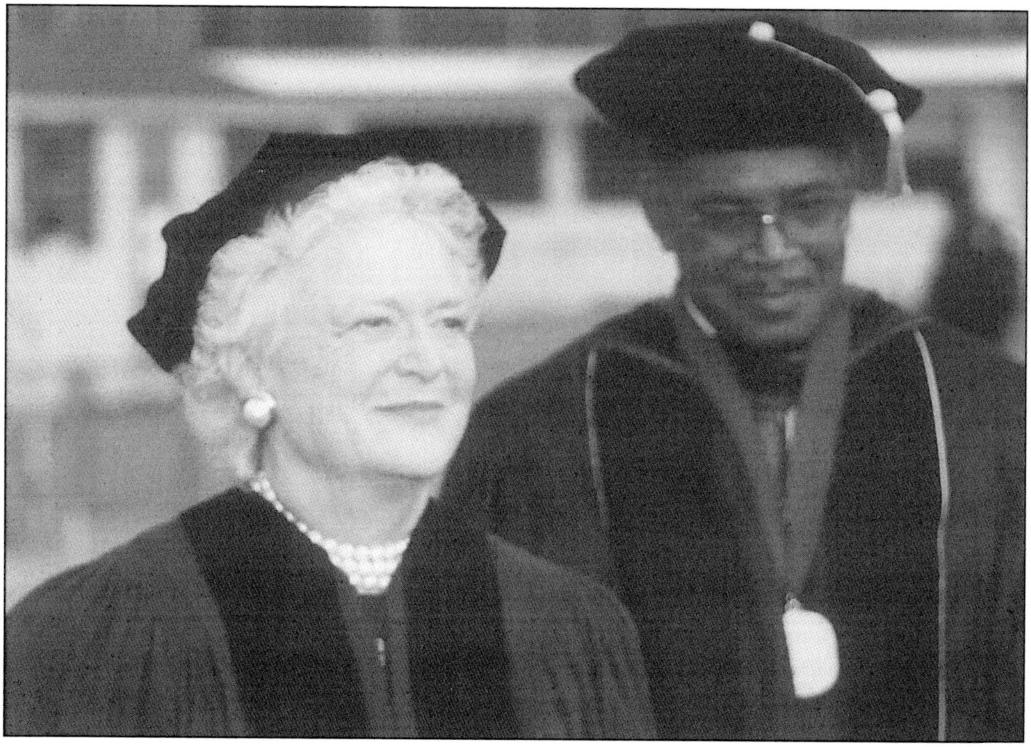

First Lady Barbara Bush, wife of President George Bush, served as speaker at the May 1991 commencement. The college conferred an honorary doctorate upon Mrs. Bush at this time.

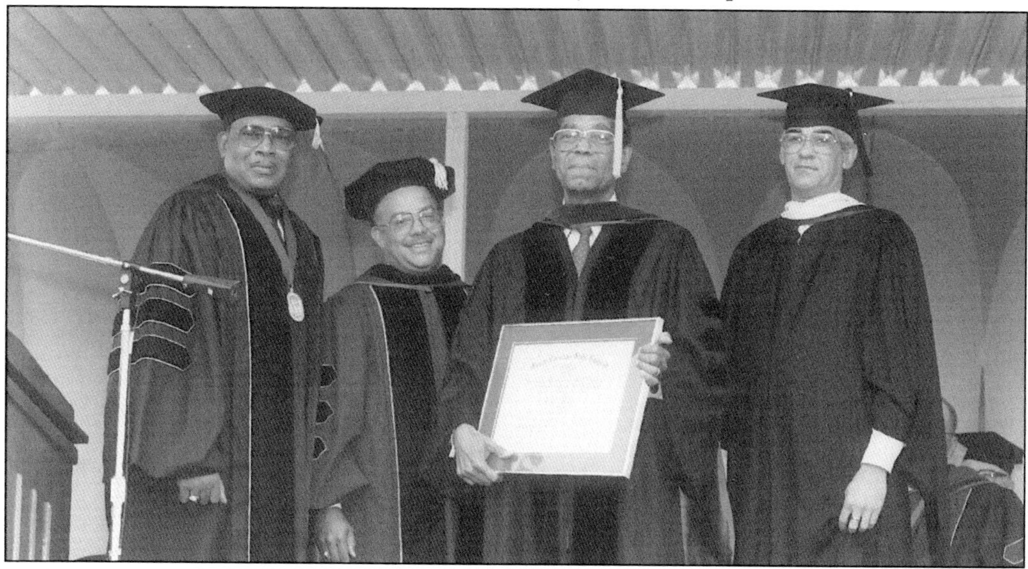

At the May 1989 commencement, an honorary doctorate was conferred upon the Honorable Matthew J. Perry, a 1951 graduate of South Carolina State College's law school, pre-eminent civil rights attorney, and federal district judge. Shown, left to right, are President Smith, Attorney I.S. Leevy Johnson (member of the Board of Trustees), Judge Perry, and Colonel John T. Bowden Jr. Other persons receiving honorary degrees were Mrs. Maude E. Callen, Mr. Harold J. Mackey, Mr. Earl E. Morris Jr., and Mr. A. Barry Rand.

Entertainer Sammy Davis Jr., a member of Frank Sinatra's Rat Pack, was the Founders' Day speaker in February 1988. Mr. Davis received an honorary degree, along with LTG Henry Doctor Jr., Mrs. Ruby Middleton Forsythe, the Honorable Ernest F. Hollings, Dr. M. Maceo Nance Jr., and the Honorable J. Strom Thurmond.

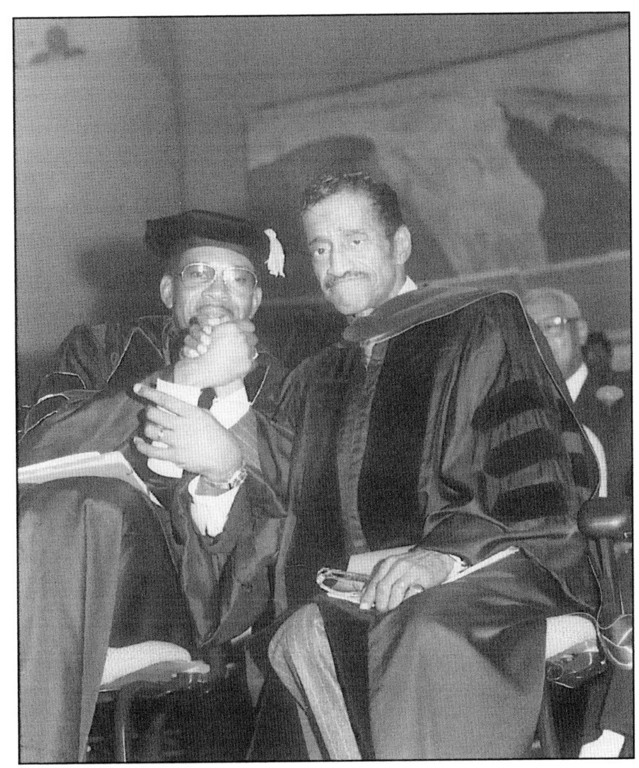

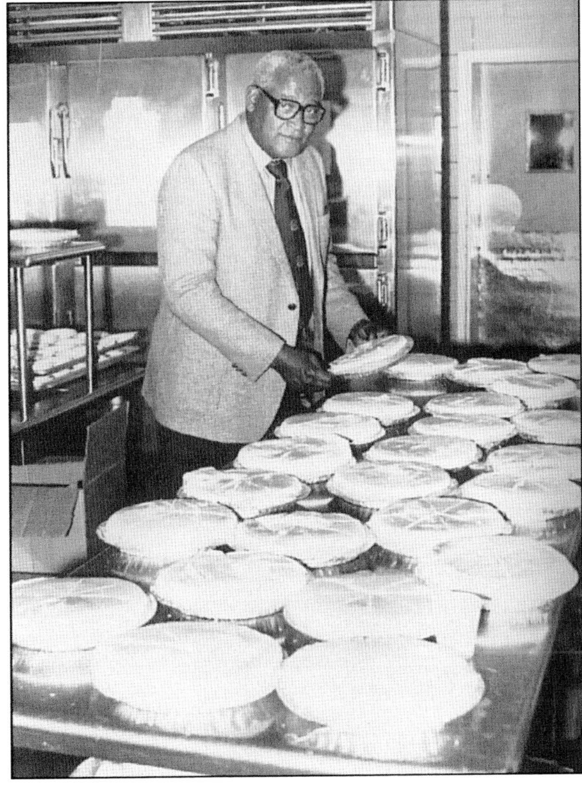

Food services director Robert S. Evans oversees the preparation of nourishment for the college community. Evans served the University community for over 40 years.

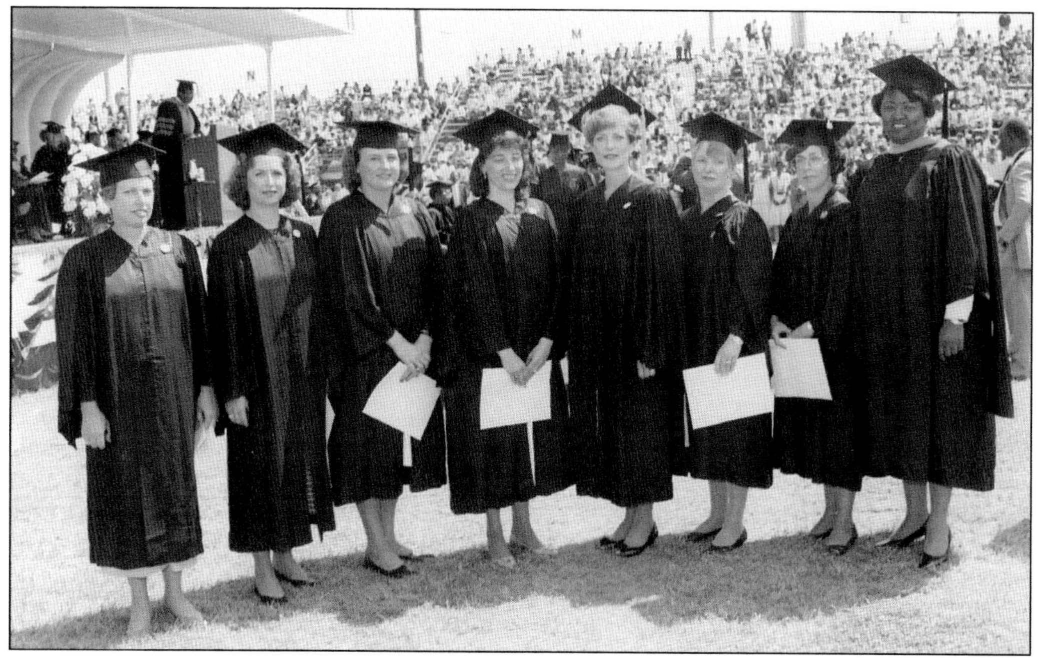

This photo shows the first graduates of the University's nursing program in 1988. Shown, from left to right, are the following: Ellsie Willis, Brenda Taylor, Peggy Phalen, Sharon Fogle, Sandra Caulder, Phoebe Fee, Linda K. Fitts, and Dr. Judy Bradley, chair. (Photo by Larry Mitchell.)

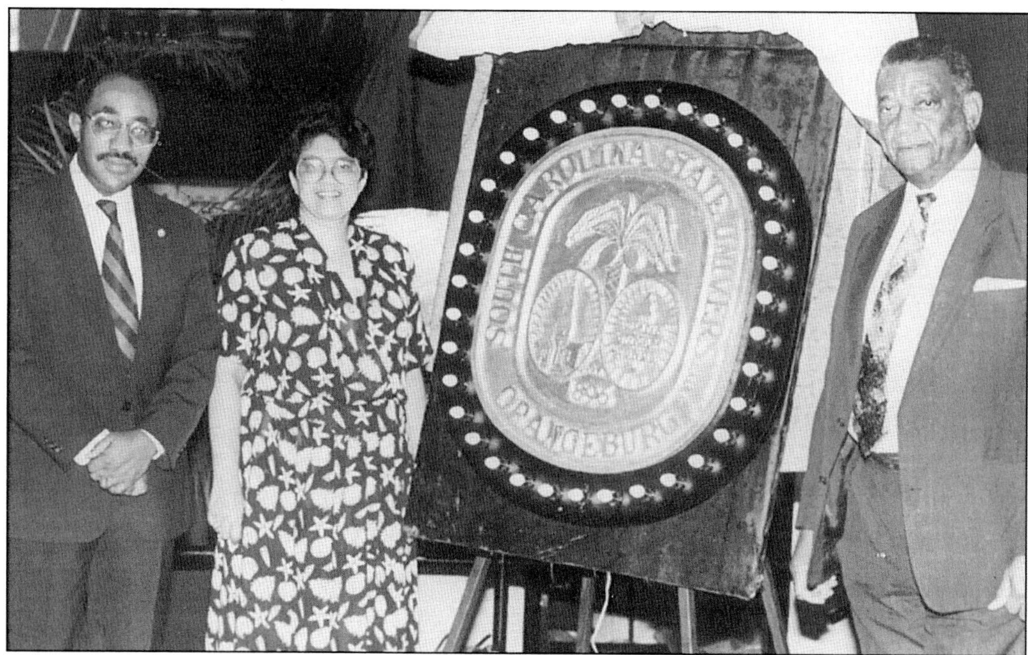

South Carolina legislators granted the institution university status on February 26, 1992. On hand for the occasion were, from left to right, Interim President Dr. Carl A. Carpenter; Audrey Q. Battiste, president of the National Alumni Association; and Dr. James A. Boykin, chairman of the Board of Trustees.

Seven

BARBARA R. HATTON 1993–1995

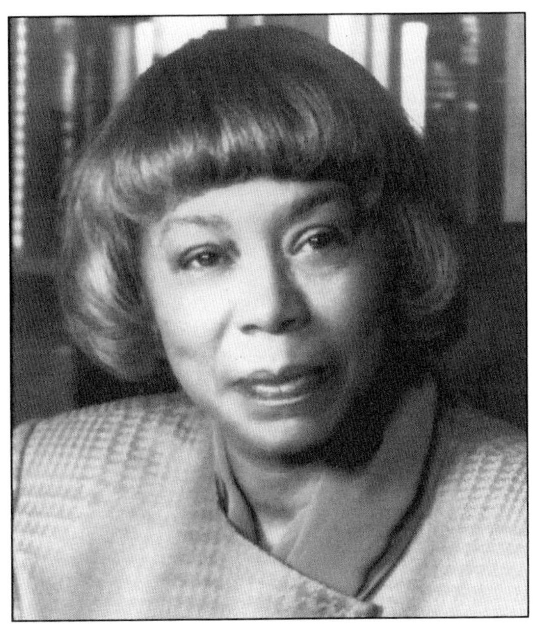

The first president of the newly-designated South Carolina State University, seventh president of the institution and the only woman ever to serve in these capacities, Dr. Barbara Rose Hatton's historic appointment in September 1992 embodied a number of the original aims of the land-grant ideals upon which the college was founded pertaining to bringing educational opportunities into a more inclusive arena.

A native of Atlanta, Hatton's credentials were exceptionally well suited to her appointment. She received her bachelor's degree in psychology from Howard University and a master's degree from Atlanta University. She taught secondary mathematics briefly at the University of the District of Columbia before obtaining the doctorate in education and the master of education administration degree from Stanford University, in California. There, she served as assistant professor of education administration and policy studies and as associate director of the Stanford Urban/Rural School Development Institute. She also received the 1993 Recognition of Outstanding Service to Education Award (ROSE), presented by the University of Southern California.

Hatton's initial foray into the complexities of the challenges in higher education in South Carolina at historic South Carolina State University were greeted with enthusiasm and support. She began her duties on January 4, 1993. During her tenure, she was instrumental in converting Felton Laboratory School into a state-of-the-art professional development school; further, her actions precipitated legislation, which was passed by the General Assembly allowing engineering technology graduates to sit for the engineering licensure examination in South Carolina; opening an office of state and community relations in Columbia; and increasing collaborations and projects with colleges, universities, and federal and private agencies. Capital improvement projects included the 1890 Extension Office Complex and the completion of the Oliver C. Dawson Bulldog Stadium and Student Center Plaza.

Hatton's sweeping restructuring reforms facilitated the propulsion of the institution toward handling the issues that will decide its impact and significance for the 21st century. Despite the brevity of her administration, the theme of "Culture, Community, and Continuity" that she established for the school is of central significance in the university's self-assessment and reorientation of its goals as it enters the new millennium.

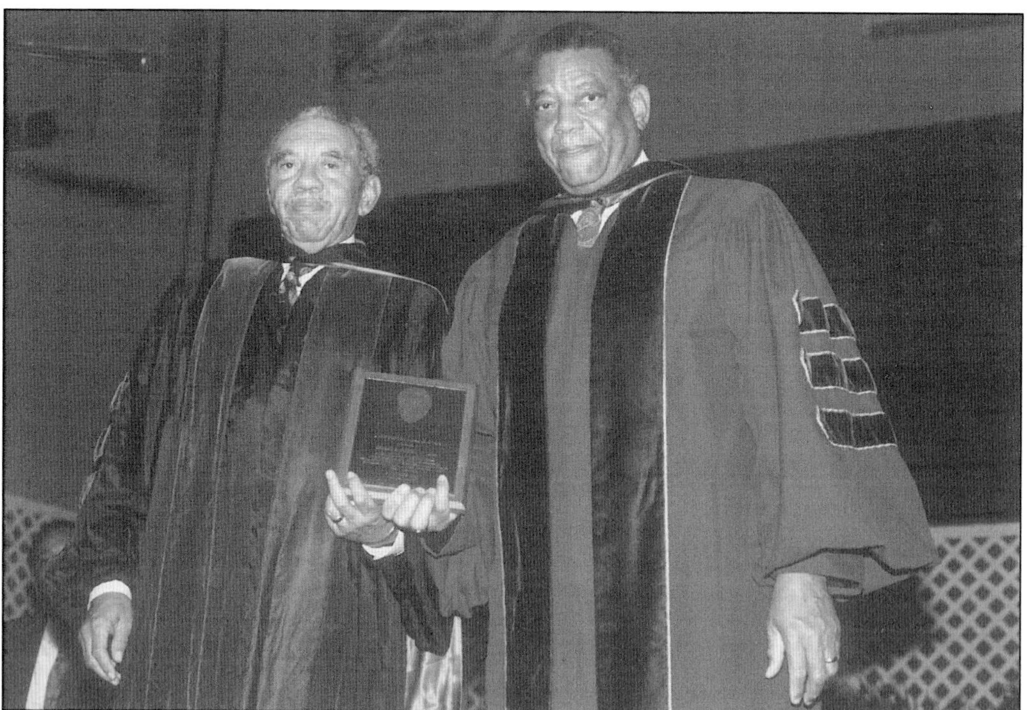

Ernest A. Finney Jr., a Claflin University alumnus and 1954 graduate of South Carolina State College's law school, was elected as a justice of the South Carolina Supreme Court in 1985 and served as Chief Justice from 1994 to 2000. He is shown here at Founders' Day in 1993 with longtime trustee Dr. James A. Boykin.

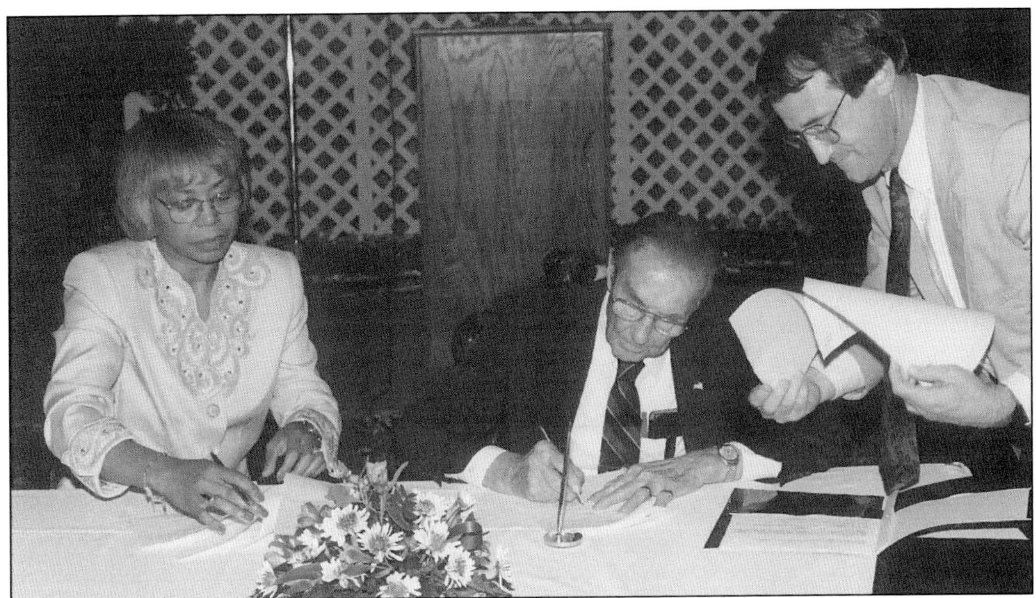

In May 1993, President Barbara Hatton and the Honorable J. Strom Thurmond, South Carolina senator, were joined by Dr. Thomas J. Stewart, assistant to the president for minority and international programs.

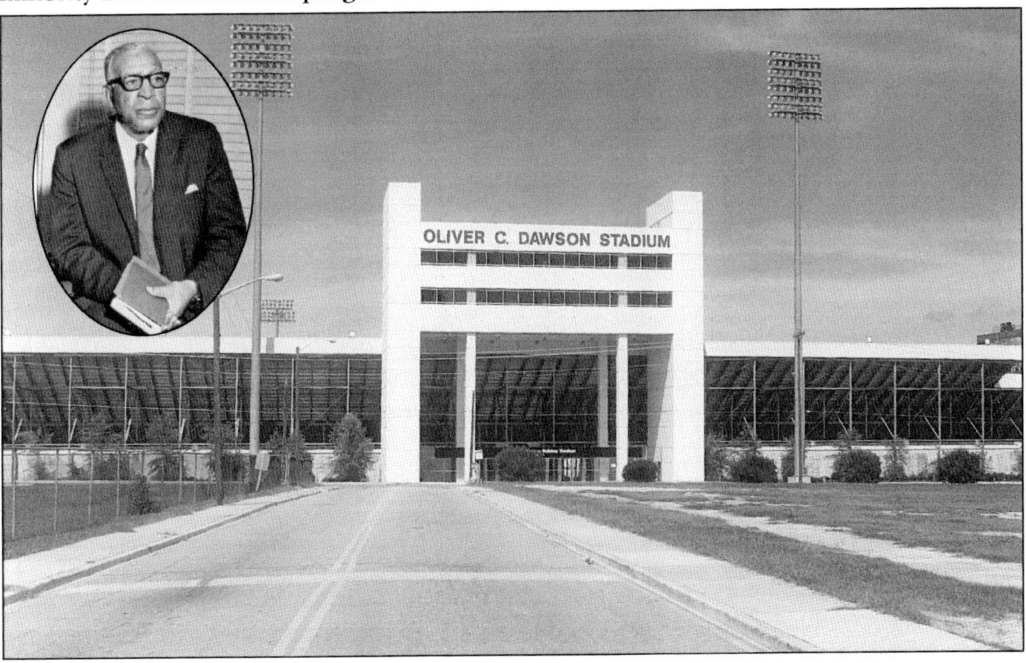

Oliver C. "Ollie" Dawson (inset) retired after 41 years of coaching and teaching at SCSU. During his tenure, he was head coach of all major sports: football, basketball, tennis, track, and golf. He coached the Bulldogs to championships in four sports. He served as athletics director for 16 years and retired as chairman of the department of health and physical education. In 1974, Dawson was the first African-American person inducted into the South Carolina Athletic Hall of Fame. The football stadium, shown here, was named in his honor in 1984 and rededicated in 1995.

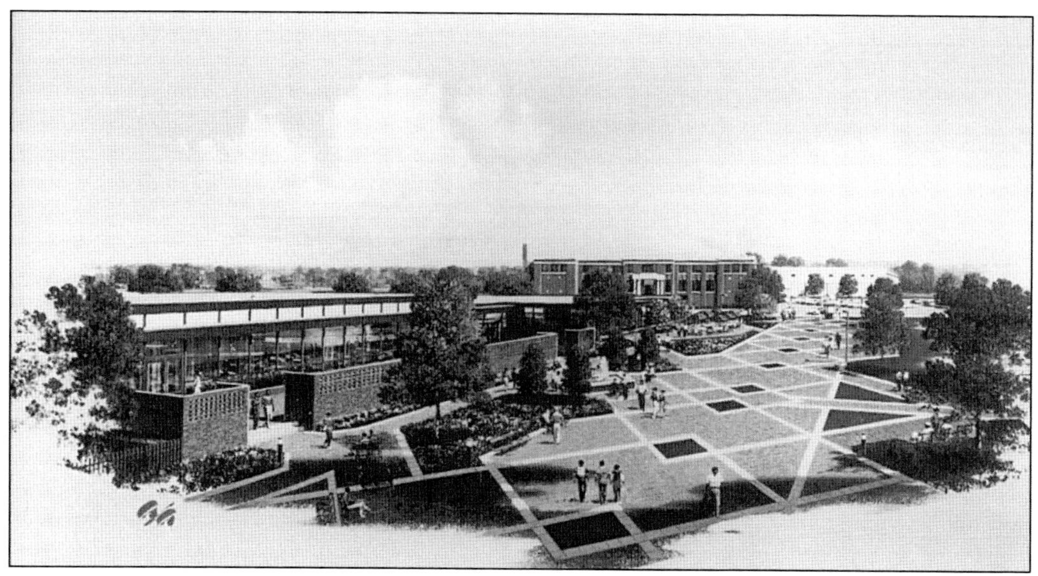

Constructed in 1995, the student center plaza (above in a drawing and below under construction) serves as a place for student gatherings, dances, debates, and relaxation. Some of its features include a water fountain, seating areas, a campus locator, and streetlights. The plaza also contains an extension to The Pitt, which enables students to eat outside on a patio surrounded by greenery and flowers. The concept for a student center plaza was envisioned in 1990 by the K.W. Green Student Union Board.

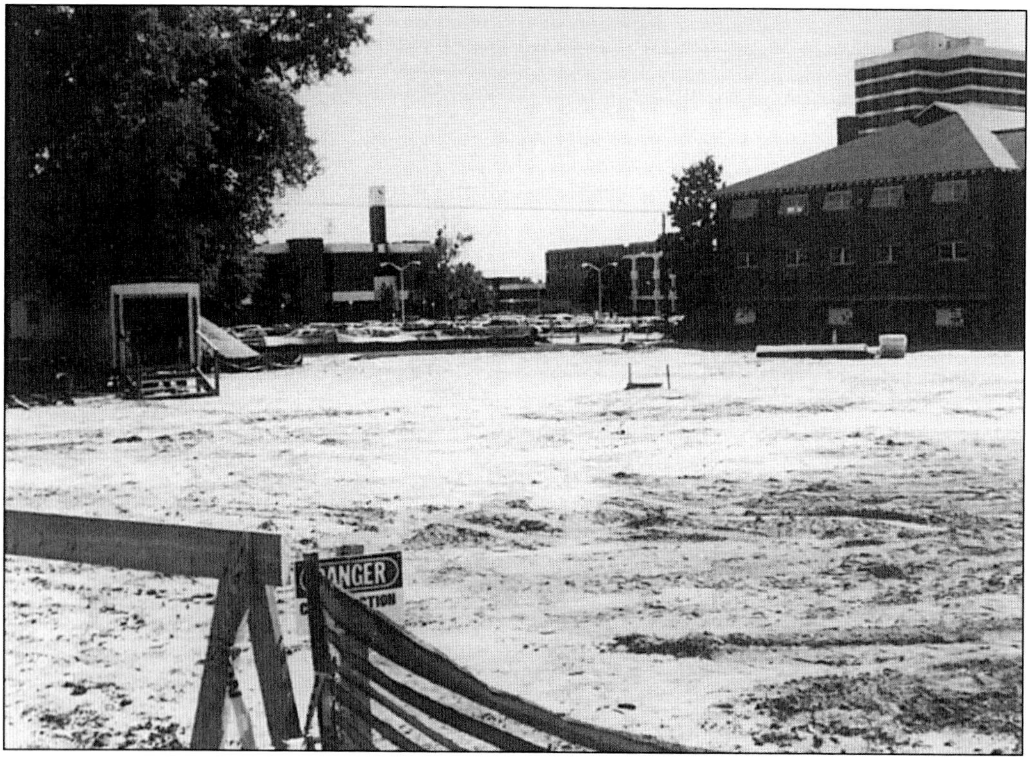

Eight

LEROY DAVIS SR. 1997–PRESENT

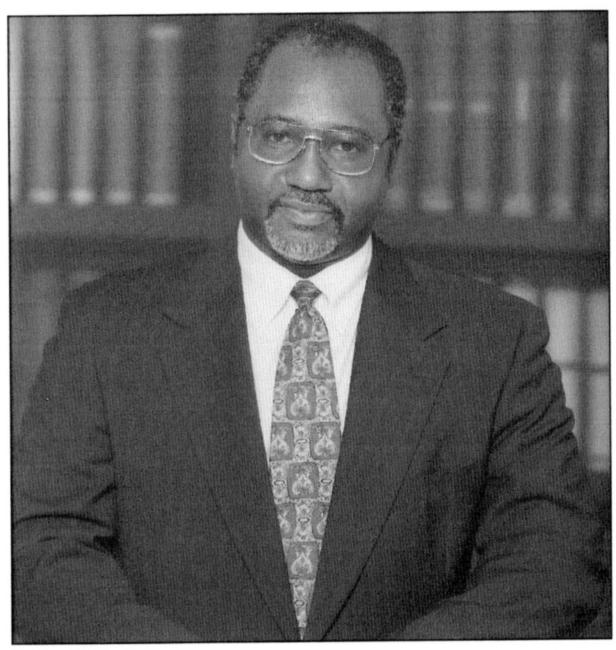

Appointed interim president of South Carolina State University on June 13, 1995, Dr. Leroy Davis Sr. brought considerable administrative experience to bear in a sensitive and complex position. A scientist by training, Dr. Davis graduated from South Carolina State College in 1971 with the bachelor of science degree in biology. His graduate and post-graduate studies were accomplished at Purdue University, obtaining the master's degree in microbiology in 1972 and all requirements for the Ph.D. in 1979. A member of the New York Academy of Sciences, South Carolina Academy of Science, American Society for Microbiology, and the recipient of many distinguished honors, Dr. Davis has published on topics including "The Biochemical Nature of Cold-Sensitivity in HIS W Strains of *Salmonella Typhimurim*," 1982, and "Altered Control of Isoleucine-valine Biosynthesis in a Cold-Sensitive HIS W Mutant," 1982. A native of Orangeburg. Dr. Davis participated in the growth of the university as vice president for academic affairs, director of the 1980 university self-study, and professor in the school of arts and sciences.

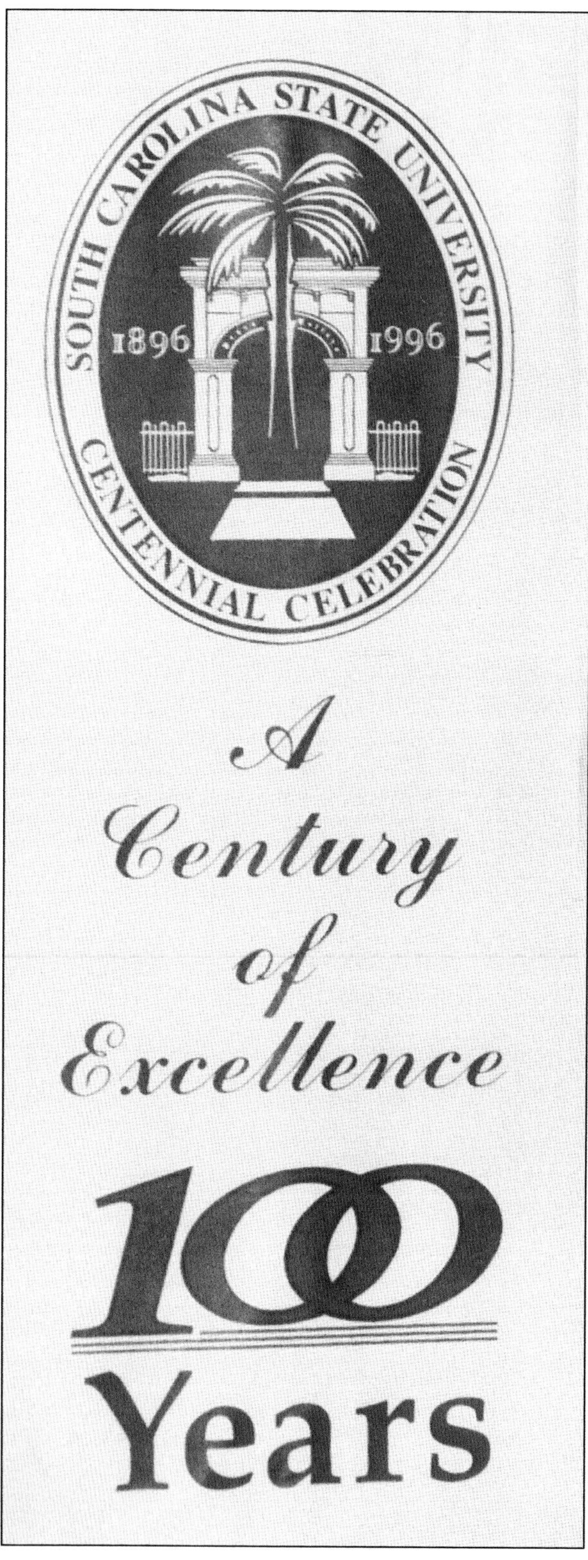

During the university's centennial year, Dr. Davis was elected the eighth president of South Carolina State University on April 10, 1996, and was inaugurated on March 22, 1997. During his administration, President Davis has established Centers of Excellence in Transportation and Leadership as part of a plan to have a center of excellence in each of the five academic schools. Under his leadership, there has been increased scholarship support to recruit more academically talented freshmen, the establishment of the first university staff senate, the implementation of a new tenure and promotion policy, increased university partnerships and collaborations, and the implementation of new community service programs in the areas of health care and economic development. Other achievements include establishing the president's service award; initiating the distance education program; and designating the first emeritus awards.

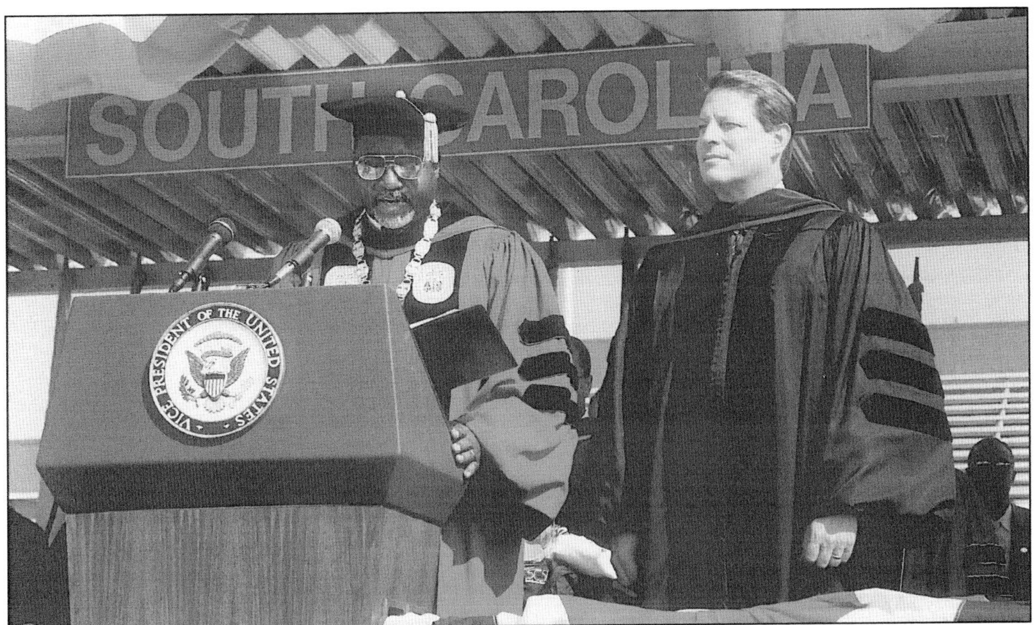

U.S. Vice President Al Gore, shown here with President Davis, served as speaker for the May 1998 Commencement. (Photo courtesy of the Office of News and Communications.)

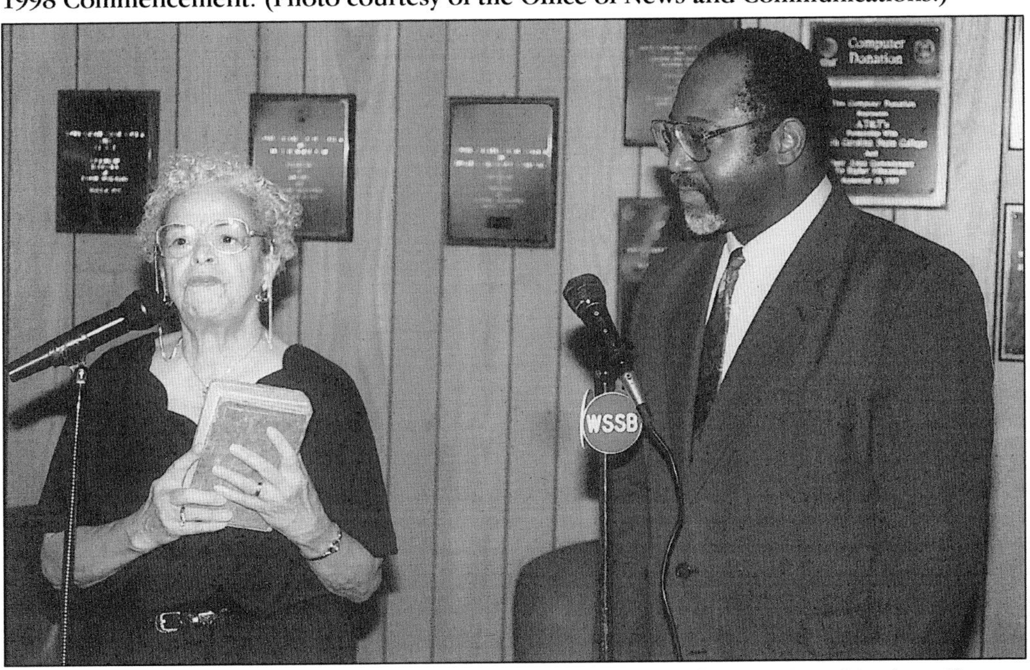

In 1995, President Bill Clinton posthumously awarded Johnson C. Whittaker (former faculty member and father of the university's third president, Miller F. Whittaker) his commission in the U.S. Army. Whittaker had been unjustly dismissed from the U.S. Military Academy in 1881. During Whittaker's court-martial, his personal Bible was used as evidence and remained in the National Archives until it was returned to his granddaughter, Cecil Whittaker Pequette. Mrs. Pequette (shown here with Dr. Davis) presented the Bible to the SCSU Historical Collection.

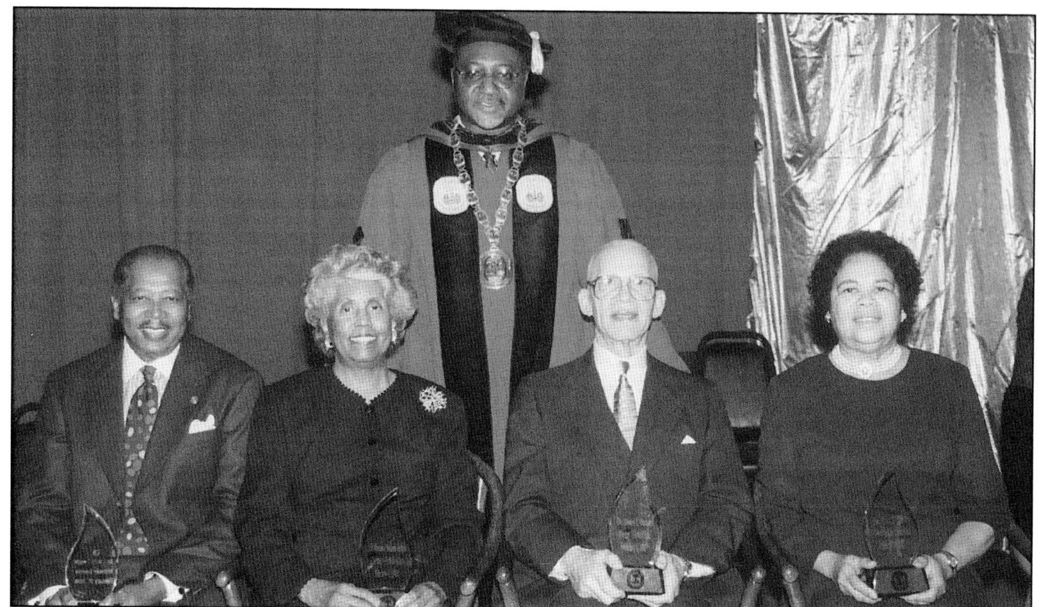

The first emeritus awards were presented on February 27, 2000, at the annual Founders' Day program. Recipients were, from left to right, Professor Emeritus, Dr. Leo F. Twiggs; Dean Emeritus, Dr. Barbara Williams Jenkins; Dean Emeritus, Dr. Lewie C. Roache; and Professor Emeritus, Dr. Doris S. Cantey.

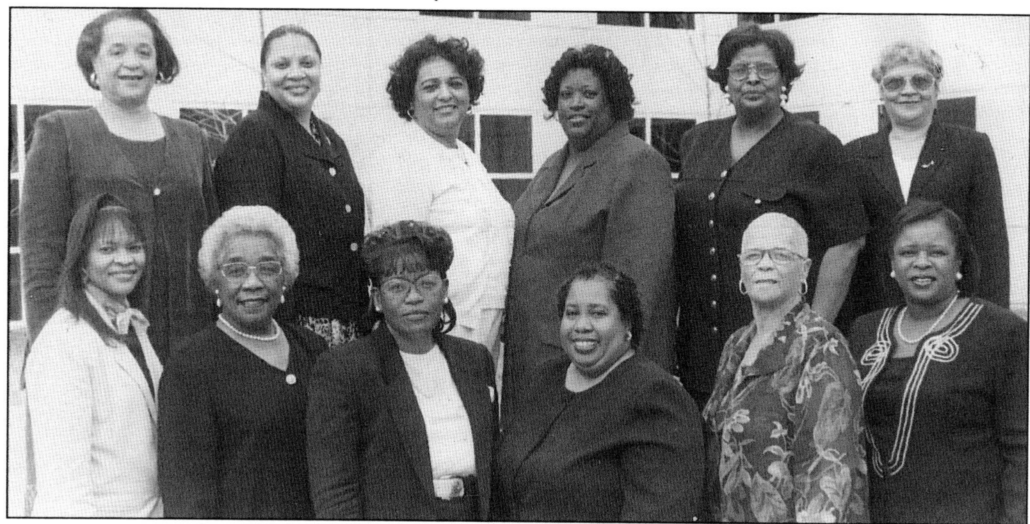

The Voices of Power is a female faculty and staff vocal group that has appeared on local television programs such as *Orangeburg Inside Out* and performed at local talent shows such as Showcase Orangeburg, the Rose Festival, the Quarter-Century Luncheon, and other campus events. Their repertoire includes Broadway musicals, spirituals, gospel, jazz, and other inspirational songs and music to fit the occasion. The group began in the late 1980s during President Smith's administration but continues to perform. Shown, from left to right, are (front row) Patricia G. Haigler, Eartha J. Corbitt, Patricia S. Holmes, Karen S. Jamison, Beverly V. Wright, and Sylvia D. Robinson; (back row) Barbara A. Vaughan (director), Carrie H. James, Delores W. Anderson, Enda C. Wade, Mable Garner, and Ruth DeLaney.

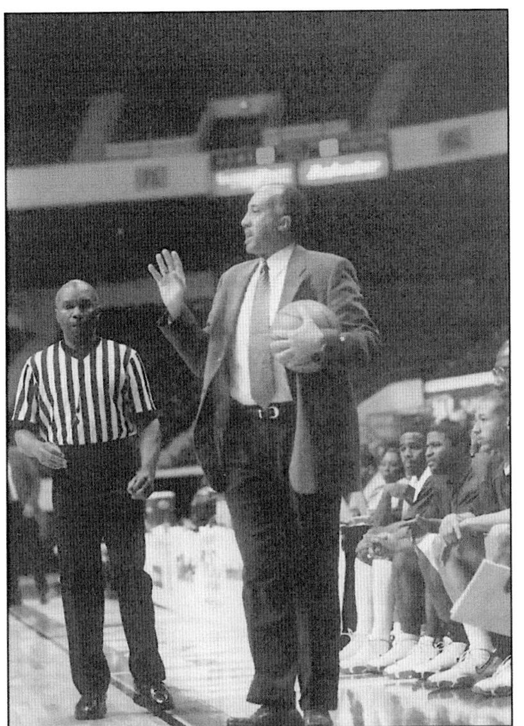

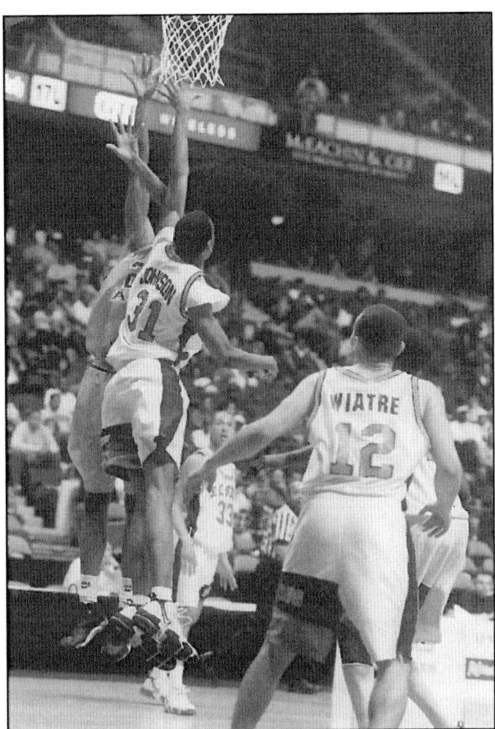

Under the leadership of Coach Cy Alexander, Bulldog basketball squads have challenged some of the nation's powerhouses, including Duke, Clemson, North Carolina State, Maryland, Brigham Young, and Villanova. They have won the MidEastern Athletic Conference (MEAC) title three times in the 1990s and advanced to play Kansas, Kentucky, and Stanford in the first round of the National Championships. (Photos courtesy of the Office of Sports Information.)

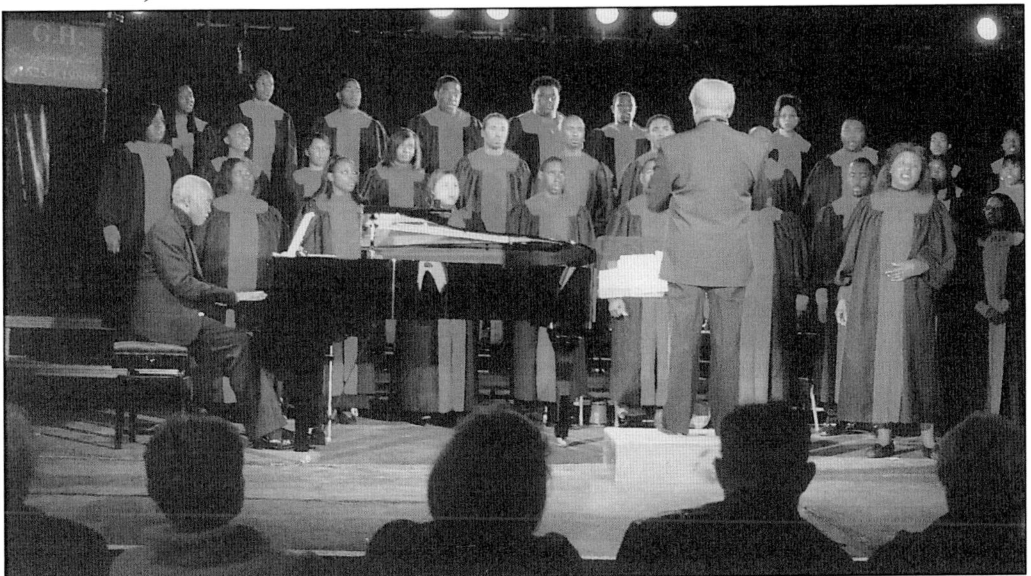

Directed by Dr. Arthur L. Evans, the SCSU Concert Choir performed in the Liverpool Cathedral, Liverpool, England, on May 25, 2000, as part of the Bollington Festival.

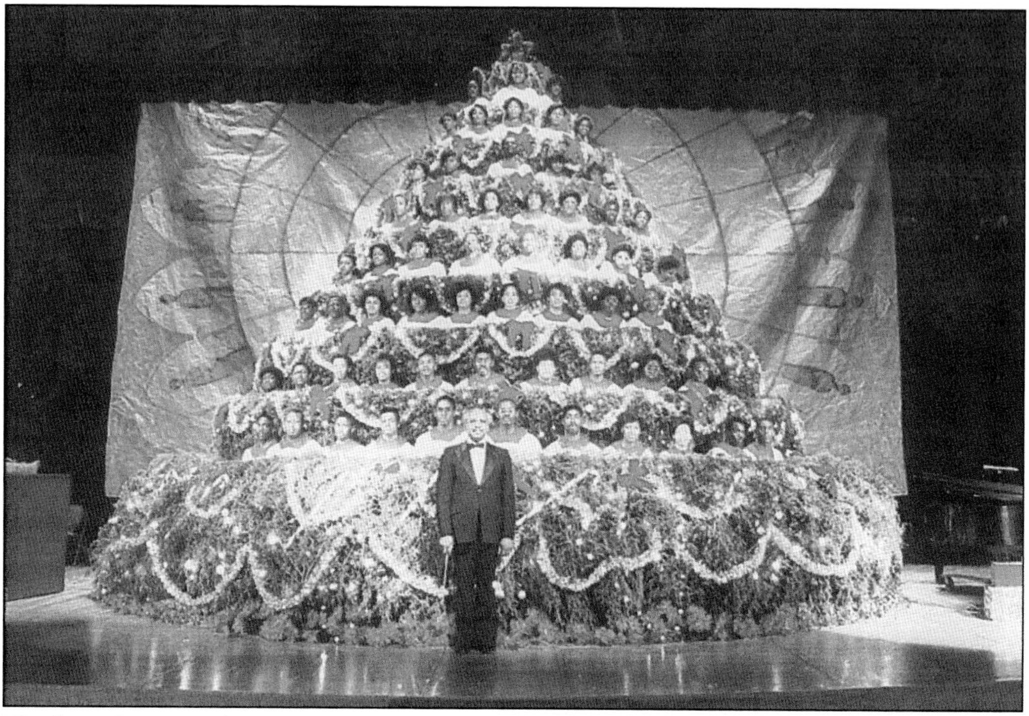

The first "Singing Christmas Tree" was presented by the concert choir under the direction of Dr. Arthur L. Evans. This December 7, 1987 image depicts the group, which continues to perform an annual program. (Photo courtesy of the Office of News and Communications.)

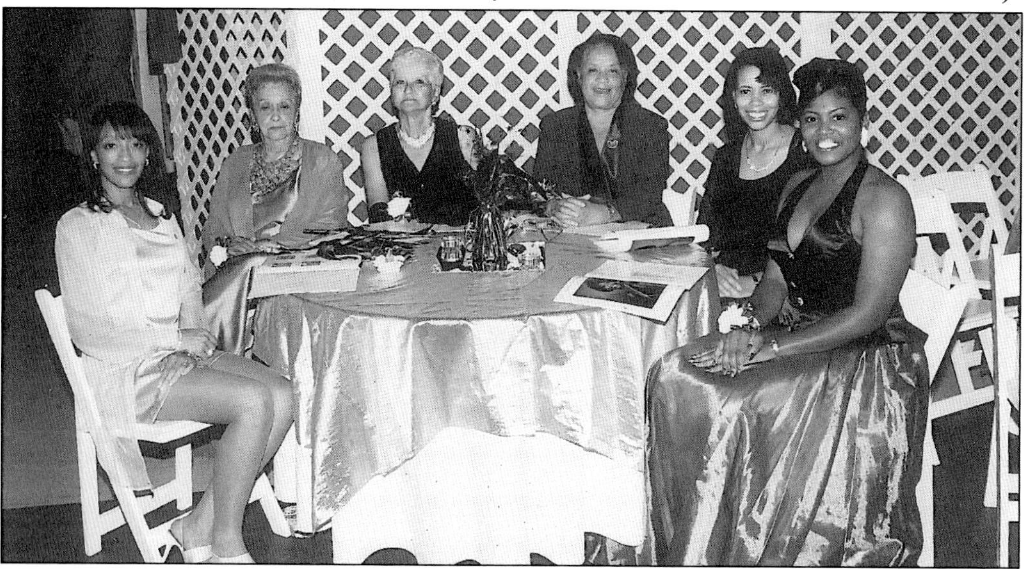

This image depicts former Miss South Carolina State College (University) queens attending the coronation of the 1997–1998 Miss SCSU, LaTonya Hickson. Shown, from left to right, are Angela Tanner Bradley (1984–1985), Gracia Watermann Dawson (1936–1937), Helen Jackson O'Garro (1940–1941), Dr. Barbara A. Vaughan (1952–1953), Hazel Armstrong Rickenbacker (1974–1975), and Jamelia L. Baylor (1996–1997). (Photo courtesy of the Office of News and Communications.)

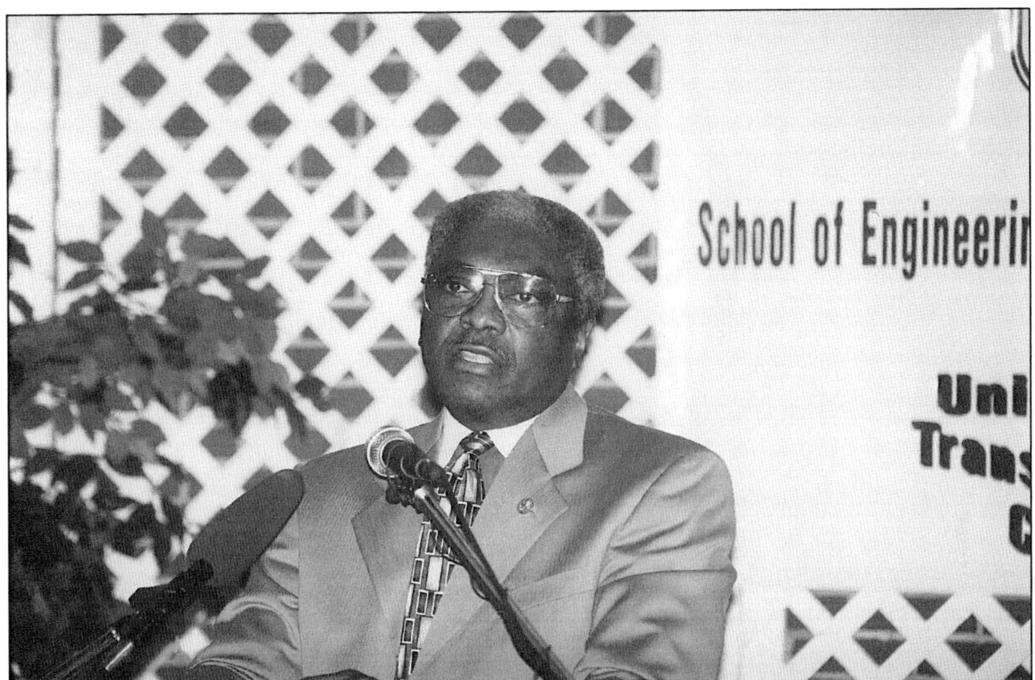

Sumter native James E. Clyburn, a 1962 graduate of South Carolina State, has represented South Carolina's Sixth District in the U.S. House of Representatives since 1993. He is South Carolina's first black congressman since George Washington Murray left the House in 1897. He is shown here at the announcement of plans to fund a $7 million matching-grant University Transportation Center, a new administrative unit of the School of Engineering Technology and Sciences at SC State. State's center is the only one of its kind in South Carolina designed to focus on current and future transportation needs. (Photo courtesy of the Office of News and Communications.)

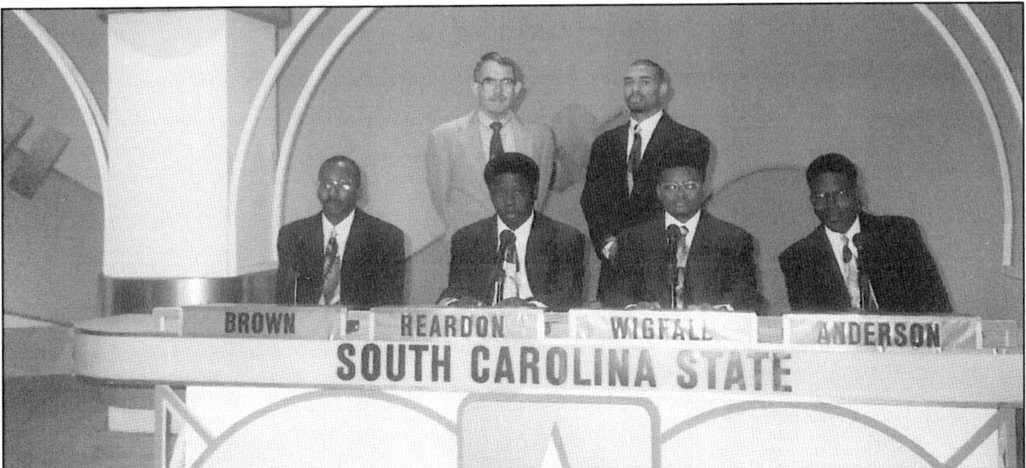

In 1995, the Honda Campus All-Star Team appeared on BET in Hollywood, falling to Norfolk State. Pictured, from left to right, are Douglas Brown, Derrick Reardon, Tyronne Wigfall, and Calvin Anderson. Standing are Coach William Hine and Corey Rogers. The 1996 team came in second in the national tournament and won $25,000 for the university. South Carolina State has participated in the tournament every year since its inception in 1989.

The GARNET and BLUE Staffer

A South Carolina State University Staff Senate Publication About, Of, And For Staff

Volume One, Number One — November, 1997

POINTBLANK!

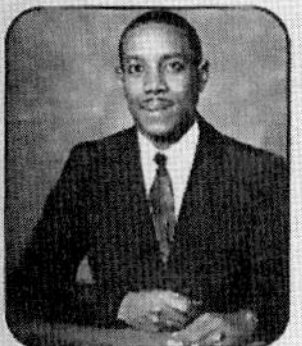

Terrence M. Cummings
STAFF SENATE PRESIDENT

*W*elcome to the inaugural edition of **The GARNET and BLUE *Staffer***, a Staff Senate publication.

The Staffer will be our voice to share information that will propel us towards *excellence*. I hope you will give us feedback as we start this unchartered course.

*M*y column, *POINTBLANK!* will develop as a straightforward, blunt, yet positive "target" about what we can do as Staff to make STATE her best.

*A*s president, I see every possibility that many of you have shared with me as I have visited your area or have talked with you. There are NO LIMITATIONS if *service*, *integrity*, and *excellence* are our guides.

I believe this Staff is destined to *shine*, and you can be among the *stars* through full membership. I solicit your support!

*R*emember, there is ***"Excellence in Unity!"***

Go Bulldogs!

Staff at STATE resurrected through new Senate

As the University's fiscal year began in July, so were staff resurrected through the newly formed Staff Senate that kicked off its beginning with an Installation Ceremony and Staff Solidarity Day on July 22.

University President Leroy Davis, Sr. installed executive officers and division representatives in Martin Luther King, Jr. Auditorium with a ceremony theme, *"To the Work: Toiling for Excellence."*

In his installation address, newly elected Staff Senate President Terrence Cummings asked staff to make three sacrifices as they toil for *excellence*.

First, Cummings asked staff to skip lunch once per week for 52 weeks beginning September 1, giving this amount to the University fund.

Cummings said if 400 staff would sacrifice $2.50 for 52 weeks, within a year, STATE would garner $52,000. He reminded staff that *"Sacrifice often comes before reward."*

Setting the example, Cummings pledged $20 per week through payroll deduction for a total of $1040, and to date, he is honoring his pledge.

Second, President Cummings asked staff to go back to their respective workplaces and fight inequity and unprofessional treatment with *excellence*, sharing with staff his parents' encouragement while a youth that *"There is no substitute for excellence."*

Third, Cummings asked all staff to embrace and support President Leroy Davis, Sr. and South Carolina State University, "like we have never done so before." Cummings said, "For this time if the President fails, so do we."

Since Staff Solidarity Day, the University has seen staff serving on committees, addressing concerns with solutions to the Senate, participating in "Dress Down Day" and Halloween, rejuvenating a "lifeless and lethargic University," and *raising the consciousness* of faculty, students, and administrators about STATE.

Nearly 130 staff have paid membership dues and the Senate has set an awesome goal to achieve full staff membership.

Cummings says, "I am overwhelmed with the excellent participation from staff, and I thank President Davis for his demonstrated courage, quality of mind, stoutness of heart, and for his self-reliance and boldness of spirit to establish the Staff Senate at South Carolina State University."

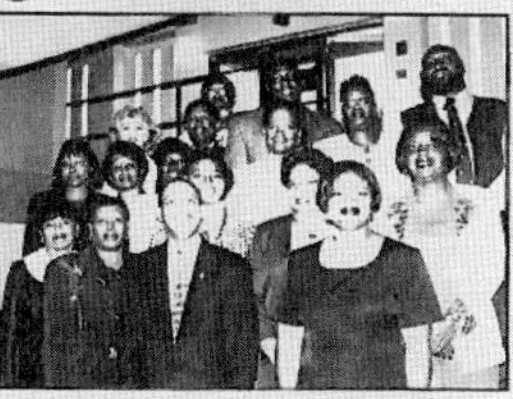

MEMBERS OF THE STAFF SENATE 1997-99

Staff talent show, GOSPELSINGOUT high on Senate event activities

Campaigning for events to bring the staff together, Staff Senate President Terrence Cummings is eager to showcase staff talent. The Senate is soliciting acts now.

Plans include a show with staff appearing as "Supremes," "Tops," Temptations," and Greek steppers. For more information, call 536.3721.

Likewise, because of the popularity of gospel music, the Senate plans a major GOSPELSINGOUT in SHM where local church choirs and gospel singers can visit the STATE campus to see what a vital resource the University is to the community. For more information, call Senator JoAnn Owens at 536.8330.

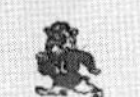

Under President Davis's administration, the university's staff senate was created. The installation of officers and representatives took place on July 22, 1997.

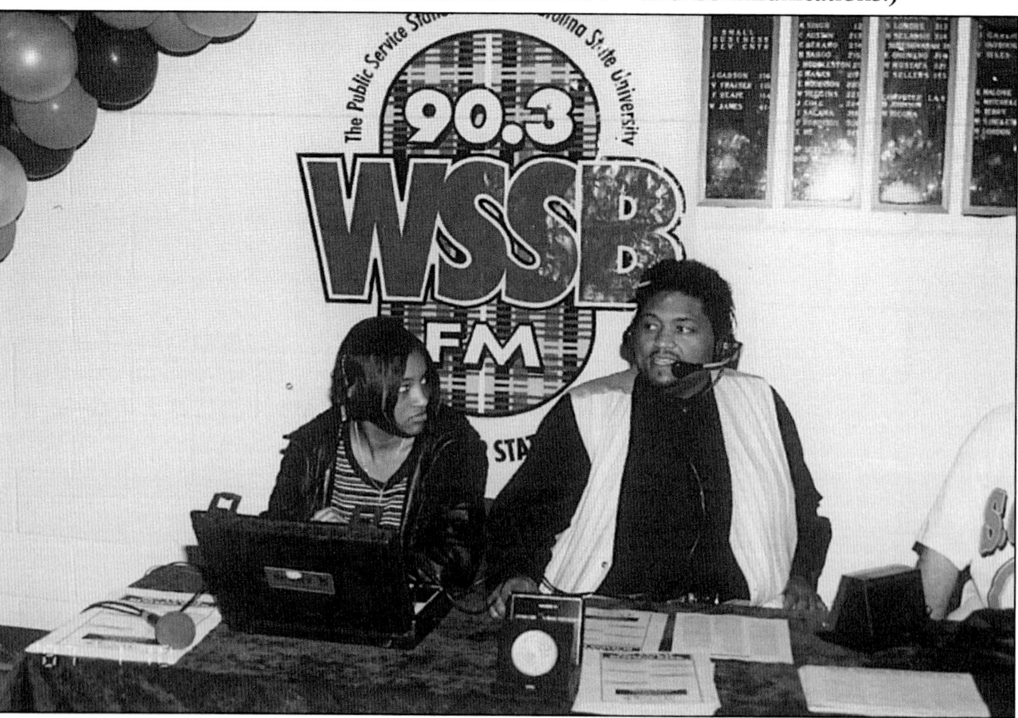

This image shows Milton E. McKissick, of State's WSSB Radio Station, and Jennifer Workman, student assistant, during business week in Belcher Hall. (Photo Courtesy of the Office of News and Communications.)

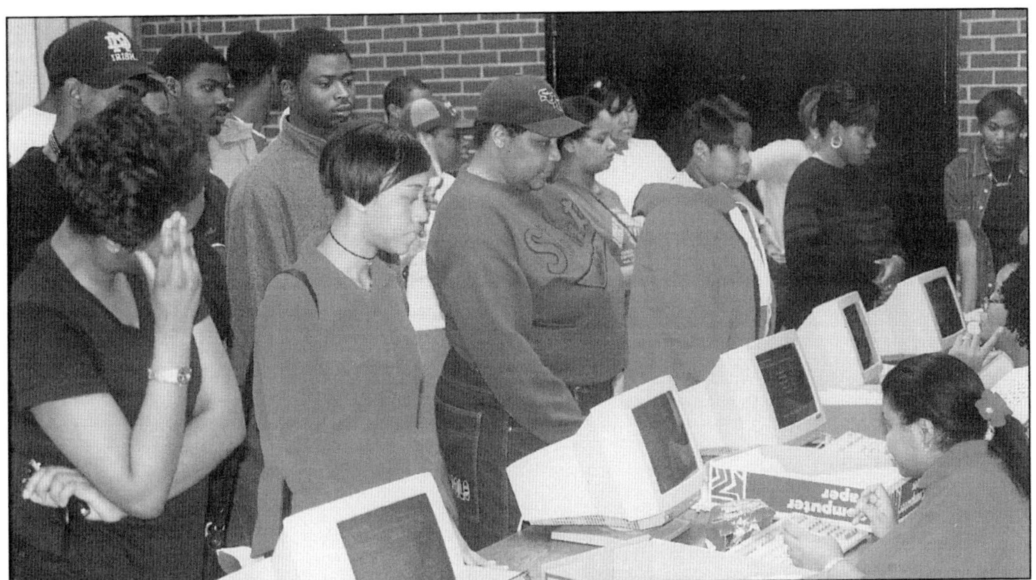

Students are depicted in this image during registration in Smith-Hammond-Middleton Memorial Center. (Photo courtesy of the Office of News and Communications.)

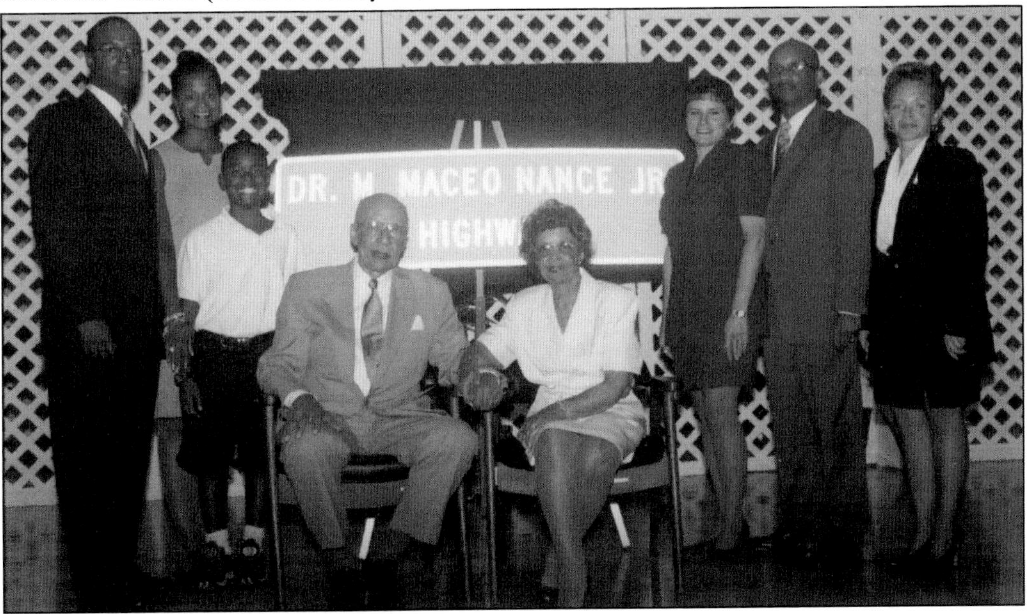

On August 22, 2000, the road in front of the University's campus—sections of which have been referred to as Magnolia Avenue, College Street, St. Matthews Road, and U.S. Highway 601—became Dr. M. Maceo Nance Jr., Highway. The S.C. Transportation Commission made the name change official on April 27, 2000. Dr. Nance was honored at a reception at the University's new Fine Arts Center. Some of the participants in the program included S.C. Representative Jerry N. Govan Jr., Governor James H. Hodges, Orangeburg Mayor Martin C. Cheatham, SCSU President Leroy Davis, and Congressman James E. Clyburn. Shown here are, from left to right, Robert Nance, Wendy Nance, Nicholas Nance, M. Maceo Nance Jr., Julie Nance, Toni Nance, M. Maceo Nance III, and niece Gloria Warner. (Photo by Larry Mitchell.)

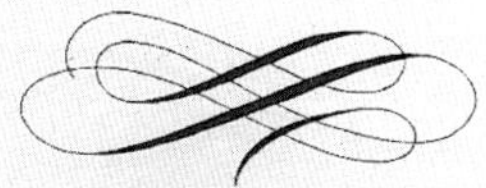

A Chronology of Selected Events in the History of South Carolina State University

1862 - President Abraham Lincoln signed into law the First Morrill Act authorizing establishment of land-grant colleges in the various states.

1872 - The Senate and House of Representatives of South Carolina enacted legislation establishing a college and institute of Mechanical Arts at Orangeburg in connection with Claflin University to be named the South Carolina College and Mechanical Institute.

1878 - The State Legislature changed the governance of the South Carolina College and Mechanical Institute and made it the Orangeburg Branch of the University of South Carolina.

1896 - The General Assembly of South Carolina by Legislative Act severed the connection between Claflin University and the state's interest on March 3.

- The General Assembly enacted legislation establishing South Carolina State College on March 3.
- The Board of Trustees of South Carolina State College held its first meeting in the City of Orangeburg and effected the organization of the new college on April 10.
- Thomas Ezkiel Miller was elected the First President of the College on June 10.
- The doors of the College were first opened to students on September 27 and the first faculty meeting was held on October 7.

1897 - The First Commencement was held on May 6. Olive Sasportas was awarded the Bachelor of Arts degree and eleven persons were graduated from the Normal School.

1898 - Morrill Hall was completed.

1911 - After serving for fifteen years, President Miller retired, effective May 31.

- Dr. Robert Shaw Wilkinson was elected Second President and assumed his duties on July 1.

1915 - State College and Clemson College entered into cooperative relations under the terms of the Smith-Lever Act whereby Negro agents were appointed to serve in the state.

1917 - Smith-Hughes funds became available to the College and the size of the faculty increased. Vocational Teacher Education was instituted.

1920 - White Hall was completed and occupied as an auditorium and classroom building. This was the first classroom building to be constructed with no living accommodations included and the last to be constructed with wooden truss.

1922 - The 25th Anniversary of the founding of the College was celebrated, and at the graduating exercises, May 24, the degree, Doctor of Laws was conferred upon Lewis M. Dunton (Orangeburg, SC), Educator and Religious Leader, Ernest E. Just (Washington, DC), Educator and Scientist, Nelson C. Nix (Orangeburg, SC), Educator and Mathematician, J. J. Starks (Sumter, SC), Educator and Religious Leader, and J. C. Whittaker (Oklahoma City, OK), Educator and Publicist.

- The Master of Arts degree was conferred upon Mary McLeod Bethune, Cora S. Boykin, Otis D. Council, Bessie E. Green, Louise F. Holmes, Lucy C. Laney, Isaac S. Leevy, William G. Nance, Martin A. Menafee, Celia D. Saxon, Herbert U. Seabrook, Miller F. Whittaker, Marion B. Wilkinson and John T. Williamson.

1927 - The Board of Trustees authorized establishment of Greek letter fraternities and sororities.

1931 - Reporting the completion of Dukes Gymnasium in 1931, President Wilkinson pointed out that student fees for the purposes collected from September 1926 to September 1930 totaled $23,006.48. An additional $15,000 was borrowed from the State Sinking Fund Commission. The total cost for the structure when equipped was $54,000. The plans and specifications of Dukes Gymnasium were drawn by John H. Blanche, Class of 1929, as a thesis project under the guidance and direction of Professor Miller F. Whittaker, College Architect and Director of Mechanic Arts.

1932 - On March 13, the faculty and entire student body were deeply grieved by the death of President Robert Shaw Wilkinson, who had been connected with the college as a member of the faculty from its founding in 1896.

- Upon the death of President Wilkinson, the Thirty-Sixth Annual Report of the President was made by Dr. Miller Fulton Whittaker who became Acting President on March 13 and was elected President on May 30.

1941 - President Whittaker reported to the Board of Trustees the completion of the manuscript on the story of the rise of State College to its present place by Dean N. C. Nix.

1946 - The Golden Anniversary of the founding of the College was celebrated.

- Honorary degrees were conferred upon Benjamin E. Mays, Robert Shaw Wilkinson, Jr., W. H. Aiken, Ernest A. Grant, and Walter Ivey.
- The Graduate Program began in September.

1947 - The Law School was opened in Wilkinson Hall (the library) with Benner Creswill Turner as Dean.

- The ROTC Unit for State College was approved by the War Department.

1949 - President Miller Fulton Whittaker died on November 14.

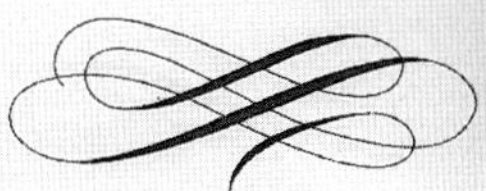

A Chronology of Selected Events in the History of South Carolina State University

1949/50- An Interim Committee of five supervised the administration of the College: K. W. Green, Chairman J. I. Washington, F. Marcellus Staley, Frank DeCosta, and H. W. Crawford.
1950 - Dr. Benner Creswill Turner was elected Fourth President on September 1.
1954 - The College inaugurated a state-wide testing program as a part of the entrance requirements and established the Guidance Center under a Director at the College.
1960 - The College became fully accredited by and a member of the Southern Association of Colleges and Schools; it also became fully accredited by the Association of American Colleges.
1966 - The School of Law at State College was discontinued with the spring session in May.
- Dr. James A. Boykin was the first South Carolina State College alumnus appointed to the Board of Trustees.
1967 - The Office of Vice President was established with Milligan Maceo Nance, Jr., becoming Vice President for Business and Finance and A. S. Belcher, Vice President for Academic Affairs.
- A Faculty Senate was organized on September 4.
- President Turner's retirement became effective June 24 and Mr. Nance became Acting President.
1968 - Henry E. Smith, Samuel Hammond, Jr., and Delano B. Middleton, in pursuit of human dignity, were killed on the front of the campus by law enforcement agents on February 8.
- November 27, Milligan Maceo Nance, Jr., was inaugurated the Fifth President of South Carolina State College and was the first alumnus of the College to be so honored.
1969 - I. P. Stanback was elected the first Black Chairman of the Board of Trustees of South Carolina State College October 6.
1970 - March 8, on the occasion of the celebration of Founders' Day, Dr. Milligan Maceo Nance, Jr. announced the initiation of the Quarter Century Club and presented plaques to the charter members.
1970/71- Celebration of the Diamond Jubilee.
- The Diamond Jubilee Convocation was held in September with the Honorable Carl Stokes, Mayor of Cleveland, as speaker.
1977 - Instituted the Presidential Scholar Awards. In each succeeding year, Gold, Silver, and Bronze Medallions have been awarded to full-time regularly enrolled undergraduate students earning cumulative grade point averages of 3.0 or better.
1979 - The "Lady Bulldogs" captured the National AIAW Championship.
1980 - The official opening of the I.P. Stanback Museum-Planetarium was held on April 27.
- Attorney I. S. Leevy Johnson was elected Chairman of the Board of Trustees of South Carolina State College.
- The Adult and Continuing Education Program was begun.
- Jacqueline E. Gilmore became the first black female to be elected to the Board of Trustees.
1983 - A program leading to the Doctor of Education degree was begun at the College.
- Established Distinguished Faculty Endowed Chairs. Applicants adjudicated by criteria established by their peers are nominated as recipients for these chairs.
1985 - The Accrediting Board of Engineering and Technology (ABET) fully accredited the following departments in the School of Engineering and Technology: Civil Engineering, Electrical Engineering, and Mechanical Engineering.
- Dukes Gymnasium, Hodge Hall, and Lowman Hall were entered on the National Register of Historic Places by the United States Department of Interior.
1986 - Albert Emanuel Smith was elected Sixth President of South Carolina State College on April 16.
- The provost system was inaugurated, and Dr. Vermelle J. Johnson was named the first Provost and Executive Vice President.
- Also named were Dr. Edward R. Jackson, Vice Provost for Academic Affairs and Dr. Milton D. Hunter, Vice Provost for Academic Administration.
- The Deans' Council was established and Dr. Lewie C. Roache was appointed as the first Chairman of the Council.
1987 - February 28, Albert Emanuel Smith was inaugurated the Sixth President of South Carolina State College.
1988 - Honorary doctorates were conferred upon Sammy Davis, Jr., LTG Henry Doctor, Jr., Ruby Middleton Forsythe, The Honorable Ernest F. Hollings, Dr. Milligan Maceo Nance, Jr., and The Honorable J. Strom Thurmond.
- Dr. Henry William Brevard, II was elected Chairman of the Board of Trustees of South Carolina State College, the first alumnus to serve in this position.
1989 - Honorary doctorates were conferred upon John C. Marous, Abelle Palmore Nivens, The Honorable Matthew J. Perry, Jr., and The Honorable Marshall Burns Williams.
1990 - Honorary doctorates were conferred upon Maude E. Callen (posthumously), Harold J. Mackey, The Honorable John W. Matthews, Jr., Earle E. Morris, Jr., and A. Barry Rand.

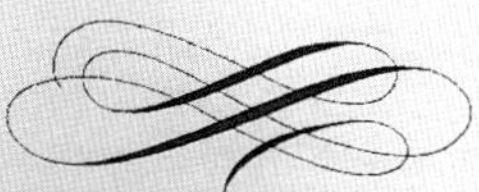

A Chronology of Selected Events in the History of South Carolina State University

1991 - An honorary doctorate was conferred upon Barbara Bush, wife of President George W. Bush.
1992 - Dr. James A. Boykin was elected Chairman of the Board of Trustees of South Carolina State College.
- Dr. Carl A. Carpenter was appointed Interim President on January 13.
- The institution was designated South Carolina State University on February 26.
- An honorary doctorate was conferred upon Rodell Lawrence.
- Dr. Barbara Rose Hatton was elected Seventh President of South Carolina State University on September 30.

1993 - The Campus Master Plan was completed and approved by the Board of Trustees.
- November 13, Dr. Barbara Rose Hatton was inaugurated the Seventh President of South Carolina State University.
- Ground breaking ceremony was held for renovating and enlarging Oliver C. Dawson Bulldog Stadium.
- The University's Scholarship Program was redesigned.

1994 - Legislation passed allowing engineering technology graduates to sit for the engineering licensure examination in South Carolina.
- Anthony T. Grant was elected Chairman of the Board of Trustees.
- Honorary doctorates were conferred upon Trudelle Willetta Wimbush, The Honorable L. Douglas Wilder, and Dr Johnnetta B. Cole.
- The first Fall Commencement Convocation was held.
- Felton Laboratory School was converted to a state-of-the-art professional development school.
- A Math-Science Hub was established to serve as a regional center to support primary and secondary science curricula.

1995 - Dr. Leroy Davis, Sr., was appointed Interim President on June 13.
- South Carolina State College Historic District was approved by the State Board of Review on November 17.
- Honorary doctorates were conferred upon Dr. Reatha Clark King, Dr. Carl A. Carpenter, John E. Jacob, William E Simms, Dr. Annabelle Spann Boykin and The Honorable James E. Clyburn.

1996 - Centennial Celebration of South Carolina State University.
- Honorary doctorates were conferred upon Chief Justice Ernest A. Finney, Jr. and Joel Smith, III.
- First Annual Scholarship Gala was held.
- Chairs' Forum established for Departmental Chairs.
- Dr. Leroy Davis, Sr., was elected the Eighth President on April 10.

1997 - March 22, Dr. Leroy Davis, Sr., was inaugurated the Eighth President of South Carolina State University.
- Established the President's Service Award.
- The Distance Education Program was initiated with the first interactive classroom in Belcher Hall.
- An honorary doctorate was conferred upon Kenneth Chenault.
- Dr. James A. Boykin was designated first Trustee Emeritus.
- The Fiftieth Anniversary of the ROTC Program was celebrated.
- Ground breaking ceremony was held for the Fine Arts Center.
- The New Nursing Program was initiated during Fall semester.
- The Posthumous Commissioning Ceremony was held on campus in honor of Cadet James Webster Smith.

1998 - An honorary doctorate was conferred upon U. S. Vice President Albert Gore, Jr.
- Groundbreaking was held for the Leadership and Skills Development Center.
- Opening ceremonies were held for The Savannah River Environmental Sciences Field Station.
- Accreditation was reaffirmed for Civil Engineering Technology, Engineering Technology, and Mechanical Engineering Technology.
- The South Carolina State University Center of Excellence in Leadership was established.

1999 - The Counseling and Self Development Center received Accreditation (IACS).
- The Child Development Learning Center received Accreditation (NAEYC).
- Accreditation was reaffirmed for the Department of Family and Consumer Sciences (AAFCS).
- Accreditation was reaffirmed for the Department of Speech Pathology and Audiology.
- Accreditation was reaffirmed for the Teacher Education Program (NCATE).
- The New Fine Arts Center was Presented.
- The University raised over $1 million in private donations.
- An honorary doctorate was conferred upon Governor James H. Hodges.

2000 - The first Emeritus Awards were presented.